ENDORSEMENTS

"Immersed in Red is a remarkably clear-eyed memoir of growing up in an American Communist family. Mike Shotwell's stepfather, Orville Olson, a hidden Communist, was a key figure in liberal politics in Minnesota in the 1930s and 1940s. Shotwell provides his memories and reflections not only on Olson but also on numerous other hidden Communists, some nationally prominent, who worked with his stepfather over the decades. His portrait of the mental world of long-term, devoted Communists is thoroughly convincing. He combines his memories of his parents and their friends and associates with his own reflections on the nature of Communist ideology based on a very wide and intelligent reading of the literature and primary sources that document the rise and evolution of Communism and like-minded totalitarian belief-systems. Readers will learn much from this book."

John Earl Haynes is the author of eleven scholarly books on American communism and Soviet espionage, most notably *The Secret World of American Communism* (Yale University Press, 1995)

"Immersed in Red provides a fascinating picture of growing up in a communist household. Mike Shotwell vividly recalls his stepfather, Orville Olson's, rigid ideological world and the numerous friends who assisted Soviet intelligence agencies in their efforts to undermine American democracy."

Harvey Klehr, co-author of Spies: *The Rise and Fall of the KGB in America* (Yale University Press, 2009)

This is a terrific read!! Immersed in Red is an intimate record of memories and meanings from one man's very personal experience of the American left's political insanity. Mike Shotwell gives us unique portraits of communists he and his family knew as friends and comrades beginning in his childhood. These memoires confirm beyond all doubt the many evolutionary links from twentieth-century Marxism, Stalinism and Leninism to the contemporary liberal-progressive movement in America. This book of unique insights spells out the congruence of irrational Soviet idealism with the modern left's criminal agenda. His personal recollections of communists, famous and infamous, give us unmatched glimpses into the left's history of stunningly destructive political and social philosophy, all of it responsible for our planet's current existential convulsions. Mike Shotwell joins the ranks of other highly intelligent men who have grown up and grown out of the madness of Marxism in all its forms. As a bonus, his insightful commentaries are just as persuasive as his accounts. Both convey an authority one can know only by having lived the lies and discovered the truth."

Dr. Lyle Rossiter Jr., Psychiatrist and author of *The Liberal Mind, The Psychological Causes of Political Madness.*

IMMERSED IN RED

My Formative Years in a Marxist Household

To Lisa

Thankyou for your interest

(also for keeping my teeth looking good)

MIKE SHOTWELL

Mike Shotwell

IMMERSED IN RED

World Ahead Press is a division of WND Books. The views and opinions expressed in this book are those of the author and do not necessarily reflect the official policy or position or WND Books.

Paperback ISBN: 978-944212-52-0
eBook ISBN: 978-1-944212-53-7

Printed in the United States of America
16 17 18 19 20 21 LSI 9 8 7 6 5 4 3 2 1

DEDICATIONS AND ACKNOWLEDGEMENTS

This book is dedicated to my wife Gwyneth, the love of my life, for her steadfast encouragement, as well as her many long hours editing and refining, while we molded the work into its final form.

In addition,

I wish to thank Prof. Paul Kengor, Ph.D. for his encouragement, his enthusiasm, his timely comments, and his help in guiding the work into publication. Without him, this book would have been exiled to the closet containing our family archives.

and finally,

I also cannot fail to recognize the many other writers and researchers including, but not limited to, Herbert Romerstein, Ron Radosh, John Earl Haynes, Harvey Klehr, David Horowitz, Lyle Rossiter Jr., Lt. Gen. Ion Pacepa, Jerry Bergman, Tim Tzouliadis, S. J. Taylor, Ann Applebaum, the eminent social commentator and author Tom Wolfe, and the great Whittaker Chambers, whose data I have plumbed and who and are, in the present and the past, so diligently and methodically unearthing the grim tentacles of twentieth-century Marxist-communist ideology . . . and exposing its dark underbelly to the sunlight for all to see.

CONTENTS

FOREWORD

PAUL KENGOR, PH.D.

My first glimpse of Mike Shotwell's compelling story was in August 2012. He happened to be reading my book, *The Communist*, on Barack Obama's mentor, Frank Marshall Davis, and he reached out to me with an email. "My own background was to have been raised by communist parents," Mike began his introduction. He told me about his stepfather, his mother, and their comrades, and small but interesting details such as the vaguely grim and oppressive overtone that accompanied their weekend cookouts and visits. But he also described the big picture in no uncertain terms. They "all had one thing in common: they were all hard core communists. And make no mistake, these were not people who wanted a peaceable replacement of our [US] leadership, they were an angry group that wanted to oust our government and replace it with Soviet leadership . . . under the banner led by Joseph Stalin."

Mike told me about his stepfather's take on the horror stories emanating from the USSR: "All of the reports of the horrors inside [Stalinist] Russia were met with scornful opposition. It was all just [dismissed as] disgusting right-wing propaganda, nonsense, and desperate tactics before the final fall and the rise of the great new racist-free proletariat kingdom. I was also informed that my stepfather would be an important figure in the new government." That is, he would be a key apparatchik in the "Soviet America" that would triumph and ally with the USSR as part of a single worldwide communist state.

And yet, to the wider public, Mike's stepfather portrayed himself as a mere good-hearted "progressive," as did many American Stalinists who quite literally swore a loyalty oath to the USSR. In fact, his stepfather, the unforgettable Orville that readers of this gripping memoir will soon meet, ran the Henry Wallace campaign for president in the state of Minnesota. Wallace ran on the Progressive Party ticket. The former FDR veep had said some really nice and really stupid things about Joe Stalin (as had FDR), which was enough for American Stalinists to flock to Wallace as their best hope in the 1948 race. Orville E. Olson was a major figure in the Progressive Party, running for governor of Minnesota on the party's ticket in 1948. As Mike puts it, Olson was "one of the principal organizers of the Progressive Party movement in 1948."

That is a glimpse into Mike Shotwell's upbringing. When liberals today scoff at the possibility that there were communist Americans who actually thought this way, Mike bristles: "Nobody can fool me about communists and their agenda. It was seared into me by systematic political brainwashing for years."

Mike was born in Saint Louis in November 1942, and grew up largely in the Midwest and California. He was raised a classic red-diaper baby. Speaking of his parents' admiration of Stalin and Mao Zedong, Mike told me, "Imagine growing up in a household where your mother and stepfather idolized two of the greatest mass murderers in the history of mankind." As a child and teen, Mike was thoroughly indoctrinated into this toxic philosophy and political "madness," which required years of introspection and real-life experience to reverse. Mike told me that he had undergone a complete "brainwashing."

The "brainwashing" included the indoctrination at a Unitarian Church in Los Angeles, where, he says, there seemed to be no Christians and not even anyone who believed in God: "I can never remember meeting a single member of the congregation that believed in God, or an afterlife, or considered themselves religious in any way." It was a pro-Russian "church" that was about not religion but radical-left politics—and about blaming and hating America.

Generally, Mike would tell me in ongoing correspondence, the communists he knew were a "miserable" and "angry" lot, his parents foremost among them (this is not unusual among communists). I once asked if it was fair to classify his parents as "un-American." Here was his answer:

> My step-father and mother were truly 'un-American.' They bitterly fought the goings-on of the House Committee on Un-American Activities, and identified with those that they felt were so unfairly singled out by these 'right wing crazies.' If somebody asked them if they were good Americans, they would have carefully explained, 'of course, the best, following in the footsteps of Jefferson and Paine.' If someone were to say to them, 'You don't sound or act like a normal American,' their chests would have swelled with pride.

Mike emphasizes that his parents never gave up the communist faith and their anti-Americanism. He describes an incident that occurred when he accompanied his aging mother as she looked for a unit in a retirement building in the luxury towers at a Laguna Beach development in southern California. "We found a perfect unit with a perfect exposure on the fourth floor that looked out at the beautifully manicured courtyard," Mike recalled. "In the background, framing the view, [were] the fluttering flags of California and America. She refused to consider the unit, confiding with a dismissive snort for the prime reason that there was no possibility that she would purchase a unit where she had to stare out at an American flag."

Mike also speaks to his stepfather's certainty that Soviet power would one day triumph in the United States: "[He] just assumed that Russia would assume control of the world, including the US. This was a Darwinian truth . . . pure Marx/Engels." He underscored: "It wasn't an issue to debate. It was a foregone conclusion. The only issue was the timeframe. This rotten, disgusting, predatory, and duplicitous [American] society would simply crumble at the feet of the proletariat and be obliterated from the world memory. Prior to '53 [the year Stalin died], it was assumed Joe Stalin would assume the reins."

Mike was taught that Stalin's Russia was the ideal, especially compared to America: "Uncle Joe was a perfect model. Weren't the Russians all lucky? After all, no society had ever progressed so rapidly." He said that his parents refused to see that they were living in an America with "the highest standard of living and the most personal freedoms that the world has ever seen. . . . All they wanted to do was obliterate it and replace it with a totalitarian, communist system."

It is crucial to realize that Mike Shotwell's shocking testimony is far from unique. It is actually standard fare for many ex-communists. I'm reminded of the words of Herb Romerstein, one of America's greatest ex-communists: "Communist Party members were loyal Soviet patriots." Mike's stepfather was most certainly just that.

Ever since our first exchange, I would occasionally email Mike and ask questions based on my research at the moment. For instance, did Orville ever meet Paul Robeson? What was his view of Nikita Khrushchev? What did Orville think of J. Edgar Hoover? Mike's answer to that one, incidentally, was a hoot:

> My remembrances of Orville's statements about Hoover were pretty much in line with his derogatory statements about American ballet dancers who he considered laughable fairies in comparison to the more manly Russian dancers that were much better trained and all married . . . I recall Orville made open fun of Hoover as a 'pantywaist' who had affairs and sex parties with his boyfriend and the close-knit circle around him. Hitler was described in the same way. In a way, the two were linked in the

> same manner. It was a way of describing to us that crazy, anti-communist people were screwed up vicious monsters who went to all lengths to disguise their insanity including destroying their foes' reputations, or secretly eliminating them. To describe it another way . . . anyone who was against communism and the great world-wide proletarian revolution was either insane, an unbalanced person such as a gay, ignorant, or just plain stupid.

Once upon a time, American communists despised homosexuals; now they are embracing them and their "LGBTQ" agenda. They do this less to love gays than to fulfill Marx's and Engels' words of two centuries ago: "abolition of the family."

All along, I knew that Mike Shotwell was recording his story in a short memoir that he intended to one day self-publish. I strongly encouraged him to keep at that book. He did. He started with a solid foundation of about 30 pages before expanding and adding as more disquieting recollections came back to him, jogged by some old name from the crazy commie past. As he did, he continued to improve his manuscript, and I encouraged him heartily.

One day in February 2016, I suggested that Mike pitch his manuscript to Geoffrey Stone, the excellent editor at WND Books, who had done a superb job the previous year with my most recent book, *Takedown*, on the left's sabotaging of family and marriage over the last two centuries. Mike did just that, and Geoff, as always, responded promptly and prudently. It led to the publication of the book by this new division of WND Books, World Ahead Press. I know World Ahead Press will do a fine job with the manuscript, which deserves it. Mike deserves it. Gee, anyone brought up the way that Mike was especially deserves it.

I am so pleased and so proud of Mike Shotwell for bringing his riveting story to fruition. I am sure that writing it must have been both painful and therapeutic. It is a tragic story but also one of hope and redemption. He has lived to tell. He is a survivor of the insanity of the far-left worldview. His story is a cautionary tale for Americans and America. The boy who was immersed in red is now a man immersed in truth. And in the end, communism and the far left can never overcome truth.

INTRODUCTION

In 1980, at thirty-eight years old, I purchased a book entitled *Breaking Ranks.* The author was Norman Podhoretz who, as editor of *Commentary* magazine, had been a leading Jewish intellectual of the political left in the decades of the 60s onward. The book began with a letter to his son, and dealt with Podhoretz's personal journey away from leftist ideology to what has been termed "neo-conservatism," and how that had come about. His eloquent writing focused on how and why his perceptions had changed regarding politics and the America he lived in. Many of the ideas he expressed had been circulating in my brain in bits and pieces for several years, but the themes he expressed so clearly resonated with me in their totality.

What did Podhoretz's leftist past and his *Breaking Ranks* have to do with me? People meeting me from my mid-30s on never knew me to be a militant political leftist; however, as a youth, from junior high through college, and followed by two years in the Peace Corps in South America (1966—68), I sat whole heartedly in the leftist camp. I actively espoused socialist and Marxist/communist thinking that I had absorbed from my home life. I wrote papers throughout my school years parroting the political ideology that I had been indoctrinated with from seven-years-old and into my late 20s and even beyond. As Podhoretz described so well, I ascribed to the articles of faith of the radical left, chief among them that "all of the miseries of the human condition could be cured by the right social and economic arrangements." I manifested that belief by brazenly defending the regimes of Joseph Stalin and Mao Zedong, thinking that was what their wonderful and grand plans were all about. I supported Fidel Castro and his revolution, was deeply opposed to US foreign policy, and generally felt that intelligent discourse and correct thinking was only articulated by those on the left. I also believed that the US military was a right-wing fascist organization; that southerners were a mean, racist lot; that religious thought was nonsense; that patriotism and flag waving was a cover up for reactionary and bigoted behavior; that the country was run by Wall Street and big business; and that real patriotism was seeking revolution requiring elimination of capitalism and replacement with Russian communism.

What my friends and acquaintances did not know was that when I was seven years old, and my parents were divorced, my mother married a prominent, though behind-the-scenes, American communist. The environment created by that union was an immersion into a political world few are aware of or can fully understand. The impact was profound, compelling me all these years later to share my experience.

Growing up in the protected environment of the United States, I really couldn't conceive of how horrifying a true revolution could be, so my outward expressions of moral outrage and leftist pronouncements were mostly just vehement, sophomoric, coffeehouse chatter. But, some doubts began to arise in those early years, as what I was experiencing in my daily life in the real world bore little resemblance to the bleak and negative narratives I received at home; nonetheless, my transition would take more first-hand knowledge and more passing years to complete.

However, adherence to my strong opinions was never encumbered by lack of experience; but you couldn't have told me that. I was one arrogant young man, who was pretty well convinced I had all the answers. My juvenile thought process mirrored a man Podhoretz wrote about, Nelson Algren, who described America, "as though it contained only two kinds of people – the exploiting (and listless) rich and the exploited (and colorful) poor."

I encountered little in the way of challenges to my strong political views. My teachers didn't question me; in fact, my high school history teacher enjoyed my dissertations. Most of my college professors were like-minded, particularly one political history professor at the University of Southern California who referred to me openly as "my socialist friend up in the back." I always received good marks from him, and he called on me a lot as an example of a scholarly and perceptive student who others should emulate.

Important people in my life. During that time, however, there were people I encountered who prompted me to reconsider some of my perceptions and beliefs. One in particular was Col. Clarence Clendenen, a professor of Western Civilization at Menlo College, where I attended my first year. He was a graduate of West Point and had a PhD from Stanford. He was in his mid-70s and taught and lived on campus. He was also a student of the American Civil War, and had fought in both World Wars. He was a quiet man who puffed on his pipe and invited students to his quarters in the evening and I went there often. Many times I was the only student present. I felt true warmth in his presence. He was the first military man I had ever met. He was intelligent, bright, experienced, had a broad knowledge of world politics, was a good listener, engaged freely in open thought and commentary, was selfless, and was a credit to his profession and life itself. He was a member of America's Greatest Generation, an American generation like no other.

Another person I met while studying architecture at USC, was a Catholic nun who was taking some art classes there. She was open, friendly, very perceptive, and a wonderful sounding board. I was moved by the conversations I had with her. But perhaps more significant was that this compassionate nun was a far cry from the anti-Catholic stereotype I grew up with.

There were two other people I remember meeting while in Peace Corps training after college, preparing to go to South America at age twenty-three. The first was a conservative political expert from the State Department, Don Barnhart, who was teaching us about Venezuelan political history. Democracy was just becoming established in Venezuela in the 1960s, after decades of autocratic rule. However, there was continuous opposition from many quarters, including the communist guerillas, and the intellectual left of the universities. I recall Barnhart predicting the collapse of the Soviet Union in the next ten or fifteen years. We all scoffed at him and what we perceived as his pathetic right-wing reasoning. As it turned out, he was off by only a few years, but correct overall when the Soviet Russian Empire economically collapsed in 1989. Earlier, Soviet Premier Nikita Khrushchev had declared the USSR would "bury" us; fortunately he was wrong.

The other individual was the Peace Corps staff psychiatrist, M. D. Spottswood, whose job it was to evaluate the characters and strengths of the volunteers, and their abilities to withstand the rigors of our next two years in South America. His findings were part of the overall evaluation process. As it turned out, 50 percent of the trainees dropped out in training, were "de-selected" by staff and peers, or terminated their service early. I worked hard to not be in any of those categories.

Spottswood was viewed with caution by my fellow trainees because he was conservative as well as religious. I had several interactions with him, and found him an impressive man who had a lot of insight into people and the broader world. Prior to meeting him, I never could have conceived that any member of the "intelligentsia," let alone a psychiatrist, could be a conservative. My conversations with him made me reflect and reconsider my thinking.

Another person who had a profound impact on my life was a therapist I saw over several years, who helped me to probe my early life, and assisted me to become the person I wished to be. He was able to bring into focus the strange life I had led through my younger years. Certainly there were others who contributed to my overall conversion, but these five stand out in my memory as benchmarks; collectively they provided moments of epiphany.

The Peace Corps. Besides the impact from these individuals, various incidents presented challenges to my long held political beliefs. While in the Peace Corps, I was asked to teach a program at the University of Caracas School of Architecture on how to use sun machines in the design process. I was well versed in the subject from my architectural education. Shortly into my tenure I was suddenly dismissed, with no official explanation. Naturally, I was confused and perplexed. Afterwards, it was explained to me by a faculty member acquainted with the decision that a group of communist professors (part of the dominant leftist faculty and administrators) determined I was being too well received by the eager students, and that reaction hadn't been anticipated. As a simple functionary teaching about a design tool, my presence was acceptable, but the results of having students look up to me as a knowledgeable and capable person was not how they wished Americans to be perceived. In addition, these same professors were convinced that I worked for the CIA and was there to foment unrest against the anti-government FALN, the active underground guerrilla communist clique that they supported.

At one dinner engagement I attended, with several Venezuelan professors present, I was questioned about my "CIA employment." I could produce no denial that satisfied them. The brilliant Peace Corp program of anti-communist President John F. Kennedy, which sent young people overseas to learn about other cultures and help out with their skill and knowledge, was, they believed, nonsensical and duplicitous. They shook their heads with disgust at my honest explanation. And to think that here I was, a devoted leftist, raised and nurtured in a Marxist household, freely espousing strong sentiments against America and our involvement in the ongoing Vietnam War, being accused of being a CIA imperialist. What irony.

Two other incidents in Venezuela affected me a great deal. The first involved projects I was working on in various outlying towns. Using a jeep that was made available to me by the governor of the state, I had to drive through the mountains to reach them. The mountains were sporadically controlled by communist guerillas, and I learned that they had destroyed a military checkpoint just a short time before I passed through. Had I encountered these forces and, very possibly, been taken hostage, I would have been nothing more than a disposable pawn in their political quest; my liberal leanings would have had no bearing on my fate. In the guerrillas' eyes, I would simply be a disgusting American capitalist piece of trash.

The other incident, not commonly known to our group, involved three Peace Corps volunteers teaching physical education, who had earlier been stationed in the same town that my former wife and I were sent to, San Juan de Los Morros, the capital of Guárico State. This, and the other locales in which I lived, were poor barrios lacking most of the common comforts that even those in the US with little economic means took for granted. Shockingly, we learned that the three volunteers were stoned by leftist high school students in the middle of the town. I was informed by our director that one of the girls had been badly hurt. Believe me, I was very cautious where I went in the town after that revelation. In fact, our neighbor, Don Jose, a man who had served time for two murders and had carried contraband over the mountains to Columbia when he was ten years old, insisted on accompanying me to the center of the town whenever I needed to go there. His reputation was formidable and few would dare to take him on.

I also befriended a traveling black American basketball team, the Harlem Stars, a mini version of the Harlem Globetrotters, who made quite a hit in the surrounding towns, leading local teams on for a half, and then squashing them at the end with their extraordinary skills. The fact that I traveled around with them for a bit and acted as their translator (they didn't speak a word of Spanish) worked in my favor to break down the racist label that the Venezuelan locals assumed I had as a white American. In fact, it was confounding to them and caused much comment. But the assumption of guilt against white Americans had a disturbing undercurrent that was all part of the ubiquitous leftist propaganda.

I had an interesting encounter that illustrates some of the unrealistic perceptions that were rampant in Venezuela (and still are). From time to time I had conversations with one of the professors connected with the University of Caracas, a well-educated engineer and an avowed communist. During one of these visits, he regaled me with back issues of newspapers showing photos of the 1965 Watts race riots in Los Angeles. Seeing the blacks protesting in conventional neighborhoods with individual houses, which was in stark contrast to the bleak hillside slums in Caracas and the rest of Venezuela, he was convinced these were photos that had been doctored by the CIA. His thinking was that racist Americans were falsely showing these rioters against faked dwellings, as if to say, "What do they have to protest about?" But at the same time, he could fully accept that American blacks were oppressed by whites, giving them ample reason to do so.

I attempted to explain the reality of the photos from my own familiarity with South Central Los Angeles and the neighborhoods in question; after all, I had lived there during my college years. I described my own experience during the riots. While still a married student, my wife and I had to escape our apartment in the neighboring area of Baldwin Hills late at night, taking our terrified stewardess neighbors with us. The Japanese apartment owner's tires were slashed in the carport, but our car, luckily, was okay. Bonfires blazed in the neighboring streets and an orange glow filled the air as we drove slowly down the street past the very attractive apartment buildings, winding our way down to Exposition Boulevard, where we met a long National Guard convoy heading toward the riot zone. I was never happier to see American military personnel in my life. But the adventure was eerie and frightening. None of us exhaled until we arrived to safety in West Los Angeles.

The issues surrounding the riots themselves were complex, but no amount of explanation by me could affect or nuance this man's preconceived notions that were further solidified when seen through the lens of communism. White Americans were racist and oppressed the black population, and that was that. I deeply resented his blanket assessment. I wasn't a racist and my ancestors weren't slave traders. In fact, they were Quakers who were among the leading abolitionists from the seventeenth century onward.

Perhaps lost in this man's view was the contradiction that blacks who weren't living in squalor would have reason to revolt while at the same time feeling it was only natural that they would rise up as a result of their lifelong oppression. He seemed to want it both ways.

All of the combined experiences in Venezuela took a chunk out of my feelings of benevolence for the communist rebels. What I had experienced was a dose of the real world. It also brought to the fore the knowledge that many of my political preconceptions were badly off-base, and that the anti- US venom of the Venezuelan leftists was wildly irrational. I also learned that I better act with caution around political zealots, and particularly with the FALN communists who painted huge graffiti banners on the whitewashed walls around my neighborhood. I found out it was one thing to intellectually espouse leftist idealism sitting in a classroom, a coffee house, or a university dorm, and quite another to come face to face with it in the real world. (A price is paid, though, for not facing reality. I think of the millions in Russia and China during the upheavals under Stalin and Mao, who would not or could not face the realities of their own changing governments and paid the ultimate price.)

In the following years, Venezuela's democracy lost its struggle, ultimately falling to the communist left, some of the very same people who terminated my seminars at the university. The result was the later communist dictatorship of Hugo Chavez. Within a short time, the democratic government had been usurped and clothed in deceptive populist jargon, just as Juan Peron had achieved in Argentina from the 40s through the 70s. Chavez re-wrote the constitution, rigidly controlled the press, stacked the Venezuelan Supreme Court, nationalized businesses, promoted hate crimes against Venezuelan Jews, characterized the US as an international bogeyman, created a national welfare state with no long-term economic foundation, and concocted a political mechanism that effectively made him president for life. I was not teary-eyed at his death. However, he has been succeeded by Nicolas Maduro, a man cut from the same cloth. The consequences for the Venezuelan people may be irreversible. Democracy is difficult to reestablish once lost.

At the end of my stint in South America, I was very grateful to finally board a Pan American jet and return to the US. I realized by age twenty-seven how precious our country and our political system were, but at the same time how fragile it could be. Nevertheless, I remained to the left in my basic political outlook.

A new beginning. After my return, my wife and I divorced and my life took on a new purpose. I began working as a consultant in the dynamic free-market business environment of this country. I was blessed with architectural projects in Mexico, Israel, and Central America, along with many domestic projects. With the responsibilities of vice-president of a development company, I not only managed design and building, but also the hiring and firing of personnel amid the ups and downs of the economy. Eager to branch out on my own, I opened my own architectural practice just before my second marriage in 1976. It was exciting and exhilarating, and sometimes unnerving. But with a growing family, my wife and I gladly took on the burden, believing in our capabilities to work hard and succeed.

Eventually, my twenty-five years of private practice segued into the area of forensic architecture, in which I acted as an expert witness in the area of construction defects. Through over two hundred cases over the last twenty-five years, I was intimately involved in the establishment of facts for proving or disproving allegations. It has also informed my attitudes towards the so-called authority that accompanies much of what passes for truth in the fields of education, science and politics.

Early in my career I also donated time to construction projects on an Indian reservation; worked in a food program connected with our church; and donated services to church building projects. I've always had compassion for the unfortunate, the sick, and those with mental issues. Our society should, and does, provide a safety net for those in need. In the 1960s, with the advent of the Great Society and the War on Poverty, well-intentioned government programs blossomed and grew, which had the unexpected consequence of creating dependency, and for many became a way of life. Unfortunately, for every truly needy person, there are many others who have learned how to take advantage of the system.

The self-empowerment I gained from knowing I could succeed in the business world through my own efforts was gratifying. My experiences with clients, contractors, business people and others bolstered my sense of what was possible within a free-market system. I encountered average trades-people who had developed their own businesses out of singular determination, honesty, and grit. I came around to the understanding that it was because of our unique form of democracy and capitalism that the US became the beacon light of the world; that we were not the grim and reckless country responsible for countless crimes against humanity, as espoused by my family, their friends, and the radical leftists I had encountered in South America.

I also came to realize that the Constitution gives people the right to pursue happiness, and the freedom to pursue their goals based on their abilities and desires. But there is no guarantee of success; things in life do not always work out and you often have to pick yourself up and start again. In contrast, nowhere in the history of the world has a nation built on socialism or communism succeeded in producing a vibrant, innovative society, upward mobility for those willing to aspire to their highest potential, and a happy populace. It is simply an ideology that does not allow such things.

Reading Podhoretz's book in 1980 really put the icing on the cake for me. It beautifully stitched together an understanding of many aspects of my prior life and my experiences that had so many parallels to this wonderful author. Since then, many other writers and researchers have opened my eyes even wider. Some of the many writers I have used as reference include Prof. Paul Kengor, an expert on the history and strategies of the left, who has spent his academic career studying communism, socialism, totalitarianism, progressivism, and the Cold War and its unsettling intrusion into American politics; John Earl Haynes and Harvey Klehr, preeminent scholars and authors who have written tomes on Minnesota politics, American communism, and the analysis of the *Venona Decrypts* and other Russian KGB documents; Dr. Lyle Rossiter Jr., a psychiatrist who has written about the destructive underpinnings of radical liberal thinking; David Horowitz, who has written eloquently on his own conversion to conservatism and the dangers of Marxist/communist intrusion into our country's institutions; Ron Radosh's works about the radical left, the Rosenbergs, and other facets of the politics of WWII; Lt. Gen. Ion Pacepa, a firsthand expert on the Soviet disinformation apparatus; S. J. Taylor's work about Walter Duranty; Dr. Jerry Bergman, whose research into the life and "scientific" studies, and religious orientation of Charles Darwin was so illuminating; and Herbert Romerstein whose literary career in regard to communism in America spanned 40 years.

In addition, I have gleaned valuable information from Tim Tzouliadis' book, *The Forsaken,* the tragic saga about American automobile workers, their families and others, who moved to Russia in the 1930s to help build the Russian equivalent of Detroit. My love of Model A Fords and my penchant for research led me to this riveting story. Many of these autoworkers were simply in desperate search of work during the Depression, but most believed they would be building and living in the new Soviet worker's utopia, as promised by Joseph Stalin. Almost all of them perished, either in slave labor camps, or were executed as enemies of the state after their usefulness ran out.

All of the writers I have mentioned are steeped in communist research in the twentieth century, and particularly the era from the late 20s to the 80s, which were the years that formed the basis for the political movement embraced by my stepfather Orville, my mother, and all of their friends who so impacted my formative years and beyond.

Uncovering the facts. My goal in writing about my early political exposure was not to produce a heavily footnoted history of American communism, but rather to concentrate on, in a far more personal manner, my eyewitness experiences and perspectives of the events of my younger life, and offer referenced historical background as required. In order to produce the work, I also relied on conversations with my stepfather and mother over many years, as well as their taped interviews, multiple books, periodicals, internet background research, references by researchers from the 25,000-page *Mitrokhin Archive*, the extensive *Index and Concordance to the Vassiliev Notebooks,* and the *Venona Decrypts.* The decryption documents are from the 1940s program released by the National Security Agency in 1995, which involved intercepting and decoding Soviet intelligence communications between Moscow and NKVD officers in the US. These are some of the American and Soviet documents that were made available for study and translation during the 1990s. The names of my stepfather and our family friends and associates are profusely sprinkled throughout them.

I have also spent some time documenting my parents' early background so that people might understand their psychological frame of mind which, in my opinion, helped propel them into the angry, dogmatic, and strange world of communism.

My involvement in this topic lay dormant for many years. It was the lead up to, and culmination of, the election of Barack Obama, and the increasing presence of the left-leaning Democratic Party which facilitated that event, that made me recognize that what I had grown up with was alive and thriving, and affecting whole new generations who have little education or understanding of this critical political movement.

What is alarming is the fluid nature of the labels and rhetoric that has allowed the far left ideology to work its way into the mainstream. And there are some very interesting factors that contribute to this chameleon-like movement. David Horowitz described the communist movement after the collapse of the Soviet

Union in 1989 as being freed from their traditional role of having to defend the Soviet government, complete with the growing backdrop of the atrocities of Stalin and the gulags. On the one hand they had been defeated; their reason for being no longer seemed viable. But as Horowitz so aptly observed, they were actually able to revamp and remold. By persistently continuing the push, they usurped, in essence, the traditional Democratic Party. By 2008 they emerged at the top of the political heap with an adoring media and academic force leading the charge.

Today, the modern Democratic Party is better described as the descendants of the Progressive Party of 1948, the far left faction whose roots were mired in a cloaked Marxist orthodoxy that promoted populist government. In fact, the term *Progressive* has become almost interchangeable with *Democrat*.

My political indoctrination was a direct outgrowth of this same movement. Leaving it behind had the effect of liberating me from a rigid set of rules that confined the soul. My life began anew when I began to see the world differently. The oppressive gloom of the left was suddenly at an end. The windows opened, and a fresh breeze was allowed to pass through the space. I felt free to prop up a Reagan sticker in the rear window of my car with pride, an immense load lifted from my shoulders.

What is painfully evident from all of my experience and research is that my step father, Orville E. Olson, was deeply involved in clandestine and subversive political activities whose aim was to replace American capitalism and democracy with Stalinist communism. Thus, he considered himself a righteous American patriot, following in the footsteps of Tom Paine and the American revolutionaries. My mother was also involved at a far less intensive, although naïve, degree. Nevertheless, her strident leftist views and support of Orville's political positions were indelibly etched in my young mind.

My hope, in the end, is to communicate the importance of learning about the roots of the modern left and persuading readers to understand the dire consequences of the natural progression of such an ideology in actual practice. At the same time, I will offer the reader a taste of the madness of the left and the politicization of every facet of life in their quest for control. I also wish to prompt conservatives to understand, as Horowitz puts it, "what they are up against."

* * *

PART I

PARENTS' FAMILY BACKGROUNDS, THE DEPRESSION, AND LEFTIST SYMPATHY

CHAPTER 1

MOTHER, FATHER AND GRANDPARENTS

I was born in St. Louis, Missouri, in November, 1942, eleven months after the bombing of Pearl Harbor and the entry of the United States into World War II. My parents remained married until I was about five years old. Within two years of their divorce, my mother remarried, which resulted in the beginning of my exposure to Marxist ideology.

My father, Henry Titus Shotwell, grew up on Long Island, NY, and my mother, Elisabeth Louise "Betty" Vonderleith, in Darien, CT. They met while students at Pratt Institute in New York City. My father graduated with a war-shortened degree in architecture, and my mother with a war-shortened degree in commercial art. They married in 1939 and, in June 1941, my older brother, Peter, was born; sixteen months later, I came into the world.

Mother's background. My mother always characterized her childhood as unhappy, stemming from having been adopted by her great-aunt and uncle at the age of three. She described them as quite cold and demanding; plus, they were of an advanced age and ill-equipped to be parents to a toddler.

The story of my mother's birth and first few years is something comparable to a star-crossed novel. In December 1916, my grandmother, Marion Lyon, an elegant 18-year-old girl, became the mistress of a 50-year-old Russian/German Baron, Edgar DeCramm (Von Cramm). DeCramm had recently arrived in the United States in order to pursue Russian government business interests. His official title was Councilor of State for the Romanov government. Besides his Russian home in St. Petersburg, he had estates in Latvia.

DeCramm was married, and his wife, Matilda, had two sons by her previous marriage, both serving at that time in the Russian navy. DeCramm also had an adult son from a previous marriage. The son and his wife were being held prisoner in Germany, where they were living when the war broke out. Matilda gained notoriety for striking up a friendship with the first American ambassador to Russia, David Francis. Her close relationship with him brought considerable scrutiny from the US State Department. DeCramm was also being investigated by the Russian authorities regarding his activities during the war. His general classification might have been that of a WWI German spy, but there is also evidence that he worked both sides, facilitating financial transfers out of Russia for both Russians and Germans.

Marion Lyon and L. Edgar DeCramm
c. 1917
National Archives

In early 1917, DeCramm "adopted" Marion, no doubt to avoid the US Mann Act, intended to stop the trafficking of young women across borders "for immoral purposes." The two traveled to Central and South America, eventually arriving in San Francisco in early 1918. DeCramm had gained the notice of the American State Department, partly due to his wife's ongoing situation, and he came under further scrutiny in San Francisco. He was soon arrested and detained at the Hotel St. Francis. His story was covered in the local papers, including the detail that Marion was in "a family way," as the *San Francisco Examiner* delicately worded it. He was eventually sent out of the country, likely due to an agreement to not reveal information about his wife's close relationship with the American ambassador.

Granddad Vonderleith and mother, shortly after her adoption, Pelham N.Y.
c. 1921
Shotwell family archives

Marion, in turn, went to Los Angeles, where my mother was born at the end of April 1918. After a year or so, Marion heard little from "the Doctor," as DeCramm was referred to in letters to her aunt that are in my possession. From the West Coast, she moved back to New York. There, abandoned by the father, and with seemingly few prospects, Marion placed her daughter in foster care. Marion's letters hint at a harsh existence, but it is a bit difficult to discern, because in 1920, records show she traveled by ocean liner "to visit friends" in Rio de Janeiro, and also ventured to Cuba. Such travel was not inexpensive.

While her daughter was still in foster care, Marion traveled to Paris looking for work in the movie industry. When it became clear that she could not support her daughter, she made the decision to follow up on her aunt's prior offer to adopt the three-year-old, and the arrangements were made. In keeping with the norms of the time, the adoption signaled a new beginning, and my mother's name was changed from Leila Lyon to Elisabeth Louise "Betty" Vonderleith. When I was growing up, Walter and Margaret Vonderleith were always recognized as my grandparents; I knew nothing of the adoption until many years later.

My mother railed her entire life against her adoptive German-American parents, about their severity, their demands on her to perform endless housework, and their lack of understanding of her emotional needs.

Her adoptive father, Walter Vonderleith, had an inward personality. He amassed an unruly collection of 40,000 volumes of books and a half-million prints during his life. But the collection was more a result of a hoarder's mentality than the product of a strict scholar. Books were stacked up six feet high throughout the three-story house in Darien, CT, and the beams of the vintage 1840 home sagged under the load. In one room, the stacks collapsed and the room became inaccessible for more than thirty years. I remember staying there during summers and following the narrow, crooked pathways through the stacked books with windrows of dust all about.

Grandparents, Walter and Margaret Vonderleith, c. 1912. Shotwell family archives

Grandfather Vonderleith, born in 1883, was always kind to me, although he was a stoic, somewhat distant, individual. I did not experience him with the same emotional baggage my mother carried. In 1961, some years after my grandmother died, he moved from Connecticut to California to live with my mother and younger brother. My older brother and I had both left for college. My grandfather handed over all his money from investments and the sale of his house in Darien to my mother, greatly relieving her of her precarious financial situation as a single mother. For this gift, however, she was quite unappreciative. She felt entitled to the money for all the perceived misery of her past. For about two years, she kept her small two-story apartment, requiring my grandfather and younger brother, Bjorn, age 10, to share the second bedroom. It was a painful experience for them both.

My mother always told me that while growing up she was clothed in ill-fitting, hand-me-down clothes for which she was still angry. I uncovered her Darien, CT, high school yearbook for 1935 in her belongings, which told a bit of a different story. She was named "The Most Popular, the "Most Attractive," the "Cutest," the "Most Original," the "Class Chiseler," the second choice for the "Best Figure," the "Best Dresser," the "Cleverest," and the "Second Best Looking." The yearbook also contained a prophecy that the young man named "The Most Dashing" would take "The One and Only" (my mother) to the Olympics. But the most complimentary description of her was that she was, "The Fairest of all the Flesh on this Earth." Photos of my mother growing up, with my grandparents and later during her college years, always showed her dressed very well, but there always seemed to be a hint of melancholy on her face. Of course, these were the Depression years, and the resulting financial strain on the family undoubtedly contributed to her outlook.

Granddad Vonderleith and mother, c. 1935. Shotwell family archives

The Vonderleiths were able to hang onto their beautiful home on Five-Mile-River-Road in fashionable Darien, even when my grandfather lost his job on Wall Street in the early 30s. However, for several summers, the family relocated to my great-grandparent's home in Pulaski, Illinois, while renting their home to a wealthy couple from New York. Through all of it, they were able to clothe and feed my mother, and send her to college. Despite these efforts, my mother remained staunchly unappreciative for the rest of her life.

In contrast, my grandfather arranged for his brother Henry, who was quite financially successful, to pay for the bulk of mine and my two brothers' college educations, to relieve that burden from my mother, who had little in the way of savings. Prior to my grandfather moving in with my mother in California, he had periodically sent her money for trips back east during the summers, and also helped out here and there during our family's many difficult financial stages.

Despite the era in which my mother grew up, it sounds as if she had far more going for her than she felt; from the entries in her high school yearbook, indicating she was popular and had a lot of friends, to marrying my father, who was the popular, good-looking class president of the School of Architecture at Pratt Institute. But she always characterized her youth as just the opposite; that she had been dealt a bad hand throughout her life. She expended a lot of energy blaming others for her perceived troubles and entangled relationships. I experienced her as being enormously self-centered and not interested in accepting responsibility for her choices and actions. In total, my mother's account of her childhood didn't entirely add up to me.

Memories of my grandmother are clouded, as she had frequent mini-strokes in her later years, which didn't allow me to accurately assess her true personality. By my mother's accounts, both grandparents were woefully unfit and unprepared for parenthood. She often stated that the most joyful times spent at home were being alone in her third-floor spacious attic bedroom, far away from her adopted parents. She repeated often that the happiest day of her young life was on her tenth birthday when they informed her that she was adopted. She also learned that her "Aunt Marion," who occasionally came to visit, was her birth mother. Her memory of being taken to speakeasies by her mother seems somewhat inappropriate today, but resonated in my mother's mind throughout her life as being colorful and fun. She also recalled the visits of her "aunt" in a chauffeur-driven Rolls Royce, and the elegant lady sitting with a parasol in the garden watching my mother play. My mother's memories as a three-year-old always incorporated a mysterious and romantic quality, and had little to do with the reality that her mother, abandoned by DeCramm, had moved to France and abandoned her as well. All of this now seems a perfect recipe for my mother's future decisions and travails.

In 2013, genealogical research revealed that Marion died in 1951 at 52 years of age. From the information obtained on her death certificate, under the name Ruth Marion MacDuff, Marion had been a homemaker married to a James F. MacDuff, and living in Oxnard, CA. She died of "alcoholism and barbiturate poisoning." In an ironic twist, our family moved to Hermosa Beach, CA, from Minnesota, about six months before Marion's death. Oxnard was only a couple of hours away. In some respects, I'm glad my mother never learned of her mother's fate, and was able to keep her mysterious and exciting fantasies alive. She would have been crushed to confront the hard reality of her mother's last years.

As for DeCramm, if he returned to Russia and his family, it's likely his properties would have been confiscated and he and Matilda would have met their fates during the revolution in a similar manner to other members of the Russian aristocracy under the brutal direction of Lenin and Stalin.

Parents' marriage. My mother and father were married in 1939, after college graduation. Their time together was short and tumultuous, complicated with, among other things, my father's emerging alcoholism, which he described as beginning at the age of twenty-seven.

In 1940, prior to the birth of my brother, Peter, my father was able to arrange an artistic endeavor for my mother, obtaining a commission through FDR's private secretary, Marguerite "Missy" LeHand, to create caricature illustrations of the president's travels, which were presented to him on his birthday. It was exciting for my mother to go to the White House more than once. Apparently, FDR was delighted with the product.

Parents, Elisabeth "Betty" Vonderleith and Henry Titus Shotwell. Wedding at Vonderleith home, Darien Ct. 1939
Shotwell family archives

I remember small pieces of early childhood with my parents, including trips to the St. Louis Zoo to visit "Joe" the gorilla. This was during the strain of the WWII years, when my architect father traveled extensively in connection with his work for President Roosevelt's Rural Electrification Administration, a creation of the WPA (Works Progress Administration). Although lost now, I remember seeing artwork that I created as a child, drawings of the skies filled with bombers and ribbons of bombs falling from their fat bellies.

I also have faint memories of Minnesota, after my parents moved there when I was about four. We lived for a period in the Francis Drake Hotel in Minneapolis. I remember visiting the Excelsior amusement park, fishing with my father on various lakes, and going downtown at Christmastime to see the decorated storefronts. My father loved the glitz of living in the hotel, and driving up to the fancy entrance with its well-dressed doorman. I also remember having dinner many times at a fancy restaurant (I think it might have been called "Charlie's") with its bar and white tablecloths. There, my brother Peter developed a taste for Lobster Bisque, and we carried live lobsters around, with bands on their claws, to show them off to the patrons. My father wanted to live at the hotel permanently. He spent time in the bar playing piano and enjoying the cocktail hours. He was self-taught on the piano but became extremely proficient during his college years playing afterhours with many of the better-known bands in Harlem night clubs. He told me he would have loved to have been a full-time musician rather than an architect.

Francis Drake Hotel, Minneapolis, MN. c. 1950.

Shotwell family archives

My brother and I reportedly spent a lot of time at the hotel unattended, going up and down the elevators, to the consternation of the management. My mother told me she hated the hotel living, complicated by the fact they couldn't really afford it. She said they also couldn't afford my father's fancy Buick, even though by now he had risen to be a partner in the architectural firm of Long and Thorshov, later Thorshov and Cerny.

Father's extended family. My father's extended family on Long Island was wealthy, and had always been quite liberal politically. Our branch descended from Quaker stock that had fled the British Civil War in the 1640s, and settled in New York, New Jersey, and later Nantucket Island. By the twentieth century the family prided itself on being fans of the Brooklyn Dodgers, and supporters of Democratic politics.

(l. to r.) Henry Titus Shotwell, Willets Shotwell, great-grandfather Shotwell, baby Peter Shotwell, Aug. 1941.

Shotwell family archives

The family grouping consisted of five intermarried families: the Mudges, Crarys, Ingersolls, Ingrahams, and the Shotwells. Mudge was a prominent New York attorney who had a private railroad car that regularly carried the gregarious, close-knit group into New York from Long Island. He was the famous lawyer that founded Mudge, Rose, Alexander (and later Mitchell and Nixon). My great-aunt Mary married Henry Ingraham, a lawyer, and their daughter, Polly Bunting, became the President of Radcliff College, and was also on the Atomic Energy Commission. (As an aside, Polly Bunting's son was one of the students on a three-masted ship that sank in the Atlantic; he miraculously survived. The incident was the basis of the movie "White Squall.") My great-aunt Mary was a major player in the reorganization of the City colleges of New York, and heavily involved in promoting public education. She had occasional lunches with President Kennedy to discuss national educational issues. Ray Ingersoll was the well thought of (so I'm told) borough president of Brooklyn and had strong ties with the Democratic Party machine of New York, particularly during the era of New York mayor, Fiorello LaGuardia. Even though the Shotwells were not in the same economic strata as others in the grouping, they were still an integral part of the extended family.

I spent many summers during my teens, in Northport, Long Island, and Darien, CT, living alternately with my grandfather and my father. The Crarys and Ingersolls owned a private island off the coast of Northport called Duck Island, and had their large summer homes there. The grounds included a softball diamond, a four-hole golf course, clay tennis courts, and little coves and inlets for their boats; an incredible private preserve. As a young boy, I remember well the annual softball games on Labor Day and Memorial Day, and meeting various dignitaries. Stories floated around that before my time there were many visits from Mayor LaGuardia, and also a singular visit from Israeli Prime Minister David Ben-Gurion. I personally recall two times quite vividly when I met and talked with the perennial socialist presidential candidate, Norman Thomas about baseball. He sat in a chair during the festivities, elegantly clad in a white suit.

Although politics was a frequent topic, this was not hard-core leftist ideology of the "working man's" Democratic Party. This was the other end of liberalism, the kind associated with the Kennedys. The politics here at play was the idealistic side of Democratic philosophy, better labeled as "benign liberalism," whose adherents would fall into the category of "limousine liberals."

What my father carried from his family as he went off to college was a benign liberal political outlook regarding helping the less fortunate, encouraging the Negroes to rise out of the oppression of the South, and other such endeavors. He gradually became more politically involved after his college years, but never at a level that could be described as socialist or Marxist. His architectural education was imbued with the liberal German Bauhaus International Style, promoting austere housing for the masses, eliminating what was perceived by the new order as the past indulgence in gaudy architectural ornamentation, and introducing modernism to the populace. This new order slowly crept into the architectural curriculums of most major universities, and usurped the old European Beaux Arts approach to design.

In his architectural profession, my father was primarily involved with business promotion, rather than design, and he was very good at it, given his gift of gab and gregarious nature. And it didn't hurt that the business needs of entertaining played well with his interests in parties, drinking, and affairs with women. Even so, I heard him say, "My ability to get business kept the firm going during the war years." He also mentioned something to me once about being involved briefly with some OSS (precursor to the CIA) airport facility on one of the Pacific Islands, but I was unable to confirm the story. He was ineligible for the military as polio had severely affected the muscles of his leg.

My father was the life of every party he attended, from his college years to the end of his life. He called everyone he met by their first name and developed friends both in the political and business arenas. For example, he became a close friend of Democratic star, Hubert Humphrey, and other emerging more conservative members of the Democratic-Farmer Labor Party. In later years, when I visited him in Chevy Chase, Maryland, he introduced me to his neighbor, Gen. Maxwell Taylor, and he was able to contact other highly placed people in the government, seemingly at will.

My father never ventured politically left of Humphrey, unlike my mother, and was always anti-communist in his basic political framework. It was a great personal loss for him when Humphrey was narrowly defeated by Nixon in the 1968 presidential campaign. He mentioned to me that, had Humphrey won, he would have been appointed the National Architect. I'm not sure if that was real or a fantasy, but with his patrician bearing and disarming friendly manner, he was able to present the proper image, despite his ongoing battle with alcohol. He lived his final years on Okracoke Island, off the coast of North Carolina, and died at age 66 of a heart attack during surgery for throat cancer at Duke University.

By delving into my parents' pasts, I've tried to create a foundation for my own upbringing. I also wished to describe my mother's general unhappiness and discontent, which played a large part in the choices she made in regard to politics, as well as her choice of her future husband. Further complicating her journey was the burden of raising two young sons, with little help from my father.

* * *

PART II

A HARD LEFT TURN

CHAPTER 2

NEW HUSBAND, ORVILLE E. OLSON

A short time into their marriage, my parent's relationship began to decline, no doubt abetted by my father's drinking, affairs, and frequent absences; but also due to the fact that he and my mother had generally incompatible backgrounds and personalities. My father, with his gregarious and refined persona, and my mother, with her generally narcissistic, humorless personality, were simply not meant for each other.

It's difficult to go back and reconstruct my feelings at that young age, but I do remember having once "run away from home." I was found by a woman quite a distance away, sitting on her front yard steps. I don't remember all of the circumstances, but it might offer a glimpse into how unhappy I was at a very young age.

Almost immediately after her marriage was terminated, and possibly before, my mother entered into an ill-fated relationship with Orville E. Olson, whom she had met, accompanied by my father, at friendly poker evenings and political events. She was not a well-educated woman in terms of academics, which may explain why she looked up to and was enamored by Orville's "bright mind." He was a dedicated communist ideologue, a good talker, and a world-class manipulator. He spouted communist doctrine and the benefits of the Russian model with ease.

Before my mother and Orville were married, I remember being brought to a political meeting in a large hall. We were put to bed in an adjoining room, and Pete Seeger sang us to sleep. Seeger, who recently died at age 94, was the popular folk singer/minstrel who was also a committed communist. He sang about and espoused leftist ideals throughout his career. One folksong I remember was about the engineer Casey Jones, on the "SP (Southern Pacific) line," but Seeger changed the final words and had Jones driving the "CP" (Communist Party) Line.

Orville had been married twice before. His first marriage produced two daughters and ended in divorce in 1937, largely due to his extramarital affairs. The discord culminated in a confrontation at a motel between Orville, his father, and brother, Bernie.

Orville's short-lived second marriage produced another daughter, born in 1937. He once confided to me that he never considered that relationship a "real marriage," because of its short duration. However, that notion would have been painful for any daughter to hear.

Orville and infidelity seemed to go hand in hand. During my mother and Orville's courtship, my mother discovered he was having an affair with "a former girlfriend," who was a secretary at the Progressive Party Headquarters. Infuriated, my mother abruptly broke off the relationship, sold her home in Minneapolis, and on a whim decided to relocate to Mexico. She purchased a new 1948 Oldsmobile convertible in the beginning of 1949, pulled Peter and me from the University of Minnesota Elementary School, and drove down through the dusty back roads to Mexico City.

Orville came down several months later and begged forgiveness. As suddenly as we had moved south, we returned to Minnesota. The two were married in 1949 and my half-brother, Bjorn, was born in 1950.

Orville's fourth and last marriage was to a woman I considered to be emotionally challenged. I understood that her family was grateful to Orville for having married her, even though it was, once again, a troubled relationship.

Orville, who loudly espoused the rights of the masses, the struggle of the "haves" against the "have-nots," and the demand for the government to care for each and every citizen so that "there would be no more want," took a less generous road with his own family. After the demise of his first marriage, one of his daughters told me, he contributed "about $100 every couple of years." He also never offered or contributed anything for the post-high school educational costs of any of his children. In my case, he did not like the fact that I was going to study architecture, as it was a "bourgeois" occupation that catered to the rich.

Orville's early life. Orville was born on November 24, 1908, the eldest son of a hardworking Norwegian Minnesota family. The family home was near the Mississippi River in a Norwegian-Swedish neighborhood. It was a strict Lutheran environment; no dancing, no cards, no liquor. I never saw him dance a step; however, contrary to his upbringing, cards, liquor, and smoking were an important part of his life.

During the twelve years I lived with him, and seeing and conversing with him over the ensuing years, I never remember Orville mentioning his mother or father. I learned about them from his interviews, and talks with his oldest daughters. They recounted that they and their parents lived for a time with Orville's father, Ole Bernhardt "Ben" Olson (1883—1938) who was fondly known by the grandchildren as "Papa." Ben Olson had no formal education, was a laborer in early life, and later worked as a clerk in the post office, rising to the position of Minneapolis assistant superintendent of mails. He was a union member whom Orville described as teaching him to "never cross a picket line" (an idea also ingrained in me in my early life). Orville's mother, Minnie A. Benson Olson, was a quiet homemaker with only an eighth-grade education. She was born in 1888 and died of cancer in 1930.

Early on, Orville became an avid reader, particularly in the areas of history and religion. By age seventeen or eighteen, he was attending a Lutheran seminary while working at odd jobs, including at the post office. During this time, he was preaching the Word and salvation through Jesus Christ at the penitentiary in Stillwater, Minnesota. In his interviews he mentioned he enjoyed hearing the *Amens* uttered by the prisoners in an Easter sermon, and admitted that he still occasionally thought about that period. He later said in a quizzical statement, "I still wake up at night sometimes, thinking about my belly's grinding and I'm thinking that I should've done such a thing. It's one of those things that stays with me all these years." He also stated, "I moved toward socialism partly because of the Bible," because the socialists were talking about "peace, love, and sharing," similar to what he had learned in church regarding the teachings of Jesus.

Orville was twenty-one when the Great Depression began. He attended the University of Minnesota for a year or so, but was unable to continue due to lack of money. Believing society should fund public education, he was angry that this benefit was not forthcoming for him. This turn of events fueled not only his evolution toward communism, but also his anti-capitalist rage.

By the age of twenty, he was no longer a believer in Christianity, and in short order substituted his religious ideology with political ideologies, beginning first with Norman Thomas style of socialism and later communism. After joining the Socialist Party, he was issued his red card, which he described as having to keep secret with his job at the post office. The deeper he entered into leftist politics, the more his anti-religious sentiments intensified, to the point where he became an avowed atheist and hater of the Christian religion, with particular disdain directed at the Catholic Church, considered to be the most anti-communist of all the faith traditions.

Interestingly, Orville always had a Bible on his bookshelf, sometimes explaining that it was "good history" and other times proclaiming that it was only there "for reference." During Orville's final weeks in a nursing facility in Santa Monica, California, he kept that same Bible on his nightstand. It must have held some deeper meaning as he certainly wasn't doing historical research then. I visited Orville many times in those last days, and a few times, at his request, I read Bible passages to him, sitting at his bedside. He listened intently, with no comment.

Orville's political history. In 1982, Orville was interviewed at length about his political history by Johnny Highkin, a son of one of his left-wing, Progressive Party friends from his Minnesota political days and later in California. The recorded interview was for a college political science class that he was taking. The unpublished interviews took place over thirteen sessions, which were transcribed by Highkin. I have studied this transcription in depth, as well as oral transcriptions from the Minnesota Historical Society, which sheds a bright light on Orville's emerging radical philosophy and the choices and actions they produced.

Describing his political life, Orville stated that he worked for Roosevelt's National Youth Administration and as an administrator of state relief funds in rural Minnesota during the mid-30s. Later, he was active in the Farmer-Labor Party as a political advisor to Gov. Elmer Benson, and during the administration (1936—38), he served as director of personnel for the Minnesota Highway Department. He referred to the highway department as a patronage job and a front for labor organizing; a good example of creating a legitimate-sounding government entity with ulterior goals. After the Benson defeat in 1938, Orville lost his patronage position, and moved on to various brief assignments including his short stint with the National Youth Administration in Washington, DC.

The following year, 1940, Orville was sent by Gov. Benson on a three-month tour covering thirty-one states in order to assess the leftist political environment of the country for the coming elections. During his travels from the Midwest to the West Coast, he met with many significant leftist leaders in the political field; the labor and maritime unions (NMU); and the progressive farming and agricultural heads. He went to pool halls, listened to political speeches, went to packing houses, spoke with railroad workers, farmers and other individuals. But one of the most impactful events occurred in San Francisco where he witnessed a Labor Day union parade comprised of sailors and longshoremen marching down Market Street in a procession that went for miles. The show of unity and the power of labor choked him up in the retelling to Highkin. After returning to DC, he wrote a report that accurately predicted the outcome of the upcoming interim elections. It was sent to the White House and was read with interest by President Roosevelt.

A second similar trip took place in 1945, when Orville traveled with Elmer Benson, Beanie Baldwin, and others to raise money for the 1946 interim elections and the National Citizens Political Action Committee, the precursor to the Progressive Party. The trip by train again covered the Midwest and the West Coast, with meetings with influential leftists, for the purpose of developing future plans for political action. Included on their schedule were visits to the irascible Harry Bridges, outspoken communist leader of the Longshoreman's Union; Anita Blaine (donor); FDR's son, James Roosevelt; CIO leaders; Hugh de Lacy (future communist congressman); the heads of the Communication Workers union, and many others.

During the war years, Orville secured work, through his extensive leftist connections in Washington, in the War Shipping Administration under deputy director Admiral Edward McCauley, concentrating his efforts on labor relations. He rose from McCauley's assistant to the role of director of recruitment for the Merchant Marine. He stated in his interviews that he applied for a commission in the army, but was turned down for "asthma and hay fever." He also stated that an FBI report regarding his leftist political involvement also prevented him from being accepted. (Earlier, in the same general vein, he claimed an FBI report had prevented him from landing a position with the Social Security Administration.)

He also claimed in his interviews that he turned down a commission offered to him by Admiral McCauley, as a "Lieutenant Commander in the Navy" with the proviso that he retain his job in war shipping. He stated he later regretted the decision as it would have provided him with a pension.

He also stated that at age thirty-six, in the waning months of the war, he asked Admiral McCauley to arrange a position for him as an ordinary seaman on a munitions convoy to Cherbourg and the Isle of Wight, as he had never been on a ship and was "scared to death of water all my life." This rite of passage took two weeks, and while he was in Cherbourg, he received word of President Roosevelt's death.

As special assistant to the deputy administrator of War Shipping, Orville received classified documents in the mornings and also spoke in detail about attending numerous meetings of the War Manpower Commission with top brass attending, including Secretary of War, Henry L. Stimson; William "Frank" Knox, secretary of the navy (also Roosevelt's vice president in 1936), James Forrestal, deputy secretary of the navy; Paul McNutt, chairman of the War Manpower Commission and War Production Manager of Sears Roebuck; Rear Admiral Emory S. Land; Admiral McCauley, and others. Orville's job was to sit behind the brass where he overheard numerous conversations of the buildup of manpower for the Manhattan Project, recalling that it was all very secretive. He also heard much conversation about a military production plant not far from Detroit where they were building 50,000 planes, and also spoke of the military's plans for the British to "take care of the North Atlantic" and "the Americans to handle the South

Pacific," machinations that Orville considered a devious ploy by the Americans to take over Britain's commercial interests in the South American region.

I have many thoughts on Orville's descriptions of his WWII years in his interviews. To my knowledge, he never had any medical issues with asthma or hay fever, no use of inhalers, no athletic restrictions, no prescriptions, and no breathing difficulties of any kind whatsoever. In his last years, his heavy smoking caused problems, but in his younger years any notion of breathing problems was a fabrication.

I am also suspicious of his claim of being offered a commission as a "lieutenant commander." He stated that thirty-six was the upper limits of the draft and that "he couldn't see the sense of running around in a uniform and being an officer in the navy and then continuing in the same job I had held previously." But, this was not entirely accurate, as forty-five was the cut-off age for the draft, making his altruistic attitude ring hollow. With no naval experience, other than a two-week voyage as an ordinary seaman, no navigational or leadership experience on the open seas, and with a distinct fear of water, the offer seems incredible, not to mention that the position is equal to that of a major in the army. A more detailed description of a lieutenant commander's duties makes it even more improbable: a "senior department officer or the executive officer (second-in-command) on many warships and smaller shore installations, or the commanding officer of a smaller ship/installation." It is more likely this enhanced history was due to some guilt that he was able through connections to circumvent the fighting war, although he was never short of negative comments about others who did the same, particularly in the case of Hubert Humphrey.

But far more important than Orville's enhanced personal military history is the fact that a man deeply entrenched in leftist politics, with a fast-growing FBI file, had access to valuable classified military information on a daily basis; was allowed to sit in on meetings with some of the highest figures in the navy discussing sensitive subjects that ranged from food and munitions shipments to our overseas military forces; was allowed to hear about the massive site in Michigan for building airplanes; and was present in meetings about secret deployment of allied naval forces in the Atlantic, as well as meetings discussing the enormous manpower and materiel increases for the Manhattan Project. The list of important subjects causes stupefaction when Orville's political history is considered.

In 1946, Orville again traveled to California, where he visited a group of Hollywood writers (many of whom were later blacklisted), and gave a talk to raise money for continuation of leftist causes. Among the group were Orson Welles, Dalton Trumbo, John Howard Lawson, Lester Cole, and others with whom he remained friendly for years. On that single visit he raised $15,000, an unbelievable sum in that era. He was also able to raise a similar amount from a private banker, which Orville used to found the Independent Voters of Minnesota. John Earl Haynes, in his book *Dubious Alliance,* cites Orville's leftist political contributions. "Communists developed another useful link to Farmer-Labor activists through Orville Olson, a secret party member . . . The contacts and relationships developed by the two (i.e. John Jacobson), proved to be of enormous value to the Popular Front over the next decade. After WWII, Orville Olson and John Jacobson emerged as two of the Popular Front's principal leaders. Olson and Jacobson also saw to it that Communists who worked diligently within the Farmer-Labor Association received a share of state patronage."

He was now not only at the top echelon of the left-wing political activities in the state, but he was also knowledgeable and well connected at all levels of the labor movement both in Washington and around the country. He was also an expert on the political intricacies of the various ethnic populations of Minnesota, knowledge that was vital for the election process. He relished the political manipulation, the subterfuge, and the masterminding that his job required in order to widen the reach of communist undertakings.

In the 1948 elections, he was appointed executive secretary and Minnesota campaign manager for the campaign of Henry Wallace, the Progressive Party's presidential candidate. Orville's primary role was to plan and implement left-wing political strategy and activities and attempt to woo back progressive members of the Democratic Farmer-Labor coalition. He also ran for governor of Minnesota on the Progressive Party ticket in the same election, even if there was no chance of winning, as the ticket had to be filled. His campaign consisted of one fifteen-minute radio speech, as all of the campaign funds had to go to Wallace.

Progressive Party cronies; Mother and step father Orville standing (upper left) Jim Youngdale, seated (4th from right), and believed to be Sol Adler seated (left center), c. 1947-48.

Shotwell family archives

The results of the election were the losses of the Progressive candidates, marking a definite setback for the communist organization. The defeat would result in the development of new tactics to achieve their goals. This will be discussed later.

Orville's extensive communist affiliations and sympathies were well known to family and friends when I was growing up, but not to the outside world, where he masqueraded as a "progressive" Democrat. When Henry Wallace asked him directly if he was a communist, Orville gave the evasive answer, "What do you think?" Wallace followed with, "Well, what about it?" Orville then responded, "Well, why don't you make a judgment on what I'm doing instead of what I'm called." Always the evader.

Orville's entire thirteen-session political interview is a paean to leftist politics, the communist cause, left-wing labor relations, and the many friends and collaborators he worked with. I had heard this information in bits and pieces for years, but the interviews stitched together the sequence of his work history and positions in a neat and tidy fashion. He exulted in how hard the communists worked prior to elections, in the precincts, distributing leaflets, and doing door-to-door canvassing. Orville described the 30s and 40s as exciting years where they (like-minded communists and left-wingers) would have the opportunity and the capacity to "change a world that was driving toward war . . . and it was possible to build a new kind of world."

The Soviet Comintern (Communist International): And how was this new kind of world going to come about and by whose direction? The US communist activity was, in fact, structured by the Soviet Communist International, or "Comintern," (1919–1943), an organization started by Vladimir Lenin in order to direct the communist movement worldwide; subservience to Moscow was a major tenet. From 1922 forward, the existing American communist parties were forced to follow the party line from Moscow. This included infiltrating established institutions in the US to further the goals of Lenin—namely to destroy capitalism the world over and replace it with socialism/communism. In his book *Defence of the Realm, The Authorized History of MI5*, Christopher Andrews, stated that their objective was to fight "by all available means, including armed force, for the overthrow of the international bourgeoisie and for the creation of an international Soviet republic as a transition stage to the complete abolition of the State."

For the next three decades or so, Americans such as Orville joined in the secretive mission to undermine the US government; some through the Communist Party USA (CPUSA), the Farmer-Labor Party, the Progressive Party, and many other leftist organizations that masked their real purpose. Some of these people worked overtly while others, like Orville, worked more secretly.

The 1921 Comintern (Communist International) *Guidelines on the Organizational Structure of Communist Parties, on the Methods and Content of their Work,* VIII, No. 53, spells out the secret methodologies for members:

> For an illegal party, it is obviously of critical importance in all of its work *to protect its members and bodies from discovery* and not to expose them by, for example, membership, registration, careless dues collection or literature distribution. Therefore, *it cannot use open forms of organization for conspiratorial purposes* to the same degree as a legal party. But it can learn to do so to an increasing extent [emphasis added].

It is important to understand the communist interpretation of socialism as distinct from communism. Again, I refer to the Comintern *Guidelines on the Organizational Structure of Communist Parties, on the Methods and Content of their Work, 1. General:*

> The communist Party should be the vanguard, the front-line troops of the proletariat, leading in all phases of its revolutionary class struggle and the subsequent transitional period toward the realization of *socialism, the first stage of communist society* [emphasis added].

Lenin also stated,

> The goal of Socialism is Communism.

Joseph Stalin's *Report on the Work of the Central Committee to the 18th Congress of The Communist Party of the Soviet Union*, March 10, 1939, outlined the program members were to follow in the transformation from socialism to communism in the Soviet sphere. He incorporated the need for a strong military, well-organized punitive and intelligence organs, vigilance against backsliding, and the importance of forceful propaganda in order to perfect Marxist principles; eradicate capitalist countries and convert them from "dictatorships of the bourgeoisie" to "dictatorships of the proletariat." Five months after this proclamation was issued to the party leadership, Stalin entered into the Russian/

Joseph Stalin's speech to the Central Committee of the 18th Congress of the Communist Party, March 10, 1939.

Nazi pact and its secret protocol to divide the territories of Romania, Poland, Lithuania, Latvia, Estonia, and Finland into German and Soviet "spheres of influence."

Orville was a staunch Stalin apologist to the bitter end with no equivocation. He subscribed to every jot and tittle of Stalin's writings and utterances, and wholeheartedly supported the Nazi-Soviet pact.

Orville often bragged to me about how difficult it was for the US to pierce Russian intelligence, but how easy it was for the Russians to infiltrate ours. This was a source of continual amusement that he understood well; after all, he was intimately aware of the extensive labyrinth of communist espionage in which he and his friends were involved. He attributed this reality to the fact that all Marxists were smart intellectuals, committed to the righteous cause, while all CIA/FBI personnel were stupid, low-intelligence reactionaries who simply did not have the brains or the fortitude to compete against the stronger foe.

When Soviet archives were opened for a period in the mid-90s, after the collapse of the Soviet Union, the extent of the financial and ideological control of domestic communist groups by Moscow was revealed in documents that have been analyzed by British researchers and also US researchers at the US Library of Congress. The *Vassiliev Notebooks* were compiled by Alexander Vassiliev, a former KGB intelligence officer and journalist, who smuggled them out of Russia. Among Vassiliev's notes, Orville is named with a description of his being a "secret communist," and "contact of Harold Glasser," whose extensive underground activities will be described in a Part III. These Russian archives have since been closed to further access by Vladimir Putin.

* * *

CHAPTER 3

MOVE TO CALIFORNIA

After the failed elections of 1948, Orville took a job as a salesman for a Minneapolis garment manufacturer called "Outdorables." He still wanted to stay involved in Minnesota politics, but the atmosphere was changing, and the hearings by the House Committee on Un-American Activities (HCUAA) were in full swing. Friends were urging him to come to California with the promise of employment with Prudential Upholstery Supply Co. in downtown Los Angeles, and my mother wanted the change as well. So in the fall of 1951, when I was nine years old, Orville reluctantly moved the family west.

One of my last memories before we left Minnesota was of the family having an impromptu celebration when President Truman fired Gen. Douglas McArthur. Despite their hatred for Truman, his dismissal of the outspoken anti-Russian, anti-communist general was roundly applauded. Regardless of my young age, my political indoctrination was already beginning, as I gleefully brought in the newspaper that carried the announcement. I had no understanding of the issues, of course, but the seeds were being planted.

Once in Los Angeles, we rented a home on the ocean strand in Hermosa Beach. During our brief stay there, I recall playing a few times on the sands with our neighbors, David and Ricky Nelson, sons of the iconic American Nelson family of *Ozzie and Harriet* fame.

A year later we settled in Westwood near the UCLA campus. This was my vision of Shangri-La—beautiful homes and nicely manicured yards, with the quaint college town with its Spanish architecture just a few blocks away. I developed lifelong friendships and enjoyed my outside world, I played Little League baseball, would go up to the old UCLA men's gym and watch John Wooden, during his early UCLA career, coach his basketball team that in later years would become so successful. Wooden's personality and Christian ethics were sniffed at in our home, yet he came to hold great personal meaning and substance for me; a man of unswerving principles who lived the life that he taught his players, and was an example to those who came in contact with him.

(L to R.) Peter, Bjorn, Orville, Mike, Hermosa Beach, CA. 1951.

Shotwell family archives

The Prudential years: In California, Orville and my mother also began a new chapter in their lives, while at the same time maintaining many of their former political friendships and associations. For the next 25 years or more, Orville was a sales manager for Prudential until his retirement in the late 1970s.

Orville was a tough, single-minded man, which was clearly on display in his work environment. As one of the salesmen working under him mentioned to me in later years, Orville was a "nasty prick." He lived to rile people, to demonstrate to them his intellectual superiority. Orville told me several times that once a salesman built up his area and was doing well, he would lop off some of the area and turn it over to others who weren't doing as well, or were newcomers. This was supposed to keep the salesman "hungry." Orville enjoyed the angry reactions of the men, and in his interviews, he justified his actions. He also confided to me that he didn't like it that the more successful salesmen were making a good deal more than he was. He had had offers to join with others in new ventures in the upholstery supply field, including one in particular which had allowed the participants to become quite wealthy, but Orville always refused. He was afraid to leave his steady job where the owners knew and accepted his radical political background. His fear was not necessarily irrational. I remember on more than one occasion seeing men sitting in cars on the street watching our house in West Los Angeles. On one occasion, in fact, I was approached by a couple of them, asking if my parents were at home; an unnerving experience for a young boy. They turned out to be FBI agents who were investigating Orville's and my mother's political involvement.

All of these things combined to keep Orville in a plodding and safe job, where he relished ridiculing his business-owner boss, whom he considered nothing more than an ignorant moron who stumbled into his money, and was raping the workers. It gave him much amusement to ridicule the gullible public and the callousness of American business when a less expensive fabric might stall on the market, but could be revitalized by a change of name, putting it in with a more expensive line and raising the price. The fact that the color, texture, or other aspects of the product might appeal more to a different segment of the public was not seen simply as a good business decision; it was the sign of capitalist greed and deception.

During his years with Prudential, he was proud of the fact that, as he described, "I became an employment agency for a lot of left-wingers from New York, and particularly out of the maritime union." One man he hired was Frank Carlson, District Organizer of the Communist Party in Los Angeles. In addition, he arranged for a Hollywood blacklisted writer, John Howard Lawson, to speak at an industry dinner for a fee of $50. Prior to this, Lawson had been the head of the Hollywood division of the Communist Party USA (CPUSA) and also served as the head of the Writer's Guild. But his finances had been hit hard after being shunned by the movie industry due to his communist activity and refusal to testify before the HCUAA, for which he served a jail sentence. So now the former high-riding screenplay writer was grateful for the fee.

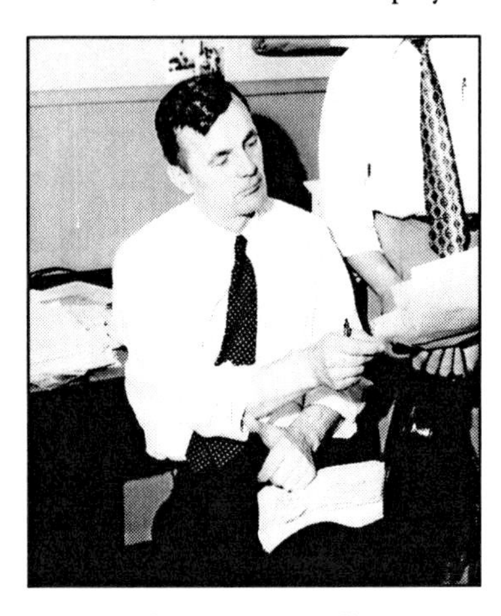

Sales Manager, Orville, at Prudential Upholstery, c. 1956.
Shotwell family archives

Orville also enjoyed giving books to his sales staff, whom he perceived as being politically uneducated. He claimed to have refrained from giving them "anything from the International Publisher, or other Communist Party literature." Instead, he included books by Howard Fast, who, for some unknown reason, he figured was non-political. The truth was that Fast worked for the CPUSA newspaper, the *Daily Worker,* in the 50s, and also wrote for the communist *Chicago Star,* edited by Frank Marshall Davis, Barack Obama's mentor. In fact, in 1953, for his service to the Soviet Union, Fast was awarded the Stalin Peace Prize by the Marxist/communist presenter W. E. B. Du Bois, and responded with gushing gratitude.

End of the marriage: Orville's and my mother's marriage lasted twelve years, ending in 1961, following angry court confrontations and all manner of mutual back-and-forth accusations.

During their court-ordered separation, Orville was caught stalking my mother, following her when she went out in the evenings, and peering through our windows at all hours. I saw him many times driving back and forth in front of our home. A restraining order was obtained by my mother's attorney and the stalking ceased. I testified against him in their divorce proceeding, as "mutual incompatibility" had not been adopted yet in California courts as a reason for divorce. I recounted to the judge how I once intervened in an altercation in our kitchen when a tipsy Orville moved toward my mother, threatening her with his fists. I'm certain I saved her from a beating by shoving him across the kitchen into the wall. He was a rough customer in an old-school fashion.

Following the divorce, my mother railed on about Orville's numerous faults and marital incompetence for the next 45 years. (However, those complaints did not include anything about his communist politics.) It wasn't until her dementia developed that her complaints faded away.

Orville's last days. During his later years, I never heard Orville repent or make any comments that perhaps he had made mistakes in regard to his political viewpoints or former political life. He was proud of his motivation to change the world.

Nearing the end of his life, he did voice some minor disillusionment with what had happened with politics in Russia, namely that people within Russia had installed some of the same type of bureaucracy that had existed at the time of the czar. He felt one of the primary reasons was what Lenin expressed, that the Russian people were uncultured (actually Lenin used the word "uncivilized"), and therefore were drifting back to old ways. Orville complained that even "ex-Reds" talked positively about Russia having been a grain exporter even under the czar, but not under the new order. He said they had forgotten the fact that the czars realized the profits from the exports after robbing the populace of the grain. Forgotten in this storytelling was the fact of Stalin's Ukrainian genocide for the same reasons.

Orville, August, 1975, at home – Age 67.
Shotwell family archives

This was a prime example of Orville's myopic views. Regardless of any chinks in his armor, Orville remained a diehard pro-Stalin and pro-Mao advocate to his death, never wavering from Marxism and the communist ideal; his fantasies remained largely intact. His health compromised by heavy smoking, he died in 1986 at age 78.

* * *

PART III

THE COMMUNIST UNDERWORLD AT WORK: ALLEGIANCE TO STALIN

CHAPTER 4

POLITICAL ACQUAINTANCES, FAMILY FRIENDS, AND RELATED PROMINENT FIGURES

What follows are short bios, along with my personal remembrances, of many of the people who frequented our home and were otherwise socially involved with Orville and my mother. Many of these people were actively involved with communist cells and intelligence gathering. The importance of this work is spelled out in *The Comintern (Communist International) Guidelines on the Organizational Structure of Communist Parties, on the Methods and Content of their Work, III. No. 12,* which stresses intelligence gathering and communications in furthering communist goals:

> Communist *nuclei* are to be formed for day-to-day work in different areas of party activity: for door-to-door agitation, for party studies, for press work, for literature distribution, *for intelligence gathering, communications*, etc. [emphasis added]

In addition, No. 8 of the same *Comintern Guidelines* states, "The Communist Party should be the working school of revolutionary Marxism."

Communist cells were part of the structure of the Soviet-directed espionage activities, and were known by various code names, including those of individuals heading them up. These cells were numerous, and many will be noted in the following pages.

The other major cog in the Soviet machine was the NKVD, the Soviet People's Commissariat for Internal Affairs, which was associated with the Soviet Secret Police, and directly executed the rule of power of the Communist Party. It was known for its political repression during the Stalin era and for activities on the behalf of the Main Directorate for State Security (GUGB), the predecessor of the KGB. (Other names for the KGB were Okhrana, Cheka, GPU, OGPU,

NKGB, MGB, and the MVD). Most notably, the NKVD ran the Gulag system of forced labor camps, where millions died from the barbaric conditions, starvation and disease. They also conducted mass executions and deportations, along with protecting Soviet borders; more broadly, the NKVD was involved with espionage, which included political assassinations abroad, influencing foreign governments, and enforcing Stalinist policy within communist movements in other countries.

Solomon "Sol" Adler: Orville's and my mother's very dear friend, Sol Adler was deeply committed to communist ideology. They both often voiced deep admiration for him and his lifelong commitment to the cause. Adler spoke several languages and was described as a "very bright man" by friends and associates. He was a chief intelligence agent for the US Treasury Department of the Roosevelt Administration in China during WWII. Whittaker Chambers correctly reported that Adler supplied weekly reports to the American Communist Party.

In 1945, Elizabeth Bentley identified Adler as a member of the Silvermaster Espionage Group. A 1948 memo written by Anatoly Gorsky, a former NKVD agent then living in Washington, DC, identified Adler as a Soviet KGB agent with the Soviet code name, "Sax" (alternately spelled "Sachs" or "Saks"). Sax appears in the Venona *Decrypts* as supplying information to the Chinese Communists, through both Gorsky and American Communist Party head Earl Browder. Adler's other KGB cover name was "Hello."

Sol Adler and Chairman Mao Zedong in Beijing. January, 1964. Courtesy, Prof. Chen Lin

Besides his contacts with US espionage groups, Adler also shared a house with Chinese Communist secret agent Chi Cha'o-ting, and State Department officer John Stewart Service, while serving as Treasury attaché in China in 1944. Service and five others were arrested the following year in the *Amerasia* magazine case. Harvey Klehr's 1996 book about the affair describes in detail the one thousand stolen government classified documents that were found in their possession, including US naval and military intelligence, British intelligence, Office of Strategic Services and US State Department reports; all involving Soviet espionage.

Adler, in his role as one of the US's leading diplomats, had attended the early meetings of the United Nations, first proposed at the secret Dumbarton Oaks Conference in 1944, where the framework was developed. He worked on the plans and organization for the conference, attended by American, Russian, English and other diplomats, which was coordinated by Alger Hiss. Hiss was later convicted of perjury and exposed as a Soviet agent when Whittaker Chambers defected and later exposed the labyrinth of the Soviet underground. More on this later.

To avoid the HCUAA hearings, Adler and his wife, Pat, defected, initially to England where he taught for a few years at Cambridge University, and then, in the late 1950s, to China. He never returned to the US. In China, he rose to be a senior advisor in the Chinese Intelligence Service where he worked closely with fellow American communist defector, Frank Coe, who had formerly been a member of the Silvermaster espionage ring and who had refused to answer questions regarding his Communist Party affiliations (he plead the fifth amendment) at the HCUAA committee hearings. In a memoir by Chen Hansheng regarding Cold War history and Chinese espionage, and in Prof. Chen Lin's memoirs, it is noted that Adler, from at least 1963 on, worked for China's Central External Liaison Department, an agency involved in foreign espionage. Adler's apartment in Beijing was also provided to him by the Liaison Department, which would indicate Adler's close working relationship with that unit.

(L. to R.), Albert Epstein, Sol Adler, Mao Zedong and Frank Coe, in Wuhan Hubel Province, China 1965.

Courtesy, Professor Chen Lin

My brother, Peter, apparently still remembering the warm feelings between Adler, Orville, and my mother, visited him in China in 1984, and later in the early 90s. Adler told Peter that he was lucky to survive the Cultural Revolution, and was able to do so due to the intercession of Chou En-Lai, who was himself under suspicion by the leaders of the Cultural Revolution.

Henry A. Wallace: Wallace was chosen to run for president on the Progressive Party ticket in 1948. He had been the third-term vice president under Franklin Roosevelt, but was replaced by Harry Truman for Roosevelt's fourth term. During the 40s, he had moved to the left of the political spectrum. He was a staunch opponent of the Marshall Plan and United States relations with Britain who favored closer ties with Stalin and Soviet Russia, making him a desirable choice as a candidate. Orville claimed in his interviews that he was not directly involved with recruiting Wallace; however, the issue is debatable. After the selection had been made, Orville was appointed as Minnesota chairman of the Wallace For President Committee.

Harvey Klehr, an expert on the Progressive Party and Minnesota politics of the 30s and 40s, wrote in a 2013 article that within the Progressive Party structure, "Wallace's chief speechwriters included such Communists as Victor Perlo, the head of the Perlo Espionage Group, David Ramsey, and Millard Lampell." Attorney's John Abt and Lee Pressman, prominent communists, were also key players in Progressive Party affairs.

Progressive Party Executive Committee (L-R, 1st row) Glen Taylor, Henry Wallace, Paul Robeson. (2nd row L-R) Rex Tugwell, Clark Foreman, Calvin "Beanie Baldwin, Albert Fitzgerald, Elmer Benson. 1948

Everett Collection Inc. / Alamy

Cambridge historian Christopher Andrew, author of *The Defense of the Realm*, as well as the authorized history of the British Secret Service, MI5, encountered references to Wallace in his study of the Mitrokhin Archive. He stated publicly in a lecture in Raleigh, NC, in 2003, that he believed Wallace was a KGB agent. Andrew continued from the podium, stating that, "Wallace's plan, had he been elected to the presidency, was to appoint Harry Dexter White as Secretary of the Treasury and Henry Duggan as Secretary of State."

Incredibly, the Mitrokhin documents list both White (KGB code name "Jurist") and Duggan (KGB code name "Frank") as Soviet agents. Unknown to the American public, both had been involved with Soviet espionage before and during the war.

In 1944, Wallace made a trip to the Soviet slave labor camp at Magadan. Unbeknownst to him, Stalin and NKVD generals had set up the Potemkin Village to appear as a volunteer labor camp. The village was staffed by NKVD personnel dressed as happy volunteers who were well-fed and content. Wallace's entire visit was coordinated by Stalin, including his being watched at all times by his hosts. The dance was well choreographed, and Wallace thoroughly swallowed the bait, believing everything presented to him.

Wallace was a badly misguided and naïve soul who, in 1951, after hearing from his friend, former Soviet spy Vladimir Petrov, about the true nature of Wallace's Soviet visit, admitted he was duped by Stalin. (Petrov miraculously survived the brutal purges of Stalin under Yagoda, Yezhov, and Beria. Even though a great number of his friends, colleagues, and superiors were arrested and executed, Petrov escaped unscathed.)

Henry Wallace, (1st row, third from left) and the U.S delegation, with guides, under image of Joseph Stalin outside Soviet Communist Party headquarters in Seimchan, Northeast Siberia, 1944

Henry Agard Wallace Papers, University of Iowa Library, Iowa City, Iowa

In his later years, Wallace turned away from his life as a Soviet apologist, became a Republican, and a supporter of both the US role in the Korean War, and Republican President Dwight D. Eisenhower.

By the time we had moved to California, Wallace had begun his "mea culpa" period, and consequently became persona non grata in our household. Orville never forgave Wallace for deserting the communist cause. The former friendship and reverence had dissolved into venomous denouncements. From the early 1950s on, Orville described Wallace in such terms as a "consummate dimwit," a "cheapskate" and a "malleable nincompoop" who was nothing more than a front man.

One can only shudder to contemplate the impact on American history if Wallace had remained vice president for Roosevelt's fourth term. The pro-Stalinist Wallace would have been eighty-two days away from being sworn in as president upon the death of Roosevelt on April 12, 1944. Luckily for the sake of the country, the anti-communist vice president, Harry Truman, stepped into that role.

During his campaign for president, Wallace was strongly supported by **Paul Robeson**, the famed opera star, all-American athlete, leading black militant, communist sympathizer, and unrepentant Stalin apologist to his death. At one point, he was strongly considered as Wallace's Progressive Party running mate in 1948. Robeson was a towering figure in our household, and his recordings and pro-Soviet political viewpoints were revered.

He was radicalized during his college years at Rutgers (1915–19), and later at Columbia Law School (1920–23), largely due to the painful legacy of segregation that he and other black Americans suffered in the US at the time. He was heavily influenced by the communist message to the black community in the 20s and 30s, which promised fairness and equality to everyone, and promoted Lenin and Stalin as the saviors of mankind.

From that point on, in both his professional and political career, Robeson identified with Soviet Russia as the superior example to follow. During a 1935 visit to Russia, Robeson was quoted in the *Daily Worker* as saying, "I was not prepared for the happiness I see on every face in Moscow . . . . It is obvious that there is no terror here, that all the masses of every race are contented and support their government." It is hard to imagine his enthusiasm given that this was at the beginning of Stalin's Great Terror and the unimaginable sufferings of the Soviet citizenry. However, he continued for years to share his effusive support during his world-wide tours and speeches.

In 1954, during the Khrushchev reign, Robeson stated, "The big lie is the fairy tale that the American people are somehow threatened by communism." Robeson's personal unhappiness may or may not have been associated with his divorcing of himself from American society, and his life spent in angry protestation, but is significant at some level. In 1961, after a wild party in Moscow, feeling empty and depressed, he locked himself in a bathroom and attempted suicide by slitting his wrists. Recurring depression was to follow him for the rest of his life.

Communist organizational poster, Jan., 1932

University of Pittsburg Digital Research Library

Soviet Premier, Nikita Khrushchev, and Paul Robeson (center) on vacation in the Crimea, c. 1960

INTERFOTO/Alamy

Perhaps to protect Robeson's reputation, leftists and Communist Party members, including Robeson's son, pointedly maintained that he was never a member of CPUSA. However, the fiction was laid to rest with HCUAA testimony in 1949 of ex-communist Manning Johnson. In addition, political science professor and writer, Paul Kengor, described the 1998 centennial celebration of Robeson's birth by noting that CPUSA head, Gus Hall, announced at the function: "Paul was a member of the Communist Party . . . a man of communist conviction . . . in every way, every day of his life. He never forgot he was a communist."

In 1952, Robeson was awarded the Stalin International Peace Prize by the USSR, and in April 1953, shortly after Stalin's death, he penned "To You My Beloved Comrade," in the *New World Review*, in which he praised Stalin, calling him "wise and good." His effusive letter also stated that Stalin was, "a man that the world was fortunate to have for daily guidance: Through his [Stalin's] deep humanity, by his wise understanding, he leaves us a rich and monumental heritage."

Even with the knowledge of the horrors committed by the Russian secret police and repressive government policies, Robeson refused to be critical of his beloved Stalin, remaining faithful until his death in 1976.

Folksinger, **Pete Seeger**, was another prominent Wallace supporter of great influence, and he was always mentioned with great affection in our household. Seeger, who admitted in later life that Stalin was a monster, and that his former opinions were misguided, still considered himself a communist up to his death.

Seeger's popular folk song group, begun in the 50s, was named "The Weavers." I often wondered what the origin of the name was since none of the members had the surname Weaver. The socialist *Internationalist Review* (Fall 1962), and other sources explained the linkage. The term was a way to pay homage to German socialist playwright, Gerhart Hauptmann, whose 1892 play, *Die Weber* (The Weavers), was about the uprising of the oppressed Silesian weavers in 1844 "against capitalism and bourgeois hypocrisy." The most famous line of the play stated, "I'll stand it no more, come what may." The epic script has been saddled with the honor of being called the "first socialist play." In the 20s, Hauptmann was honored by the Soviets for his work regarding the plight of farmers in Russian famines.

(L. to R.) Pete Seeger, Henry Wallace on airplane during the Progressive Party campaign through the South, Sept. 1948.

Library of Congress

What was not publicized by leftists was the fact that Hauptmann applied for membership in the Nazi Party; signed a German loyalty oath; had a heavily annotated copy of *Mein Kampf*; was a founding member of the eugenics organization, the "German Society for Racial Hygiene"; and had written a play in 1902 whose main character rejected his fiancée due to concerns about her genetic makeup and the potential effects on their children.

Calvin Benham "Beanie" Baldwin was a major figure of the Progressive Party, the assistant director of the CIO-PAC and was also a close-working associate of Orville. The *Venona Decrypts*, deciphered and updated in 2009, show Baldwin as a "secret communist" and "KGB US line." His wife, Lillian Traugott, also worked for Soviet Intelligence.

I recall Beanie Baldwin only faintly, but Orville made it clear that they shared common political views. After the 1948 election failure, Baldwin went on to be campaign manager for Vincent Hallinan, Progressive Party candidate in 1952. Prior to this, Hallinan served time in jail for perjury and contempt of court resulting from the trial of the communist head of the Longshoreman's Union, Harry Bridges, another acquaintance and associate of Orville. Later, Hallinan also served time for fourteen counts of tax evasion. In 1953, after Henry Wallace's political transition from left to right, he blamed Beanie Baldwin for the communist domination of the Progressive Party.

Calvin C.B. "Beanie" Baldwin seated at desk. C. 1948.

Library of Congress

Baldwin's name was always near the top of the list when Orville reminisced about his closest associates during his Minnesota political days.

Nat and Johnnye "Janet" Ross were old friends of Orville's. After he and my mother got together, they socialized frequently with the Ross's, both at our home and theirs.

Nat Ross joined the Communist Party at age twenty-four in 1928, and Janet joined in 1934 at the age of twenty-five. Janet's brother, Don West, was also a prominent Communist Party icon in the south. Authors Harvey Klehr and John Earl Haynes documented the Ross's activities in their three books, *The Secret World of American Communism; Venona: Decoding Secret Espionage in America;* and *Dubious Alliance: the Making of Minnesota's DFL Party.* Nat was head of CPUSA activities in the Deep South in the early 30s, and directed communist activities in the Dakotas and Minnesota from 1935 to December 1938. After a four-year assignment in Moscow, he returned (1943) as State Secretary of the Communist Party in Minnesota and served until replacement shortly after World War II by Carl Ross (no relation).

In an article he published for *The Communist,* in 1938, Ross quoted Earl Browder, head of the CPUSA. "We should constantly study our Party documents, and not leave them to gather dust on our shelves. We are the bearers of American culture and civilization and we must use every hour to qualify ourselves for that noble and historic role."

In 1939, at the tail end of Stalin's Great Terror, he and Janet moved to Moscow, where Nat was awarded a prestigious and important position in the Communist International (Comintern). The Comintern, in the words of J. Peters, head of the communist underground, ". . .is the international organization of Communist Parties in all the countries of the world and the World Congress was composed of delegates from all parties . . . and is the highest authority of the Communist Party Organization."

The Voorhis Act, passed by Congress in 1940, required political organizations controlled by foreign powers to register with the Justice Department. The CPUSA, being directed by the Soviet Comintern, was forced to officially relinquish that tie. However, Nat Ross's secret report to the Presidium of the Executive Committee of the Comintern guaranteed everything would stay the same: "Despite the current law . . . the entire party membership . . . will be drawn still more closely together, under the banner of the Communist International."

I recall hearing from Orville about one of the Ross's experiences in Russia, traveling through war-ravaged areas immediately after the Battle of Stalingrad, passing frozen bodies stacked like cordwood on the sides of the roads, and their sleeping in a shelter formed with frozen bodies packed over with snow to form the walls.

While living in Moscow, Janet was the communist *Daily Worker* correspondent. She used the pen name Janet Weaver in her articles. Her brother, Don West, also assumed the pen name Jim Weaver for much of his work. As with Pete Seeger's singing group, both Janet and Don incorporated the name Weaver as a paean to Hauptmann's play.

Janet Ross had access to journalists and American embassy diplomats. She became one of the principal informers to the Soviets during the war years of 1941–43, and her sensitive reports were sent by George Dimitrov, head of the Comintern, directly to Foreign Minister Molotov and the NKVD. Dimitrov referred to her as, "Our American correspondent, comrade Janet Ross." She was a devoted Stalinist and considered by the communists as a "Soviet patriot." Her duplicity is recorded in Herbert Romerstein's book, *Exposing Soviet Espionage and America's Traitors.*

Janet was also involved with political theater in Minnesota, which had its roots in Germany and the Soviet Union in the 1920s, and was fueled by a new generation of American playwrights brought together by leftist political activists. The most important leftist group was the Theater Union Players, consisting of members of the Socialist Party, the Socialist Workers Party, and the Communist Party.

In his interview, Orville recalled something his dear friend Janet had said the day before at a reunion of old political friends in California. She remarked, "They [the communist left] had a sense of doing something really meaningful for people."

It is almost impossible to wrap one's mind around the true meaning of Janet's statement. The Ross's were engulfed in Soviet policies with the sworn purpose of dominating the world, and they were ready to give up their lives for it. So "doing something really meaningful" meant bringing down the government by any methods required and replacing it with their ideal, the reality of which amounted to one of the most horrifying regimes in the annals of mankind. Their imperiousness was evident in their embracing the lofty self-assessment that they were the "bearers of American culture and civilization," for which they gave Stalin and the Soviets their all. That was their "noble and historic role" and they did "use every hour to qualify" themselves for their designated tasks. In the end, they felt no remorse for their actions.

Roger S. Rutchick was not only a close friend, but was our family attorney. FBI files indicate that Rutchick was a key figure in the American Communist Party (CPUSA). My mother claimed that, regarding political issues, Rutchick was the "brains of the outfit." I found this comment a bit ironic, as it seemed to undercut Orville's own self-image and position of authority as one of the three chief strategists of the Farmer-Labor Party. Born in Poland, and six years Orville's senior, Rutchick attended Macalester College in St. Paul, Minnesota. In 1933 he was appointed Assistant State Attorney General. From 1936–38 he was Gov. Elmer Benson's secretary, and used his position to cover for and protect internal communist activities.

When we relocated to California, Rutchick was left in charge of shipping much of the family's furniture to our new location. A dispute arose when Rutchick held back some of it for himself; he claimed it was payment for past work performed for Orville.

John "Johnnie" Jacobson was a political ally and another member of Orville's close inner circle. He worked under Orville as the assistant director of personnel at the Highway Department in Minnesota, and the two became long-term friends. Orville referred to Johnny as a "born teacher." My remembrance of him in my early youth was as a friendly, good-natured man, and we looked forward to his company.

It is stated in the *Vassiliev Notebook*, however, that Jacobson, like Orville, was a secret member of the Communist Party. He was also the regional director and national representative of the CIO Political Action Committee (PAC). In Orville's interviews, he recalled an FBI agent interviewing him about Jacobson's communist activities, apparently not having been briefed about whom he was talking to.

Meeting with members of the Independent Voters of Minnesota (l. to r.) Senator Claude "Red" Pepper, V.E. Mickelson, Orville E. Olson, Campaign Director of the DFL Party, John M. Jacobson.

The Minneapolis Star, Fri. Oct. 18, 1946

Elmer Benson: Another key figure in Orville's life, and in a sense a political mentor, was former Minnesota governor, Elmer Benson, who took office in 1936 upon the death of leftist Democratic Governor Floyd B. Olson. Benson continued the liberal policies of the prior governor, but went even further to the left and lost badly to liberal Republican Harold Stassen in the 1938 gubernatorial elections. Benson described himself as being a "radical," an "unreconstructed leftist radical," and an "early socialist sympathizer." He was an "ardent foe of capitalism" and offered strident support of communists, and Joseph Stalin in particular, up until his death in 1985. Benson was quoted in an interview two years before he died saying, "Stalin did some things that were pretty rough. But maybe, just maybe, if he hadn't done it, maybe the nation would have been taken over by the worst enemies of mankind—the Nazis." This was dubious justification, to say the least.

Elmer A. Benson, campaigning for governor of Minnesota, c. 1936

Minnesota Historical Society

Benson was a political enigma of sorts. According to John Earl Haynes, who has written extensively on the subject, "There is nothing in Benson's public statements or his private papers that show any significant interest in Marxism-Leninism." However, "from 1936 onward

Benson was one of the CPUSA's most steadfast high-profile political allies. What stands out most in his papers and rhetoric is his loathing and hatred for big corporations and big finance. And perhaps this was his tie to communism."

Prior to US involvement in World War II, Benson was an outspoken opponent of our support of Great Britain against Hitler's Germany. This position directly resulted from the secret August 1939, German/Russian non-aggression agreement (Ribbentrop/Molotov Pact) which guaranteed that neither country would ally with or aid an enemy of the other country. It also included the secret protocol that divided the territories of Romania, Poland, Lithuania, Latvia, Estonia and Finland into Nazi and Soviet spheres of influence. The Germans broke the short-lived pact by invading Russia on June 22, 1941. Benson abruptly reversed course and was now a re-born anti-Nazi and proponent of Roosevelt's support of Great Britain. He never fully explained his change of heart, but it was clear that his pro-Russian sympathies governed his positions, as it did for Orville and other die-hard Stalinists. Initially, the German/Russian pact's very existence was denied as western fabrication. Later, with evidence that was impossible to repudiate, the pact was characterized in a positive light as a brilliant ploy by Stalin to gain time for war preparation.

As mentioned, Orville served as Benson's director of personnel for the Highway Department, but his self-described clandestine purpose was conducting behind-the-scenes activities involving labor organizing. In addition, both men were intimately involved with the 1948 Henry Wallace campaign. Benson's role during that time was as the National co-director of the Progressive Party and he was also instrumental in the merger of the Democratic and Farmer Labor parties.

Baldwin, Olson and Benson, St. Louis, 1945

Benson's ardent anti-capitalistic rhetoric and political posture was not on display in his personal financial dealings, where he operated as an unmitigated capitalist. After he left office, he organized a group of wealthy investors who, with the information gleaned from his former role as commissioner of banking in Minnesota, bought up the best of bank-owned prime farmlands, forfeited by bankrupt farmers, at extremely low prices. He accumulated significant wealth from these dealings.

From my perspective, accumulated from years of conversations with Orville, I'd always assumed that Benson was, in fact, a communist, albeit secretly.

His support of the communists was unwavering, and he even elevated secret communists like Orville to positions within his administration. (It was not, however, a secret to Benson.) During speeches, Benson bragged about the thick file the FBI had compiled regarding his political activities; it was his badge of honor. Considering all of the adulation heaped on him by Orville and my mother through the years, and our periodic pilgrimages to the Benson farm, if Benson were not an official communist, he was as close as anybody could be without applying the label; and, as has been shown here, Orville simply did not have non-communist friends.

In recalling Benson, Orville felt that his abrasive confrontational nature had not allowed him to achieve the long-term leftist political goals that they were fighting for. As a result, he was soundly defeated by liberal Republican, Harold Stassen, in the 1938 elections. Had Benson been more inscrutable in his dealings, Orville surmised, he could have been far more politically effective.

Frederick "Blackie" Myers: Myers, a dedicated communist, was heavily involved with Harry Bridges and the International Longshoreman's Association battles on the docks in the 1930s and 40s. He was a vice president and one of the principal organizers of the National Maritime Union (NMU), which was founded in 1937. He also served on the National Committee of the Communist Party (CPUSA) and openly declared his membership.

On a fairly regular basis, we visited the Blackie and Beth Myers family in the San Francisco area. On one such trip sometime in the mid-50s, I remember my mother and Orville giving them money to buy shoes for their family. Myers was known to be perpetually broke, partially due to his penchant for alcohol. I recall my mother not being happy with the arrangement because it created a hardship for our own family.

Charles "Charlie" (Krivitsky) Kramer also moved to California from Washington, DC, in the early 50s, with his wife, Mildred. He was one of Orville's closest political allies. I recall many weekends spent with Kramer and his family, including events at the Unitarian Church. We also often visited their home in the West Hollywood area. They, in turn, would visit us at our home in Westwood, and later at our home in Sherman Oaks for summer pool parties.

Evidence of Kramer's membership in the Communist Party USA and his contacts with known Soviet agents comes from several sources: the direct testimony of Whittaker Chambers, Elizabeth Bentley, Lee Pressman, and Nathaniel Weyl; the Venona decrypts; the *Vassiliev Notebooks*, and the Moscow archives of the SVR (Soviet Foreign Intelligence Service that replaced the KGB).

Kramer also wrote a biography at the NKGB's (Soviet state security agency later folded into the NKVD) request in 1944, which is included in the Vassiliev transcripts, where he described doing Communist Party work beginning around 1928, and officially joining the Communist Party in 1930. Mildred, joined the party in 1934 after serving for several years as a courier. In addition, Hope Hale Davis in her book, *Great Day Coming, Memoirs of the 1930s,* describes attending her first Communist Party meeting at the Kramer's apartment, which was led by Kramer and Victor Perlo:

Charles "Charlie" (Krivitsky) Kramer testifying before the HCUAA. 1948.

Charles explained that "we would try to limit our knowledge of other members, in case of interrogation, possible torture." Kramer explained that as members they were expected to contribute money to the CPUSA. "Basically that would be ten percent of our salary."

Kramer worked for far-leftist Florida senator, Claude "Red" Pepper; was a member of the National Labor Relations Board; and held other positions within the FDR administration. He was also identified as an NKGB source in several World War II intelligence cables that were partially decrypted in the course of the Venona operation, and released in 1995–96.

He appeared under three cover names, "Plumb," "Lot," and "Mole." The last identification was confirmed in notes on the "Mole" file made in the early 1990s by Vassiliev. In addition, Kramer was identified as a member of the Perlo and Ware espionage groups. According to the Soviet archives, Charles Kramer was instructed to try and recruit Robert Oppenheimer, head of the Manhattan atomic bomb project, as a spy, but reported back to his Soviet handlers that Oppenheimer was a "liberal" and not a communist.

On May 6, 1953, when Kramer was called to testify before a Senate subcommittee on the judiciary regarding "Interlocking Subversion in Government Departments" in relation to the Administration of the Internal Security Act and other Internal Security Laws, he refused to answer any questions about his communist background.

I never met the Marxist economist, **Victor Perlo**, but since Orville worked closely with him in the Progressive Party campaign, and many of our family friends were involved with both the Perlo and Ware Espionage Groups, I am including both histories.

Victor Perlo was born in 1912, the son of Jewish parents who had emigrated from Russia. In 1933, he joined the Communist Party while a student at Columbia and remained true to his ideology for life. At 25 years old, he went to work at the liberal think tank, the Brookings Institute. He was a contributor to the communist press under pseudonyms, and secretly assisted I. F. Stone in gathering information for exposés. He headed the Perlo espionage group of agents in the US, which included a Senate staff director. The ring supplied the Soviet Union with economic, political and military intelligence, including data about US aircraft production. He infiltrated the US Department of Commerce where he prepared economic data for the Secretary of Commerce, Harry Hopkins, who was one of Franklin Roosevelt's closest advisors. Records in the KGB Archives, based on examination by Allen Weinstein and Alexander Vassiliev in *Haunted Woods,* describes the extensive data passed on to the Soviets.

Victor Perlo, head of the Perlo Espionage Ring, testifying before the HCUAA, 1956

At the Division of Monetary Research, Perlo served with Harry Dexter White, Frank Coe, a member of the Silvermaster espionage group who fled to China to join Sol Adler and other American expatriates in the early 50s, and Harold Glasser. The Russian archives have irrefutably identified White, Coe and Glasser as Soviet agents; and Harry Hopkins, if not an agent, was a fellow traveler and devoted friend of Soviet Russia. In 1948, Perlo obtained a position as an economist for the Progressive Party and was instrumental in developing the party platform.

Spartacus Educational reported that Victor Perlo divorced his wife, Katherine in 1943. In April 1944, she sent a letter to President Roosevelt naming her husband and several members of his group that included Orville's close friends, Harold Glasser, John Abt, Nathan Witt, and Charles Kramer, as Soviet spies. Unfortunately, they escaped FBI arrest which would likely have curtailed their espionage activities. The anti-communist historian, Kathryn S. Olmsted, has argued, "Possibly the FBI discounted the tale of what they considered coming from an unstable, vengeful ex-wife." Perlo died in 1999, a devout Stalinist/Marxist to the end. After being fingered by Elizabeth Bentley in 1947 as head of the espionage group, Perlo plead the Fifth the following year before the HCUAA, and again in 1953, before the Senate Committee on Internal Security.

Harold Ware, the son of Ella Reeve "Mother" Bloor, one of the earliest members of the Communist Party USA (CPUSA), was educated in communism from youth and spent many years in the Soviet Union. He also fell in love with farming at a young age. He later used his expertise, and his and his wife Cris's association with the Quaker Society of Friends of the Soviet Union to arrange equipment, expertise, and manpower (including themselves) to be shipped to the Soviet Union for use in the development of communal farming during the years of the Soviet famine (1946–47).

He returned to the US with funding from the Comintern to finance Communist Party organizing among the farmers. A member of the Communist Party from the early 20s, he attended the Lenin School in Moscow, an institute for the study of sabotage, revolutionary organization, and espionage. When he returned to the US, he wrote secret reports about US food production that were sent to the Comintern, receiving praise from Lenin himself. In the 1930s, Ware worked for the Agricultural Adjustment Administration (AAA) department of the federal government and helped set up the Washington Soviet underground apparatus under J. Peters that included some of Orville's close associates, including Charles Kramer, and the attorneys for the AAA, Lee Pressman and John Abt, who had a great influence on US policy at several levels.

Harold Ware, head of the Ware Espionage Ring, c.1935.

Tim Davenport collection, Hoover Institution Archives

The Ware Espionage Group was a secret arm of CPUSA, and was also an adjunct of the Soviet NKVD. By 1934, a year before Harold was killed in an automobile accident, the Ware group had about seventy-five members and was divided into about eight cells, one of them headed by Charles Kramer and Victor Perlo. They were first recruited into Marxist study groups and then into the CPUSA. Besides Kramer, Pressman, Abt, and Perlo, other prominent, verified communists associated with the group included Alger and Donald Hiss, George Silverman, Marion Bachrach, Nathanial

Witt, Nathanial Weyl, and Harry Dexter White who became FDR's director of the Division of Monetary Research in the United States Department of the Treasury.

Each of these agents not only provided classified documents to Soviet intelligence, but was involved in political influence operations as well. Membership was highly secretive, with many enrollees eventually infiltrating into higher levels of the United States government during World War II.

Harold "Hal" Ware, head of Society of Friends of Soviet Russia, (dark hat, rear seat) and Crista "Cris" Ware holding steering wheel, visit to Toikino near Perm at the foot of the Ural Mountains in Soviet Russia. June 18, 1922

SPUTNIK / Alamy

Another close political ally in the Farmer-Labor Party (later the Democratic Farmer-Labor Party, DFLP) was **James "Jim" Youngdale**. Along with Nat Ross and Orville, the three were the chief political strategists for the DFLP. Youngdale was described as a "protégé" of Elmer Benson. He ran in Minnesota's 7th District as a DFLP candidate for the US House of Representatives in the 1948 elections and was narrowly defeated, receiving 47.5% of the vote. He was a professor at Mankato State College (now known as Minnesota State University, Mankato), and wrote books on populism and Minnesota radical politics. Orville always referred to Jim as a person he mentored. He was young, vigorous and likeable, and struck me as one of the more congenial persons in Orville's crowd of friends.

Youngdale's political fortunes were pretty well shattered after the 1948 Minnesota elections when Hubert Humphrey emerged dominant with a strong anti-communist platform. Nevertheless, he remained a committed leftist for the rest of his life. I'm uncertain whether Youngdale had a Communist Party affiliation; however, it bears repeating that I cannot remember a single close friend of Orville's who did not have some kind of association with the Party and the left.

Harold and Faye Glasser had frequent contact with Orville and my mother, and though I have little personal recollection of them, Harold and Faye were always held in high esteem and were frequently mentioned in conversation. The Venona decryptions state that Harold, who worked in the US Treasury Department under Soviet agent Harry Dexter White, was a "Soviet source/

agent," whose KGB code name was "Ruble." Orville was described in the *Vassiliev Notebooks* as being "a contact of Harold Glasser."

Elizabeth Bentley further identified Harold as a member of the Perlo espionage group. The *Vassiliev Notebooks* also state that Harold's wife, Faye, was a Soviet courier between the KGB Station and her husband.

Harold Glasser, former Treasury Dept. economist, testifying before the Senate Internal Security sub-Committee, April 23, 1953.

In 1945, Pavel Fitin, the deputy head of the NKVD and director of Soviet Intelligence during WWII, stated that Glasser felt slighted when others he worked with received Stalin's Order of the Red Star; however, it is quite possible he received the honor later.

Fitin stated in Soviet records, "Our agent RUBLE, drawn to work for the Soviet Union in May, 1937, passed initially through the military 'neighbors' and then through our station, valuable information on political and economic issues."

Glasser's intelligence found its way into thirty-four special reports to Joseph Stalin and other top Kremlin leaders. Fitin continued, "To our work RUBLE gives much attention and energy (and) is a devoted and disciplined agent."

Glasser also worked for the United Nations Relief and Rehabilitation Administration (UNRRA). Sometime in 1937, while still working for the UNRRA, Glasser was clandestinely transferred to the underground Soviet Main Intelligence Directorate GRU (*Glavnoe Razvedyvatel'noe Upravlenie*) to report on US government activities.

Glasser's transfer was affected by a Hungarian, Alexander Goldberger, known by the various aliases, "**J. (Joseph) Peters,**" "Sandor Goldberger," "Isador Boorstein," "Steve," and "Alexander Stephens." He became involved in communism during the Russian revolution, and emigrated to the US in 1924 where he became an organizer for the Communist Party. J. Peters, as he was commonly referred to, established and directed the CPUSA underground apparatus in the US from the early 1930s to 1938. His specialties were in surveillance, exposing infiltrators, protecting Party records from seizure, disrupting leftist movements not loyal to Stalin, and maintaining contact with the embedded Ware espionage group. Peters was a delegate to the 6th Congress of the Communist International. Rather than answer to a summons by the

HCUAA in 1948, Peters defected to Communist Hungary, where he died in 1990.

Solomon "Sol" Lischinsky: Orville met Sol and his wife Melva in 1939 in Washington, DC, where he went seeking work after the defeat of the Benson administration in 1938. Their strong friendship lasted until their deaths in California in the 80s. Along with my mother, the four were considered best friends. Sol was a warm, kind, humorous man, and had a smile that lit up his face. Of all of my parents' friends, Sol was the one I most looked forward to seeing, both at our home and at his family's Spanish-style apartment in the Fairfax area of Los Angeles. A mathematician by training, he tutored me a few times in my high school years, and was patient in dealing with my frustrations in that realm. He loved tennis, playing frequently, and was also a casual businessman who at one point purchased a small business that manufactured plastic weaning cups for babies. I recall him grousing about having to go to the casting factory and staple cellophane bags for shipment.

Sol was the least overtly political of all of Orville's friends, or so it appeared to me as a young man. As an adult, I was able to have political discussions with him that were blessedly not bound up in party doctrine. In fact, during one discussion, he volunteered that he was grateful that there were "bright men in Washington that were able to manage the country's finances." It was quite a shock to hear something positive about the US government from any of Orville's and my mother's friends.

I had only been aware of one politically related incident involving Sol, and that was his move, with Melva, to a dirt farm in Virginia to escape the Washington political scene. He had also worked for the United Nations Relief and Rehabilitation Administration (UNRRA) and served as the head of the Balkan Department of the UNRRA during the FDR administration.

Although he was out of the limelight of politics when I knew him, the revelations I was uncovering about the rest of our family friends made me decide to look further into Sol's background. I discovered that his early years, during which he became friends with Orville, were every bit as taken up with communism as the others. I discovered his name in the Venona Project archives, which stated that in 1942 he worked for the Select Committee Investigating National Defense Migration of the US House of Representatives (the Tolan Committee). The Dies Committee discovered that practically all staff members on the Tolan Committee, excluding the congressmen, were either members of the CPUSA or followers of the Communist Party line. In his Washington years, Sol was a member of the Perlo group of Soviet spies. His KGB code name was "Rock" (ROK) which was appropriate, as he was a thick, strong man.

When Sol and Melva left the farm in Virginia for Los Angeles in the early 50s, they retained ownership of the property and turned the land over to sharecroppers. When the first phase of Dulles International Airport was built on land adjacent to Sol's, he didn't sell. However, when his property was needed for an expansion runway, he relented, making a financial killing which allowed him to live comfortably for the rest of his life.

My mother remained close friends with Sol long after her divorce from Orville. They even became business partners in the ownership of an apartment building in Hollywood (a decidedly capitalist venture). Their camaraderie was evident in their years-long ritual of working on crossword puzzles together over the phone. I know she missed his company greatly after his death, as did I.

John Toussaint Bernard was yet another close friend and associate of Orville and my mother. He was a former congressman from Minnesota (1937–39), and a native of the French Island of Corsica. Bernard was born in 1893 and was Orville's senior by 15 years. He did not run for office until 1936, when he was elected as a member of the Farmer-Labor Party and served only one two-year term. He was known during his brief tenure for casting the sole vote against the US resolution banning arm sales to both national and rebel forces in Spain during the Spanish Civil War when the US government was attempting to remain neutral.

Bernard's personal secretary in Washington was Marion Bachrach of the Ware Espionage Group, who was the sister of communist John Abt. Marion later rose to the next-to-highest rank in the Communist Party (CPUSA).

During his time in politics, Bernard steadfastly denied being a communist or a sympathizer, even though at the time, the outspoken freshman congressman was inserting *Daily Worker* articles into the congressional record. The truth came out later in life when in 1977, at a party in Minnesota honoring Bernard and attended by CPUSA leader Gus Hall, Bernard accepted his Communist Party card. Nat Ross, the Minnesota communist leader, claimed he was the person who convinced Bernard to run for office.

John Barnard (r) with author's mother; Harry and Elspeth Highkin with sons, John and Greg (rear). Author in the foreground. Hermosa Beach, 1952

Shotwell Family photos

A photo taken by Orville when John Bernard was visiting in 1952 shows the family and a few friends out on the sand in Hermosa Beach, California. I recall Bernard's visit was a joyful reunion. Later, in retirement, Bernard moved to Long Beach, California. Bernard's name was often mentioned by Orville as a stalwart who stood tall against Fascism and US foreign policy.

Also included in the photo are Orville's and my mother's close friends Harry Highkin and his wife Elspeth. Their son, Johnny, Orville's interviewer, informed me his parents met at a Communist Party meeting in Minnesota. Highkin was a professor at Cal State Northridge, and a fellow leftist who idolized Orville. In addition, during the 1948 Progressive Party Campaign, Highkin made a lasting friendship with Henry Wallace, their mutual interest being horticulture.

Many years later, as a favor to Orville, Highkin agreed to take in my younger brother, Bjorn, following severe family difficulties at home. He was trying to help, but it proved to be an uneasy task. Harry mentioned to me that it was the biggest mistake of his life. By that time, Bjorn was into heavy drug usage. Highkin died in his home in Kailua-Kona, Hawaii, at age 89. His seven-line obituary made it clear that he was a "devout atheist."

Leading West Coast Communist Party activists: Front row, l. to r., Phillip Connelly, Mrs. Rose Kusnitz, Frank Carlson, Dorothy Healey. Back row, l. to r., Frank E. Spector, Henry Steinberg, Ben Dobbs.

Frank Carlson was another close friend of Orville's who was a district organizer and Chairman of the Communist Party's Defense Committee for the Los Angeles CPUSA. Orville spoke about him to me often and also mentioned in his oral interviews that he had hired him at Prudential Upholstery Supply Co., another example of his habit of employing fellow communists who were having a difficult financial time during the 50s. Carlson, a Polish immigrant whose given name was Solomon Kolnick, emigrated to the US, Americanized his name, and in 1946 and '47 became the top man in the Wisconsin Communist Party. He also founded a communist newspaper, *The People's Voice,* which the

Milwaukee Journal (Sept. 1, 1951) described as targeting the black populace with the aim to "incite to class and race hatred."

In 1951, Carlson was arrested by the FBI, along with twelve other leading West Coast Communist Party leaders, including **Dorothy Ray Healey** (Connelly) and were charged and convicted of "conspiracy to overthrow the government by force." Healey, who was dubbed "The Red Queen of Los Angeles," was another favorite of Orville's whose friendship and support of the USSR was strong throughout the 50s, but who fell out of Orville's favor by 1974 when she resigned from the CPUSA and joined the "New American Movement," and later in 1982, the "Democratic Socialists of America," the party of Bernie Sanders. Healy stated in her later years during a *Los Angeles Times* interview, "My hatred of capitalism, which degrades and debases humans, is as intense now as it was when I joined the Young Communist League in 1928." In 1957, technicalities regarding the Fifth Amendment resulted in the Supreme Court overturning the convictions for all twelve, much to the pleasure of the communist movement.

Carl Ross was another close friend and confidant of Orville's, and the two remained in contact for years after their Minnesota political days together. Ross, a self-educated author and leftist historian, interviewed Orville in California in 1984 in conjunction with the Minnesota Historical Society's program to document the state's radical political past. The interview centered on Orville's personal history, but was more focused on the workings of the pre-war Benson administration and the manipulation by the powerful leftist factions on Minnesota politics; they also discussed the political conditions that brought the demise of the Progressive Party following the 1948 elections.

Minnesota radicals, Vincent R. Dunne (L) and Carl Ross at a meeting of the Twin City Labor Forum, c. 1957

Minnesota Historical Society

Ross was deeply embedded in communist activities. During an interview with John Earl Haynes in 1977, Ross described himself as "the chairman of the Minnesota Young Communists in the mid-30s, head of the National Young Communists League during World War II, and led the Minnesota Communist

Party in the late 40s." He left the Communist Party in the mid-1950s shortly after the death of Stalin.

Vincent Ray Dunne was another political associate of Orville's albeit with complications, as he was the head of the Socialist Workers Party (SWP), a Trotskyite faction of the Communist Party that was opposed to Stalin. Dunne was, at the same time, strongly committed to perpetual communist revolution against capitalism and the US. During an interview in 1959 by the leftist magazine, *The Militant New York*, Dunne described how he was stirred by the radical movement shortly after the 1917 Bolshevik Revolution and joined the Communist Party. Within the next ten years, he was elected to two terms on the Minnesota District Committee of the Communist Party. He became a cause célébre in 1941 when he was convicted under the Smith Act, along with seventeen other SWP leaders. The law forbade membership in any organization that advocated the violent overthrow of the government. Dunne served sixteen months in prison for his treasonous actions, but when released he continued his outspoken views against the "evils of capitalism and the desirability of socialism." He mentioned that reading Darwin was a "big factor in his thinking," strongly affecting his decision to becoming a revolutionary, a topic that will be addressed later.

John Abt, a self-described communist for fifty years, spent most of his mid to late career as chief counsel to the Communist Party USA (CPUSA). In prior years, he was the chief of litigation for the Agricultural Adjustment Administration (AAA) from 1933 to 1935; assistant general counsel of FDR's Works Progress Administration (WPA) in 1935; chief counsel to Senator Robert La Follette Jr.'s Civil Liberties Committee from 1936 to 1937; and special assistant to the United States Attorney General from 1937 to 1938. He was also an attorney for the then leftist-infiltrated Congress of Industrial Organizations (CIO). After 1940 the CIO made moves to dampen the powerful Communist Party influence on the union's political agenda.

CIO attorney John Abt, fixing wage rates. Ansley Hotel, 1939
Textile Industry Press photo

During his legal career, Abt was also an important figure in the covert CPUSA Ware Espionage Group. This ring had been engaged for some time in espionage for Communist Party head, Earl Browder, and as described earlier held regular clandestine meetings at Abt's apartment with other members, including Victor Perlo, Charles Kramer, Harry Magdoff, Edward Fitzgerald, and Abt's sister, Marion Bachrach, who became a high-ranking CPUSA official. John Abt's KGB code name was "Bat," and he was considered an espionage risk by US intelligence. He was also described in KGB records as a Soviet intelligence contact/agent.

After the death of Harold Ware in an automobile accident in 1935, Abt married Ware's widow, Jessica Smith, further emphasizing his ongoing connection with the espionage community. Interestingly, due to Abt's prominence for defending leftists, Kennedy assassin Lee Harvey Oswald unsuccessfully attempted to have John Abt represent him.

Lee Pressman also worked hard for Farmer-Labor Party activities. Orville described Pressman as "a very bright man who I knew well." He also was a member of the Ware Espionage Group, with the code name of "Vig." He was general counsel for the CIO from 1933–1948. In 1950, Pressman testified before the HCUAA that he had been a secret member of the Communist Party USA in 1934 and 1935 and, although no longer officially a party member, he was a firm ideological Communist from 1936 to 1950.

Lee Pressman testifying before the HCUAA, 1950

Harris and Ewing Collections, Library of Congress

In his testimony, he named Charlie Kramer, Nathan Witt, and John Abt as communists, and also members of the Ware Group. On the surface he appeared to have abruptly changed his political allegiance; however, recent KGB documents point to the fact that he secretly continued cooperation with the KGB long after his testimony.

The Marxist scholar and economist, **Abe Harris,** was an important working associate of Orville's through the Benson administration and the later Progressive Party years. He had been a close friend of former Minnesota governor Floyd Olson from childhood. After the death of Olson, Harris was instrumental in the political rise and transition to the governorship of Elmer Benson.

Orville stated in his oral interview that Harris was an economist, and had been a former boxer who came from a tough Jewish neighborhood in North

Minneapolis. He also became the general editor of the Farmer-Labor Association newspaper, the *Minnesota Leader,* which was used to promote Benson's Popular Front policies, a loose coalition of left-wing elements including communists, radicals and socialist organizations. Harris hired Ruth Shaw, wife of one of Minnesota's leading communists, as his secretary; she spent much of her time organizing a Popular Front faction among Farmer-Labor women's groups which dove-tailed with Orville's and John Jacobson's interests. In later years, Harris modified his far-left position, but his previous significant influence was valuable to the leftist battles of the era.

Abe Harris, economist.

Additional associates: The transcripts of Orville's interviews divulge many additional names of associates, acquaintances, and political confederates. Some among them include **Louis Budenz,** a former editor of the *Daily Worker* whom Orville originally lauded, but later angrily denounced as "selling out the communists"; **John Coffee**, leftist congressman from Washington State; and **Rex Tugwell,** the most influential ideologue of economic planning of the Roosevelt administration (New Deal) and a leading liberal proponent of the welfare state; **Clarence Hathaway**, prominent longtime member of the Communist Party's governing Central Committee from the 1920s through the early 1940s, and an editor of the *Daily Worker.*

Also mentioned at length in the interviews was Orville's buddy and poker-playing friend, **Leo Huberman,** who was the co-founder of the Marxist publication *Monthly Review*, along with his close friend, economist **Paul Sweezy**. Huberman taught at Columbia University and Sweezy at Harvard (later fired for his political extremism). Sweezy was considered the dean of radical economics, and more than any other single person kept Marxist economics alive in North America. His book, *Monopoly Capital,*

(l. to r.) Paul Baran, Paul Sweezy, Fidel Castro and Leo Huberman, Cuba, 1960

written with Paul Baran, is considered the cornerstone to his contribution to Marxian economics.

Huberman was a prolific writer on socialist and communist revolutions with particular interest in China, Cuba and South America. He was called to testify before the McCarthy Senate Committee in regard to communist-related activities and State Department overseas information centers. Orville often cited Huberman's book, *Man's Worldly Goods,* as a good primer for young people to understand socialism. In addition, Huberman was a close friend of communist Sol Adler, who fled to China to work with Mao and Chinese Intelligence. Orville's comment about Huberman was that he was "a hell of a guy."

Commentary: It was no idle move for Orville and his communist friends and associates to join the Communist Party in the 20s through the 50s and even later. Specifically, one had to pledge oneself to revolution and the overthrow of capitalism; to give up your life, if required; to pledge to defend Leninist socialism; and pledge to work for the triumph of Soviet power in the U.S. The full text of the above abbreviated statements, authored by J. Peters in the *Manual of Organization*, is found in the section entitled "House and Senate Investigations of the 40s and 50s."

I have to laugh when I hear people today try to minimize Communist Party membership in the past as youthful folly or casual involvement. Pledging one's life in the fight to erase capitalism and install Soviet power in the U.S. is no small decision. It was deadly serious, traitorous behavior, and one had to prove oneself to attain and retain that membership card.

* * *

PART IV

COMMENTARY ON OUR LEFTIST LIVES

CHAPTER 5

ORVILLE'S VIEWS ON A MULTITUDE OF TOPICS

Orville's political ideology dominated the atmosphere in the home, in all of its bizarre permutations, while my tight-fisted mother directed the day-to-day operations and kept the lid on the powder keg that was the family. However, her own rigidity and concepts of political righteousness combined with Orville's political severity to create an environment where no independent thinking outside of their narrow little box was acceptable.

Patriotism: I was taught early on about the strictly held beliefs that would inform my thinking through my developing years. Regarding the founding fathers, Hamilton was out; Jefferson and Paine were in. Jefferson and Paine were often quoted, albeit selectively, excluding references to the Almighty, religion in general, slavery, and other topics which might have complicated Orville's vision of history ("his-story"). His fertile mind created a curious blend of Jeffersonian thinking with communism. In fact, freely using Jefferson quotes to justify his line of thinking, Orville often described himself and other communists as patriots. He also believed that if Jefferson and Jesus (the man, not the deity) had lived in the present, they would certainly have been ardent communists and, by his definition, would be supporters of Joe Stalin in Soviet Russia and Mao in China. One can only imagine Jesus and Jefferson conspiring to produce the inhumanity of Stalinist Russia.

The American military: By Orville's reckoning, the American military was an organization with a shameful reputation; absent from this characterization was any recognition of courage and sacrifice in the American Revolution, World War I, or World War II. This was always contrasted with the Russian and Chinese armies that were formed to fight the injustice of the past royals and corrupt capitalist leaders and were, consequently, purer. When a uniformed American soldier was encountered on the streets or in film, Orville was hardly able to conceal his contempt. He went even further regarding the Korean and Vietnam Wars, praising both the North Koreans, Ho Chi Minh, and the Vietcong, and deriding the "corrupt" American army efforts.

The military's treatment of the American Indians was always front and center with communist propaganda campaigns and I heard an earful over the years. It was a regrettable collision of greatly different societies, with the Indians coming up the losers . . . suffering through broken treaties, death, displacement, and degradation in many areas of the country. While America can be criticized for its actions in this regard, communists attacking America for its treatment of the Indians is the pot calling the kettle black; their propaganda programs conveniently overlooked their own Russian extermination program of indigenous tribes. Anne Applebaum states in her 2003 book *Gulag*, "At some level, the Bolsheviks, like all educated Russians, would have been aware of the Russian Empire's subjugation of the Kirgiz, Buryats, Tungas, Chukchi, and others. The fact that it didn't particularly concern them---they, who were otherwise so interested in the fate of the downtrodden---itself indicates something about their unspoken assumptions."

Compassion: Orville personified a phrase I have often heard when describing the left: "They love the masses and hate the individual." That sounds like an oxymoron, but well describes my stepfather. Foreshadowing the "identity" politics we see emphasized today, the "loved" people were the downtrodden of society who were exalted in all aspects of daily life; the Jews, the Negroes, the anti-war students who were being persecuted in the universities across the land, the dock workers, the Chinese, the Russian workers, political exiles, farmers, the poor, those behind bars, as well as anyone who had an axe to grind with the establishment, and possibly the most significant of all, the "humiliated" workers who "toiled for a decent wage." If you tuned in, Orville surmised, and examined the rotten underbelly of the nation, you could hear the suffering and yearning for a new order.

Compassion for those in need of assistance and representation is indeed important. But Orville's focus was purely political and accompanied by indignant anti- US pronouncements and hand waving. If it furthered "the cause," then these groups served that purpose.

Further illustrating Orville's focus on the generalized population, those in prison were not really guilty of their crimes, but were, instead, victims of oppression, likely having had to steal bread to survive. A crime committed by a leftist or a poor person, particularly a black or a Mexican, couldn't be a true crime either. After all, the whites had enslaved the blacks, and the US had stolen much of Mexico from the Mexicans. These groups had a right to strike back. The society was to blame for making the person or persons commit the acts, and the society should be on trial. In our home, American society was on trial each and every minute of every day.

There is an inevitable downside to the unqualified "love for the masses" view, which simply lumps countless "downtrodden" groups together; there is no room for discussing variations among individuals or circumstances; complexities of societal or political behavior, poor choices made by governments or individuals; or anything short of blanket assessments. If you aren't seen as wholeheartedly on the side of the "oppressed," you are an unfeeling and less-than-intelligent nobody. (I am struck, in describing this that it pertains quite well to the current leftist narrative about "cold and uninformed" conservatives as well.)

Trust: When faced with the individual, Orville's tone changed. He trusted few and was suspicious of anyone whose politics he couldn't affirm. For Orville to engage in a discourse, the person had to be vetted and found to be "politically good." Even then, there would likely be shortcomings. For example, a person might be liberal, but if they weren't pro-Russia or pro-Mao, they might have good intentions, but they probably weren't too bright. For example, Hubert Humphrey was a liberal; however, he was reviled for his anti-communist politics, and Kennedy was in the same league. Anyone supporting revolution, and displaying vilification of the United States, was "very political," meaning morally and politically righteous. Dealing with individuals was problematical; keeping them from straying outside Orville's prescribed comfort zone required a lot of energy.

As for friendships for Orville and my mother, there were basically no other candidates beyond the political ones; few people passed the test. Using round numbers, removing Republicans represented 35% of the adult, voting population. Religious people who weren't Republicans caused another 20% reduction. Most southerners accounted for an additional 20% or so (not counting blacks), and the additional percentages of soft-headed liberals, businessmen, wealthy people, military personnel, Catholics ... my, the figures do add up, possibly even 100%. Who was left? Practically no one, with the exception of four or five close friends, and when you looked closely, they too had a few chinks in their armor.

Pursuit of the ideal: To Orville, in line with Stalin's and Mao's methodologies, anybody and anything that stood in the way of the pursuit of the cause had to go; be it people or institutions, it was all fair game. This rotten society had to have its eyes gouged out, its carcass flayed, before being crushed under heel and burned. The new communist empire under Joseph Stalin would build its foundations on the ash heap of Western Civilization. Any way to get that message out was acceptable. Lying, cheating, and fabrication were all acceptable to achieve the end ("The ends justify the means."). Lenin's own quote is also apropos, "a lie told often enough becomes the truth." The communists were consummate experts at the art of the lie, with disinformation programs that were state of the art.

As the years went by, though, Orville realized it likely wouldn't happen during his lifetime. But it surely would come, he believed, and be the ultimate historical vindication for his and his friends' boundless work; in a way, he saw himself as an apostle.

Who's "in" and who's "out:" Within our proscribed home life, the Russians were always praised, as were those who opposed the perceived vile US domestic and international policies, and the enslaved and oppressed multitudes clamoring for liberation all around us. The heroes were Joseph Stalin, Karl Marx, Vladimir Lenin, Mao Zedong, Fidel Castro, Che Guevara, The Hollywood Ten, Paul Robeson, and even black boxers such as Joe Louis, Ezzard Charles and Archie Moore. The same was not true for white boxers. According to Orville, Rocky Marciano, the undefeated Heavyweight Champion (49-0, with 46 knockouts), was an imposter and never would have beaten any of the blacks in their prime. The same was true in baseball: Jackie Robinson, Roy Campanella, and Willie Mays were all great, and far superior to Ruth, DiMaggio, etc. Being white somehow tainted and diminished them as athletes and men.

Not surprisingly, people not included in this list were the towering figures of Eisenhower, Churchill, and Marshall. Eisenhower was characterized as a buffoon, a low-IQ idiot who ascended to the position of Supreme Commander of the Allied Forces during WWII only because of the Peter Principle. In addition, the fact that America demanded that the Allied forces be commanded by an American, as a condition of entering the war, was seen by Orville to be patently unfair. To leftists, the real leaders were Montgomery and the Russian generals, who did the dirty work in the battles in Africa, and battling the Germans in the Russian winter. While that cannot be diminished, the Americans battling to regain the islands in the South Pacific, the invasion of Normandy, and the dreadful fighting across Europe, was downgraded in importance. The American generals, Patton and McArthur, were sub-par generals and egomaniacal nut cases.

The post-war rebuilding of Japan and Europe: The version of post-World War II history that I was taught concerning Japan held little resemblance to reality. In Orville's mind, and within Soviet propaganda, the reality of Japan's unprovoked attack on the United States, and all that followed, was now overlooked, and the Americans were substituted as the villains.

In the aftermath of World War II, the rebuilding of Japan presented a problem for leftists, namely because the hated McArthur spearheaded US efforts and performed so well in converting Japan from a feudal war-like society to a modern democratic nation with strong support even inside Japan. He promoted the development of democracy; suspended Japanese laws restricting political, civil and religious liberties; ordered the release of political prisoners; and abolished the secret police. He announced a general election to be held in April 1946, only seven months following the surrender. He also called for the Japanese Diet (Parliament) to pass a new election law to provide for free democratic elections, including, for the first time in the history of Japan, the right of women to vote. In addition, under MacArthur's direction, the growth of labor unions was encouraged, large landholdings were broken up and the education system was reformed. All of this was unheard of in the history of post-war relations.

But that is not how the American left saw it, nor did their compatriots in Russia. A new focus for hatred of America had to be established. The new line of propaganda was that the Japanese were the suffering scapegoats of the war, the ones on whom the US dropped the atom bomb. And here at home Japanese-American citizens had been exiled to internment camps.

The reality was that after Pearl Harbor, the west coast was readying for a Japanese invasion. It was a frightful and unnerving period of time. Also not to be forgotten in the historical context was the devastating list of Japanese atrocities that had transpired; the brutal invasion of Manchuria; the death marches; the horrors of the Solomon Islands, Guam and Iwo Jima; the slaughter, torture, and beheading of American prisoners and civilians. To Orville and his comrades, these issues faded into insignificance.

The Japanese internment camps here at home, set up with unanimous congressional support, were a result of the fear and hysteria of the time. Contributing to this was the inability of Americans, in general, to understand the insular Japanese culture that had evolved in the United States. The total number of those sent to the camps was approximately 110,000. To the honor of the Japanese-Americans, many young men enlisted out of the camps, and there were those who were heavily decorated for bravery in combat and in the air force.

American society, over the next half-century, recognized the injustice, particularly as no Japanese civilian was ever convicted of espionage. But all of this took time to sort out in the post-war, evolving American culture. The irony of course was the ongoing espionage and clandestine communist activities by the American left that caused them no moral dilemma.

But seeing the big picture and weighing the complexities was not in Orville's playbook. He joined in the left's unending cries of American arrogance over the bombings of Hiroshima and Nagasaki; as an unnecessary slaughter of innocent people. Left out of the equation was the calculation of lives that would be saved by avoiding an invasion of mainland Japan (100,000 or more); a calculation based on the understanding and observation of the Japanese war tactics of fighting to the last man. Culturally, they were determined to not let up without something forcefully bringing them to a halt. While the merits of Truman's decision will always be subject to some amount of second-guessing, the left embraced their indignation as a further rallying cry in the ongoing battle against the United States.

The rebuilding of Europe by the US after the war, by implementing the Marshall Plan, was essentially an American plan for world domination that radiated evil. The reality was that the US role in rebuilding the war-torn countries was part altruism and part practicality to help bring the world out of poverty and war and avoid the punitive measures of WWI that paved the way for the rise of Hitler. But none of this figured into the ever-present leftist dialogue that turned a blind eye to the Soviet economic take over and subjugation of Eastern Europe. This was deemed justified as a protection against future German invasion and therefore beyond criticism.

In the years after the war, Orville's contempt was heaped on anyone who purchased a German product, or car such as a Mercedes or Volkswagen; they were automatically Nazi sympathizers. (Interestingly, the same disdain didn't apply to buyers of Japanese cars in later years.) The terms *fascist* or *Nazi* covered far more people than Hitler's political ruling party; *reactionary* was another slur often used. These terms were used to describe people across all facets of American life who opposed the communists.

Who were the "useful idiots?" Both Lenin and Stalin were reported to have referred to US liberals as "useful idiots," seeing them as tools in their quests for world domination and destruction of the West. Many in Hollywood and the media played into that scheme wonderfully. In the end, Stalin would have had one solution for all of the western "bourgeois" liberals who worshipped him . . . elimination once their usefulness ran out. It is my belief that Orville could never process the idea that he might be in that group. In fact, he treated those he considered lower caliber liberals in the same context . . . they were no more than simpletons who would vote the right way and could be easily manipulated. It's quite possible he saw himself as something of a blood brother with his communist friends and the Russians; they would fight the battle together and reign supreme.

Religion: Friends of mine who were from religious families, particularly Catholics, were frowned upon as deluded imbeciles whose faith was a sham. Christianity was the "opiate of the masses," the common Marxist/Leninist theme. It was an evil institution that was a worldwide fraud that preyed on old ladies and guilty men readying themselves to meet their maker and wishing to buy their way into heaven with their ample wills. The Catholics were reputed to be the richest institution in the world and were an international financial force in the capitalist world, therefore, their interests were self-serving and their anti-communist history was only to protect their ill-gotten gains. But they would sooner than later receive their due when the inevitable new regime took over. Woe to the church and their ignorant followers.

Newspapers: Newspapers were politically black or white, with the *Daily Worker* being the embodiment of truth, while conservative publications were filled with lies. The US military was a despicable collection of misfits who promoted fascism and US imperialism. Gen. George Marshall and his European rehabilitation plan, as discussed, was a favorite whipping boy. Added to the no-count list was the Salvation Army, or anyone involved with a church food program. In fact, any church's benevolent activity or charitable assistance to have-nots or people down on their luck, was jeered at as being nothing more than a feel-good move to salve the guilt of white parishioners. These stupid people were using a garden hose on a forest fire, which their capitalist greed and corruption had ignited in the first place.

"Big business:" Singled out with particular vitriol was the omnipresent, underhanded world of "big business." Within that realm, all manner of conspiracies abounded, according to Orville, and all aimed at keeping the oppressed populace uninformed and under heel. One had to be ever watchful because the conspiracies were disguised in many forms. For-profit businesses were suspect; whether they provided products or services that were desirable or useful to the public was of no consequence. Money was seen as dirty and the capitalist, free enterprise system rotten to the core. Private business, large or small, had as its purpose the maintaining of the status quo, along with the subjugation of "the workers." A friendly business owner, who viewed employees with respect for their contribution to the success of the enterprise, was a gross oxymoron, not to be believed. Everybody knew, so it went, the real truth that the huddled masses were kept groveling in the mud, forced to kiss the rear ends of the new oligarchs of the business world. "Oligarchs" was one of Orville's favorite terms, originally used for the former Russian nobility, but now employed to label "rich people" in general. The notion of pervasive conspiracies came naturally to Orville; after all, conspiracy and deception were the foundation of communist activities designed to infiltrate daily American life. Having internalized that belief from his personal life history, it was a small step to assign that behavior to all opposing institutions.

The theme of "big business" found its way into nearly every conversation (disregarding the fact that over 95 percent of businesses in the US are categorized as "small"). Reactionary powers in Washington, DC, were the shadowy figures that controlled the purse strings of America and the world. These figures were the enemies. However, there were exceptions. Author and philanthropist,

Corliss Lamont, was one. He inherited money from the J. P. Morgan Empire, was radicalized in the 30s and 40s and remained so to his death in 1995. He praised Stalin and anything Russian, was the chairman of the National Council of American-Soviet Friendship, Director of the American Civil Liberties Union, and founded and subsidized the publication, *Marxist Quarterly*. Anita McCormick Blaine, heiress to the International Harvester fortune, was another exception; she was a heavy contributor to the Progressive Party.

Both of these philanthropists became heavily involved with the Henry Wallace campaign, the anti-McCarthy movement and other leftist causes throughout their lives. But it is amusing to note that neither ever considered the idea of forgoing their "ill-gotten" inherited fortunes in view of the suffering and injustice all around them. In Lamont's case, he lived well despite the "criminality" of American business that helped amass his father's vast fortune. Instead, both Lamont and Blaine were content to remain wealthy and privileged, in stark contrast to their socialist idealism.

* * *

CHAPTER 6

ORVILLE AND REVOLUTION

Societal "cleansing:" The lectures and adulation of Stalin and Mao were unending. To Orville, these communists were men of enormous personal courage and great wisdom. When confronted with their brutal legacies, Orville dismissed any negative talk as Western propaganda; still, he did subscribe to the belief that a certain amount of societal cleansing was necessary as a part of world revolution. The people that would have to be eliminated in the US during and after the revolution would be the obstructionists to the new society; a certain number simply would not conform.

In later years I would occasionally meet Orville for lunch at Rancho Park Municipal Golf Course in West Los Angeles. I would ask him about Stalin's then well-publicized party purges and he would counter with a question such as, "Weren't the Americans far worse?" To suggest a comparison was stunning and nonsensical; yet, Orville continued to twist the facts to fit his ideal vision. One time he did admit that Stalin in his last year or two was "a little off," but saw that as essentially irrelevant. In the final run, any minor weaknesses were overshadowed by the great things that he accomplished for the Russian people . . . the fastest-growing economy and the most benevolent society of all time. I do remember being unnerved by his seemingly unhinged statements, but I kept asking questions and plumbing his thoughts. He never really knew that my political viewpoints had evolved far away from his by the mid-1970s. I cringe to think that, had Wallace won the 1948 election, Orville would have been in an influential position to further Soviet ambitions.

Ayers and Dohrn: There were two personalities who played a significant role in the evolution of leftist thought and actions moving into the 1960s. They were the domestic terrorist pair, William "Bill" Ayers and his wife Bernardine Dohrn, who had formed the Weather Underground cult, with the goal of creating societal chaos that would lead to the overthrow of the government. They were responsible for a bombing spree of the US capitol, the Pentagon and several police stations in New York, as well as the death of one of their own who blew himself up making a bomb in his condominium. To further advance their objectives the Weathermen sought to establish a "white fighting force" to be allied with the "Black Liberation Movement" as well as developing alliances with other radical groups to achieve "the destruction of US imperialism and achieve a classless world: world communism." Orville's view of them was of a younger generation demonstrating their frustration with "the system" and taking matters into their own hands for the greater good. In the same vein, my mother strongly supported the Black Panthers and their allied political agenda.

The relationship between the Weather Underground's history and my experience with Orville was highlighted by the reports of FBI investigator, Larry Grathwohl, who infiltrated the Underground and learned firsthand about their terrorist activities and goals. These eerily mirrored what I heard from my stepfather in regard to their plans of massive re-education camps of the Chinese and Russian variety, to be implemented after the revolution and takeover. The most horrific aspect of the WU's blueprint was the estimation that some 25 million people would not readily go along, or submit to "re-education programs," which would result in their elimination for the good of the new society. Orville's figures were in the range of 10% or 15%, roughly corresponding to the Underground figures. The hideous scenario depicted by the Underground was simply an accepted necessity of a Marxist revolution.

Most distressing today is the fact that Ayers and Dohrn have moved into the mainstream of society; Bill Ayers is a former tenured professor at the University of Illinois at Chicago, and Dohrn, remarkably a member of the legal profession, sits on important committees and boards of the American Bar Association, and is an Associate Professor of Law at Northwestern University. To this day, they are unrepentant and unremorseful for the carnage they caused. Ayers has stated, "I wake up every morning thinking about how I'm going to end capitalism."

Ayers' and Dohrn's world view contained a disturbing undercurrent of truly antisocial behavior. Incomprehensibly, the group showed admiration for the deranged killer Charles Manson and his equally disturbed "family." In 1969, Ms. Dohrn delivered a speech at a "War Council" meeting organized by the Weathermen and attended by about four hundred people. In it, she made reprehensible comments in regard to some of the victims of the Manson murders, specifically Sharon Tate and her friends, and Rosemary and Leno LaBianca. She was quoted as saying, "Dig it! First they killed those pigs [Tate's friends] and then they put a fork in pig Tate's belly . . . Wild!" This was followed by a similar exuberant statement about the inhuman butchering of Rosemary and

Leno LaBianca, which concluded with, "Far Out!" In 2008, Bill Ayers tried to characterize her remarks as "ironic" and that she was just trying to make a "political point." This remark is all the more disingenuous and distasteful given the horrors it is meant to rationalize.

More recently, Bill Ayers has been associated with Barrack Obama, although both have tried to minimize the relationship. The two served on the board of the Annenberg Challenge in Chicago, no doubt interacting in their respective capacities. And Obama held a political fundraiser in Ayers' living room. It is evident they were more than just "neighbors."

Orville not only expressed support for the Weather Underground, but also for Huey Newton and the Black Panthers. They were yet another example of the populous being fed up with capitalism and American foreign policy, and therefore striking back in the name of justice. The pot was finally boiling over and America was getting what it deserved. Not surprisingly, growing up in this environment was topsy-turvy and bewildering.

* * *

CHAPTER 7

CULTURAL MARXISM

I include this section as it deals with the bridging of the economic Marxism of my youth to the more modern form that blossomed in the 1960s, the newest chapter in the never-ending movement toward the left's unrealistic utopian ideal. Although Orville had a stake in the new left, he remained for the most part an old-school economic Marxist, but my mother more easily embraced the changing culture. I followed suit, easily moving into this new milieu.

Two of the splinter groups of classical Marxist-Leninist ideology, the socialist Fabian Society born in England, and the cultural Marxist Frankfurt School in Germany comprised the emerging New Left that would massively impact our contemporary society.

The Fabian Society: The Fabian Society was formed in January, 1884. The basic philosophy of the society was derived from earlier wealthy elitist socialist thinkers many of whom were connected with the British East India Co. In the late nineteenth and early twentieth centuries, leading members of the Fabians included the science fiction writer, H. G. Wells, Sidney and Beatrice Webb, and George Bernard Shaw, author of *Pygmalion* and other plays. Shaw, the Irish playwright, became the outspoken leader of the Fabians, using his plays as vehicles to disseminate his political, social, and anti-religious ideas. His stances on public issues were often controversial: promoting eugenics, denouncing both sides in WWI, enthusiastically supporting Mussolini's 1922 seizure of power in Italy; and praising him as "the right kind of tyrant." In the 20s, he hailed Lenin as the "one really interesting statesman in Europe," and toasted Stalin at a dinner party in Moscow stating, "I have seen all the 'terrors' and I was terribly pleased by them." Shaw's admiration for Mussolini and Stalin demonstrated his growing belief that dictatorship was the only viable political arrangement. When the Nazi Party came to power in Germany in January, 1933, Shaw described Hitler as "a very remarkable man, a very able man."

Author, Clare Ellis, writing about H. G. Wells, stated that he remained a staunch socialist throughout his life. Wells himself, in his 1926 book, *The World of William Clissold*, wrote that the New Fabian Republic he envisioned would be "a classless World State run by an intelligent minority . . . it will be more like a world-religion . . . and become the new human community." He further declared, "We can weave a world system of monetary and economic activities, while the politicians, the diplomatists, and the soldiers are still too busy with their ancient habitual antics to realize what we are doing." One again, we see deception guiding the left.

Ellis reported that the Fabian's mascot was a tortoise, depicting their slow grinding methodology for achieving their goals by the use of "stealth, intrigue, subversion, and the deception of never calling socialism by its right name." As with Wells, the government George Bernard Shaw envisioned would be led by a Fabian socialist dictatorship. Two stained-glass windows designed by Shaw depict first, a wolf disguised in a sheepskin holding aloft the Fabian Society banner, and second, a scene of people "praying and worshipping a pile of books which advocate the theories of socialism." In 1895, influential Fabians, including Shaw and the Webbs, set up a branch of the University of London, namely the London School of Economics and Political Science, which became a means to foster Fabian Society aims. Today, the London School is one of the leading social science institutions in the world, and the foundations can be seen in Britain's Labour Party, their founding members in 1900 having largely come from the Fabian Society. In the United States, the influence of Fabian transplants is apparent in the slow, grinding movement toward leftist ideals of a national welfare state, coupled with the vilification of capitalism.

The Frankfurt School: In Germany, the Frankfurt School evolved out of a 1922 conference in Moscow at the Marx-Engels Institute. From these origins, the ideas of these Marxist philosophers were developed, resulting initially in the founding of the Institute for Social Research, a deceptively innocuous title.

Georg Lukacs, one of the early prominent members of the movement, was born in Hungary to a wealthy family. Distant and problematic family relationships contributed to his melancholy and angry worldview. He embraced Marx's view that the family was to be destroyed, a tenet he encouraged to further his societal aims. He reportedly stated that the traditional bourgeois family gave off the reeking odor of "swamp gas" and that "women were the enemy." An apparently depressed personality, he also had a "Dread of the destructive influences of happiness."

Besides Lukacs, the group included Herbert Marcuse, Wilhelm Reich, Max Horkheimer, Erich Fromm, and Theodor Adorno. Together they believed in "compulsory promiscuity, one-parent families, premarital sex and homosexuality . . . " which all struck deeply into the core ideas of family and child-bearing as mainstays of Western society. Much of this philosophy resulted from combining Marx and Engels with Sigmund Freud under the umbrella of a new philosophy dubbed "Freudo-Marxism." Frankfurt School historian and writer, Ralph de Toledano, aptly noted, "The Freudian Marxists realized that sex could be a devastating instrument if prompted to run rampant. Anyone that fought against it was condemned as a part of capitalist depravity." It should be stated, however, that parts of this doctrine were far beyond even Freud's tolerance. Toledano tells us that Freud referred to the adherents as "morally insane," and felt that their ideas were "complete lunatic."

These predominantly Jewish philosophers gained increasing importance to leftist ideology during the 30s, but at the same time, with the rise of Hitler, the leaders of the Frankfurt School realized they would have to leave Germany. In the United States, the socialist, Marxist-inspired educator, John Dewey, with financing from the Rockefeller Foundation, became their angel when he was able to affect the transfer of many standout members of the group to welcoming top universities such as Cal Berkeley, Princeton and Brandeis; but the most prestigious recipient was Columbia University in New York and their well-known Teacher's College. Thus was born the slow, unrelenting shift to the left of American academia.

The cultural Marxists bypassed Marx and Lenin's ideas of violent revolution and instead concentrated on developing alternate and insidious ways to impose their ideology; thereby furthering the collapse of western society. Their new path would be a "long march through the institutions."

These left-wing academics and intellectuals looked to the universities, the arts, Hollywood, and the media, as their new targets, rather than the Marx/Engels focus on "the working man." The new approach was not based on economic class warfare, which they felt was too restrictive, but rather a system that would demolish capitalism by attacking the cultural framework of western society and its traditional norms and institutions.

Wilhelm Reich, often characterized as an unadulterated charlatan, nevertheless, commanded great respect with the neo-Marxists and to this day still has followers. He was an early bright star working under Freud, but left that camp to follow his own theater lights. The core of Reich's theory was that one's physical inability to surrender to orgasm was the underlying incubator of neurosis which, if not dealt with, eventually turned people to fascism and authoritarianism. At his Orgonon Institute in Maine, he became absorbed in researching what he believed was the cosmic force of orgasms. This energy, which even to the present has never been identified in any scientific experiments, was integral with his overarching concepts of repressed human sexuality as the basis of human psychological problems. Very briefly put, Reich believed that he could capture this "energy" within the confines of his invention, the Orgone Accumulator, and a person who spent time sitting in this phone-booth sized box would experience its curative powers.

Around 1970, I came in contact tangentially with this famous contraption. Early in my professional architectural career I met a prominent Hollywood personality and actor who, with his wife, were contemplating a large addition to their home. During my initial visit touring through the home, I was instructed to tiptoe quietly down the hall and not enter one of the bedrooms. At the time, I didn't think much of it, assuming someone was sleeping there and I would simply see it later. When I returned to take the measurements I needed in order to do my design work, the client reluctantly allowed me into that room. He led me in complete silence; the room was low-lit and filled with boxes, piles of clothing and other family bric-a-brac. But in the middle of the room stood a black voting-booth type structure. The client explained that it was an Orgone box and that it radiated immense energy from somewhere out in the ether. He asked me if I had ever heard of Wilhelm Reich, and he was impressed when I answered in the affirmative. I must say it was a bit discomfiting seeing a grown man fairly quivering from forces of uncontrollable energy he firmly believed were emanating from this box. My experience, complicated by the client's unwanted advance during a meeting, in the form of a hand on my leg, made me not unhappy that the project did not proceed.

After Reich made claims that the energy from the Orgone Accumulator could cure cancer, the FDA charged him with fraud and ordered him to cease manufacture and sales of his product. He ignored the order and was subsequently jailed in 1954 where he died three years later. Far from being the end of interest in this unproven phenomenon, you can still find instructions online for building your very own Orgone box.

It is remarkable that the noted individuals of the Fabian Society and Frankfurt School movements, with their express goals of eroding and ultimately destroying Western society, enjoyed such intellectual adulation and regard.

"Critical Theory:" The other mainstay that evolved from cultural Marxism and the Frankfurt School is well described by Toledano: "The destruction of the West, from which a phoenix-like Marxist Utopia would arise, was to be achieved by the combination of Neo-Marxism, neo-Freudianism, Pavlovian psychology, and mass brainwashing, wrapped up in what is euphemistically known as "Critical Theory." This theory, spread far and wide through the world's universities, is an innocuous sounding concept that gives the impression of being an intellectual study that results in plumbing fundamental truth. Though it has taken many forms since the 30s, one fairly succinct definition from Max Horkheimer is that any theory is critical insofar as it seeks "to liberate human beings from the circumstances that enslave them."

A more precise description is Clare Ellis's quote from Raymond V. Raehn's book, *The Historical Roots of Political Correctness,* which describes Critical Theory as, "essentially destructive criticism of the main elements of Western culture, including Christianity, capitalism, authority, the family, patriarchy, hierarchy, morality, tradition, sexual restraint, loyalty, patriotism, nationalism, heredity, ethnocentrism, convention, and conservatism."

The fruits of the spread of Critical Theory were exemplified by the activities of the afore-mentioned Bill Ayers and Bernadine Dohrn and their neo-Marxist adherents, as well as student activists such as Communist Party member, Angela Davis, Jerry Rubin, Abbie Hoffman, Tom Hayden, the Black Panthers organizers, Huey Newton and Bobby Seale, and many thousands of others who were part of the sexual/cultural chaos of the era. The fuel for this fire was derived from the ugly undercurrent of cultural Marxism.

Paradoxically, in 1985, Jerry Rubin and Abbie Hoffman traveled together for a series of debates billed as "Yippee vs. Yuppie." While Hoffman remained an activist who occasionally got arrested for civil disobedience, Rubin had become a Wall Street millionaire, thanks in part to investing in Apple. Rubin's position was that activism was hard work and that the abuse of drugs, sex, and private property had made the counterculture "a scary society in itself." He also said, "We activists in the 1960s eventually lost touch with ourselves." He maintained that "wealth creation is the real American Revolution and what the society needed was an infusion of capital into the depressed areas of the country." Abie Hoffman, still involved with drugs and liquor, and diagnosed with bi-polar disorder, committed suicide in 1989 with an overdose of phenobarbital tablets.

The instability of Hoffman's personal life, like so many others in the same period, found an outlet that propelled him to the forefront of the student protest era, where he was seen by fellow students as pointing the way to a new and healthy world. Sadly, it was revealed to be a deadly, negative, skewed vision of a failed ideology. But pressing on, most of the leftist leaders continued with their idealistic agendas; some, like Ayers, Dohrn, and Davis even became respected, albeit unrepentant, teachers and university professors.

During the turbulent years of campus unrest in the 60s and 70s, Marxist Herbert Marcuse became the acknowledged "guru" of the free-love lifestyle, and the student movements of Germany, France, and the US. He criticized capitalism, modern technology, historical materialism and entertainment culture, arguing that they represented new forms of social control. He regarded man's erotic nature as the true liberation of humanity, thus inspiring the utopian dreams of Rubin, Davis, Hoffman and other Marxist student leaders.

James Glaznov, in his book, *The Left's Romance with Tyranny and Terror,* stated, "Herbert Marcuse, often termed the 'father of the New Left,' outlived the rationale for the leftist hatred of the abundance of freedom in American society. Marcuse coined the term 'repressive tolerance' to describe the way capitalism enslaves people by making them happy and free. Because capitalism satisfied its citizens' material needs, it distracted them from what they should be enraged about: their captivity."

It is difficult to imagine another more twisted and arcane logic for a political philosophy, but it resonated with the fired up students of the 60s, along with the hopelessly inoculated Marxist left. Once again, as we heard from Lukacs, there is an inbred loathing of the "destructive influences of happiness." What they embraced was tyranny and terror, the title of Glasnov's book ... and societal repression, exactly mirroring the dictatorial regimes of Stalin, Mao and the socialist monster, Adolph Hitler.

One of the rallying cries of the post-Woodstock "free-love" era (1968), the year I returned from my Peace Corps stint in Venezuela, was the song by Stephen Stills whose refrain reverberated with the free-love philosophy of the Freudo-Marxists, "If you can't be with the one you love, honey, love the one you're with." The lyrics are thought to have been adapted from a song in the 1947 musical, *Finian's Rainbow*, co-written by the socialist/blacklisted writer, E. Y. "Yip" Harburg, whom Orville would get together with on West Coast trips, and Fred Saidy. Harburg's lyrics were "When I'm not near the girl I love, I love the girl I'm near."

This stands out as an example of the discreet ways that leftist Hollywood writers could interject, but disguise, their leftist political viewpoints. Author Russ Kick in his book, *Everything You Know About God is Wrong: the Disinformation Guide to Religion,* states, "The wildly successful *Finian's Rainbow* was produced in 1947 . . . as a socialist attack on capitalism and racial inequality." In the same book, he quotes musical librettist, Peter Stone, "*Finian's Rainbow* was . . . extraordinarily political, (but) the audience had no idea of that . . . if you ever want to reach people with a political tract, go study *Finian's Rainbow.*"

Ironically, my father's second wife, dancer-actress, Joan Skinner, was a star of one of the early productions of *Finian's Rainbow,* along with the black folksingers, Sonny Terry and Brownie McGhee. I remember being taken to the theater to see the grand production. Whether my father or Joan were aware of the underlying purpose of the play would be little more than conjecture; however, my father often related to me that during a stretch of time in the late 40s, he put up the communist songwriter, Woody Guthrie, in his home. My father's sympathies were definitely on the left side of the aisle, but likely due to his personal issues I did not experience him as being actively political.

Another prominent representative of the cultural Marxist movement is Angela Davis. Growing up, she was surrounded by the communist milieu through her mother's role in the Southern Negro Youth Congress, an organization influenced by the Communist Party. Introduced to socialism and communism at Elisabeth Irwin High School in New York (the high school level of the communist Little Red Schoolhouse), she joined the youth group, Advance.

While attending Brandeis University, she fell under the spell of, who else but Herbert Marcuse, whom she met at a protest rally during the Cuban Missile Crisis. Angela later said about Marcuse, "He taught me that it was possible to be an academic, an activist, a scholar, and a revolutionary."

She spent time in Europe during her college years, where she became involved with the radical Socialist German Student Union and the Students for a Democratic Society (SDS), as well as the Student Non-Violent Coordinating Committee (SNCC). Back in the US, she joined the recently formed Black Panthers. Davis was an active member of the Communist Party USA, running for vice-president in 1980 and 1984. In 1972, the Soviet news agency, TASS, reported that Davis had been awarded the Lenin Jubilee Medal, a high Soviet honor. She also received the International Lenin Peace Prize in 1979 for her contribution to worldwide communism and traveled there in July of that year to accept the honor.

In 2014, UCLA, the institution that fired Angela Davis in 1970 for her activities related to her membership in the Communist Party, brought her out of retirement to teach a spring-quarter graduate seminar in the gender studies department, titled "Critical Theory and Feminist Dialogues." The school followed up their adulation of Davis in the fall when they festooned the campus with Angela Davis banners that carried the caption, "We Question." Despite a lack of evidence of her own questioning in regard to the brutality of the regime she so admired, Davis now appears to be among the ranks of Ayers, Dohrn, and others sporting the title of "esteemed professor."

When asked during an interview with the *Los Angeles Times* whether she thought democracy was a good chassis on which to build a political system, Davis answered, "I believe . . . democracy needs to be emancipated from capitalism." Although no longer a party member, she still "maintains a relationship (with CPUSA) and believes . . . that capitalism is the most dangerous kind of future we can imagine."

Orville was sympathetic to the cultural Marxist camp, but not actually involved in that realm. He didn't take up the causes of the counter culture with its drugs and emphasis on sexual liberation. He was distinctly opposed to Freudian psychology, believing it to be castrating, debilitating, and a waste of good proletarian money. So his focus remained on Soviet Russia and the economic side of communism.

My mother, as described earlier, bought into the psychiatric world of Freud, Erich Fromm, and their associates with abandon. I recall seeing Fromm's books on our living room coffee table. She also eagerly supported the protests of the SDS, SNCC, and CORE, often participating in rallies. Angela Davis, too, was held in high regard as a significant leader of "progressive causes." My younger brother, Bjorn, sometimes joined her in these activities, which took place in downtown Los Angeles, the Federal Building in West L.A., and on the campus of UCLA.

For my part, I vividly remember reading Ernest Jones's three-volume biography of Freud almost nonstop. I became motivated to write down all of my dreams in order to practice self-analysis. On one occasion when I had a dream, I arose from my bed and carefully wrote it all down. Imagine my surprise the next morning when I found nothing on the pad of paper . . . so much for my amusing experiment.

* * *

CHAPTER 8

THE DOCTRINAIRE WORLD OF THE ARTS

For my mother and stepfather, literature, music, the arts, and architecture all resonated with dogma and political rigidity, in the sense of being either "good" or "bad." For example, only certain books by certain leftist authors were credible. Unless a book or article was in adulation of leftist principles, it was a product of right-wing, bourgeois propaganda. Certain playwrights like Albee and Richard Yates were acceptable because they opposed, satirized, and ridiculed the Eisenhower-era American ideal of family life, with the hardworking American male as the head of the household.

Author Lincoln Steffens was, with many others, at the fore in the literary category. He met and fell under the spell of Lenin and condoned the atrocities taking place in the Soviet workers' paradise, believing them necessary to bring about the great changes to come. Writers of the past, such as Mark Twain and Harriet Beecher Stowe, the author of *Uncle Tom's Cabin,* displayed liberal social perspectives and were therefore admired. On the other hand, if a person enjoyed reading mystery novels, or a conservative press, they would be brushed off as an uneducated sap; definitely not part of the "intelligentsia."

Modern architecture was the only acceptable form of design. The primary example of this was the Bauhaus school in Germany, which was founded by German architect Walter Gropius in 1919. Initially an art school, and later encompassing architecture, it grew out of the emerging socialist narrative that, in part, disdained anything considered "bourgeois." In the broad architectural sense, this meant doing away with unnecessary external ornamentation, but in reality anything that deviated from the rigid philosophy would be given the moniker "bourgeois." Gropius's cooperative ideal envisioned the architects, artists, and designers all working together, rather than individually, as part of a compound devoted to serving the new workers' paradise. He even issued his own manifesto that outlined the acceptable forms of artistic expression that reflected the revolutionary era. The woodblock illustration on the cover depicted a cubist cathedral by Lyonel Feininger which was drafted into service as a symbol of the Bauhaus, creating problems when the institution later came to be dubbed "the Cathedral of Socialism."

The history of the Bauhaus is many-faceted and complex, navigating politics, personalities, ideologies and more. But the most apparent legacy was its architectural style, the forerunner of what became known as the "International Style," followed by "post modernism" and other antiseptic variants. A learned and succinct commentary on this subject is the 1982 book by Tom Wolf entitled *From Bauhaus to Our House.* Also worth reading is an article by Hilton Kramer for *The New Criterion*, June 2016, entitled "At the Bauhaus: the fate of art in "The Cathedral of Socialism."

Due to the changing political landscape with the rise of Nazism, the Bauhaus was closed down in 1933. Gropius immigrated to the United States and was invited to head the Architecture Department at Harvard University. His architectural métier was embraced with relish, ushering in not only the austere and sterile International Style to this country but also the compound mentality of conformity in design, the powerful echoes of which have endured to the present in the majority of architectural programs offered today.

Both my father and mother enthusiastically responded to this school of design having been steeped in its study through Pratt Institute. The architectural publication "Pencil Points" turned its attention to Bauhaus designers, and consequentially changed its name to "Progressive Architecture" to align itself with the progressive movement. In the 40s and 50s, my mother decorated her homes in that style with bare hardwood floors and austere naugahyde-covered foam furniture.

The anti-bourgeois focus as manifested in uniform worker housing never translated to the US. Ironically, however, the Bauhaus-inspired style became quite desirable with the one segment of society that could afford to hire architects . . . the derided bourgeoisie.

Photography as a modern art form was acceptable, as was the multi-faceted work of Picasso and other modern contemporary artists. These "forward thinkers" made the realistic painters of the past obsolete and absurd. You wouldn't waste your time, for instance, going to the Huntington Library and seeing works of John Constable or Gainsborough, or Van Dyck. They were passé, and their works were definitely not equal to the social message of Picasso, who extolled the virtues and bravery of the Lincoln Brigade in the Spanish Civil War. Furthermore, the talents of classical artists were wasted painting the corrupt gentry and royalty of Europe, the evil barons of the past whose vestiges would be erased in the new order.

The music in our home was a diet of politically left folksingers like Pete Seeger, Burl Ives, the Almanac Singers, The Weavers, and Woody Guthrie. Paul Robeson's, "Ballad for Americans" and his songs from *Showboat* were often listened to. Russian composers and the Red Army Chorus also filled the living room with their heavy Russian accents offering renditions of the "Volga Boatmen" and "Oh no, John." Much of the artists' music was fun and enjoyable, including charming songs my children adored and loved to hear over and over; and for the general public it was simply entertainment, with no political associations. In my home, however, they were presented and experienced through the lens of politics, as was everything else.

"Drill ye Terriers, Drill" was one of the popular, left-galvanizing, labor folk songs recorded by Pete Seeger. Of particular enjoyment was the line that, after the explosion in the mine, the drillers were "docked for the time they were up in the sky" by the ruthless capitalist bosses and their overseers. All laborers were elevated in status and characterized as suffering, indentured slaves held under the boots of cigar-chomping, bigoted, criminal industrialists. The characterization was strictly black and white: laborers were noble, oppressed victims; the business owner, or "boss," was greedy, heartless, and labeled the oppressor.

Television, then in its infancy, came with its own grading system, good or bad, depending on the politics associated with the program or the actors. Few programs were deemed acceptable, particularly those with actors who had testified about the existence of communist activity in Hollywood during the HCUAA and later the Senate McCarthy hearings. Comedians like Jerry Lewis or Red Skelton were not well received; they didn't deliver an appropriate political message. Skelton in particular was considered a dimwitted moron who wrapped himself in the American flag and prostituted himself before the House Committee. Shows like *Ozzie and Harriet* that showed happy families, nicely dressed people, well-groomed children and orderly life, all of this was nothing more than pap, manufactured by big business interests to distract from the underlying lie that was American life. The irony was that, having played with the Nelson kids on the beach, we could see for ourselves that they were just regular kids like us, and yes, they did seem happy.

Other disliked TV and movie personalities included such names as Gary Cooper and Walt Disney, who testified and offered names of suspected communists. As a result, we never were taken to Disneyland. Actors such as Adolph Menjou, John Wayne, Ginger Rogers, Barbara Stanwyck, Robert Taylor, and Charlton Heston were seen as reprehensible scum. Their anti-communist positions made them nothing more than sell-outs and corrupt scabs, and filled Orville and my mother with disgust.

Hollywood movies and comedians had to have some form of leftist political overtone to be considered good, and anything else was just frivolous drivel that pandered to the ignorant masses. Watching a movie comedy or stand-up act for the sake of diversion and a few laughs was a ridiculous waste of time, but great pains were taken to take us to see old Charlie Chaplin films such as *Modern Times*, where he made fun of the monotonous work in industrial factories, or old Marx Brothers movies such as *Duck Soup* and *Horse Feathers*. Neither Marx nor Chaplin were ever directly associated with the Communist Party; nevertheless, they were tireless leftists with FBI files who danced on the periphery, supporting numerous leftist causes.

A few other comedians could also penetrate Orville's and my mother's humorless personalities, such as Mort Saul, or Victor Borge sliding off his piano stool. These confirmed leftists were hilarious, bright, and right on target. The Smothers Brothers were considered very profound when they launched into their anti-US foreign-policy routines.

Even the seemingly innocuous world of ballet contained political overtones. Orville believed that Russian male ballet dancers were the epitome of masculinity, who exemplified the superiority of Russian art; they were real men. American male ballet dancers were "fairies"; aberrant products of Western decadence. How would he have described, I wonder, the world-renowned dancers Rudolf Nureyev or Alexander Godunov?

* * *

CHAPTER 9

HOUSE AND SENATE INVESTIGATIONS OF THE 40s AND 50s

The House Committee on Un-American Activities (HCUAA) began investigations into suspected Nazi infiltration of the government in 1938. The committee was bipartisan, however, the leading members were Democrats. From mid-1949 and into the 1970s, the committee became better known for investigating alleged disloyalty and subversive activities on the part of private citizens, public employees, and those organizations suspected of having communist ties. The hearings focused on communist infiltration into many aspects of American life, from labor unions to government and beyond. The basis for the hearings was the fact that it was illegal to advocate, either publicly or privately, the overthrow of the government by revolutionary violence. The House was performing its due diligence in its role of protecting the country.

The House investigations are often confused with the Senate hearings involving Sen. Joseph McCarthy, which began in 1950. Both committees were involved in investigating allegations of communist infiltration into various government departments, the military, and other areas of the society. Many of McCarthy's accusations during the Senate hearings allegedly lacked clear evidence at the time, and his rather bombastic personality contributed to public distrust. In fact, his image became that of a paranoid, clownish bufoon who saw communists under the bedsheets, inspired by the *Daily Worker* and other sources of communist propaganda. The oft-used term "red scare" became inextricably linked with McCarthy's name, defining the era. Ironically, since the release of the Soviet NKVD and KGB documents, much of what McCarthy suspected turned out to be accurate. This new information has been largely ignored by modern journalists and academics, but is readily available today.

The American public had no difficulty with, or objection to, the original government inquiries of the HCUAA, leading up to WWII. The target was clear, with Hitler and his followers voicing goals that were repugnant and commonly derided by the American public. But when the investigations later focused on communists and an equally brutal regime, the tables turned. Soviet disinformation, a willing press, and behind-the-scenes efforts by the left, succeeded in making the anti-communists the target, and placing the American justice system on trial. The communist community even rearranged the acronym for the Democratic-controlled HCUAA, to read "HUAC" to describe the committee members and supporters as the "Un-Americans," and turning criticism away from themselves. The tactic was quite successful, and the sentiment endures today, however unfairly.

Having acknowledged his deep involvement with pro-Soviet work during his interviews, Orville admitted he was "scared stiff" at the thought of being called to testify before the House Committee. Nevertheless, he was proud of his friends who not only invoked the Fifth Amendment, but also refrained from implicating others on the witness stand. It is an interesting aside that Orville mentioned in his interviews that he kept records, but that some of them had been burned. As Orville never experienced any of his homes being burned down, I assume he destroyed any incriminating evidence he had (reports, notes, letters, accounts of meetings, etc.) that might implicate him or others in Communist Party or other subversive activities.

To understand what forces lay behind the activities of the American Communist Party and allied groups at this time, and why the government felt the pressing need to engage in these hearings, it is useful to see what the official communist documents guiding these activities contained; the "instruction manual," so to speak.

In 1935, J. Peters, head of communist underground activities in the US, authored the Communist Party's *Manual of Organisation,* which included certain obligations to the party that members were required to fullfill. Section 1. *Fundamentals of the Party Program,* used words from a Lenin pamphlet that stated, "for revolution it is essential, first, that a majority of the workers . . . should fully understand the neccessity for revolution *and be ready to sacrifice their lives for it* [emphasis added]."

The document also states in the same section, "socialism can be won only through revolution." Another quote in Section 1 states, "The Communist Party is armed with the teachings of Marx, Engels, Lenin and Stalin. These teachings are a powerful weapon in the hands of the communist Party."

The section entitled *The Role and Aim of the Communist Party*, also in Section I, states,

> The Communist Party of the U.S.A. leads the working class in the fight for the revolutionary overthrow of capitalism, for the establishment of the dictatorship of the proletariat, for the establishment of a Socialist Soviet Republic in the United States, for the complete abolition of classes, *for the establishment of socialism, the first stage of the classless communist society* [emphasis added].

Section 4. *Party Membership and Cadres – What Are The Conditions For Membership In The Communist Party?* The oath states,

> I now take my place in the ranks of the Communist Party, the Party of the working class . . . I pledge myself to rally the masses to defend the Soviet Union, the land of victorious socialism . . . *I pledge myself to remain at all times a vigilant and firm defender of the Leninist line of the Party, the only line that insures the triumph of Soviet Power in the United States* [emphasis added].

In a section entitled *Who are the Professional Revolutionists*, the document states, "A professional revolutionist is a highly developed comrade . . . who gives his whole life to the fight for the interests of his own class . . . From these comrades, the Party demands everything. They accept Party assignments - the matter of family associations and other personal problems are considered, but are not decisive. If the class struggle demands it, he will leave his family for months, even years. Nothing can shake him."

Clearly, the methodolgy and focus of Soviet communism, as enacted by the policies of the Comintern in Soviet Russia, was the exportation of communism, with Moscow at the center, leading to political domination of the world. The United States of America was the primary target, being the embodiment of western, capitalist culture.

Earl Browder, head of the Communist Party of the US between 1932 to 1945, stated in 1934, "We arm ourselves with the political weapons forged by the victorious Communist Party of the Soviet Union, with the mighty sword of Marxism-Leninism, and are strengthened and inspired by the victories of socialist construction won under its Bolshevik leadership headed by Stalin." He also stated, "Our World Communist Party, the Communist International, provides us the guarantee not only of our victory in America, but of the victory of the proletariat throughout the world."

William Z. Foster, longtime head of CPUSA, spoke openly of CPUSA's goal of creating a "Soviet America," the topic of his 1932 book of the same name.

Sen. Hamilton Fish, questioning Foster in 1930, asked, "If they [Communist Party members] had to choose between the red flag and the American flag, I take it from you that you would choose the red flag, is that correct?" Foster's answer was succinct. "The workers of this country and the workers of every country have only one flag and that is the red flag . . . the red flag is the flag of the revolutionary class, and we are part of the revolutionary class."

Beginning in 1940, the legislature passed various laws aimed at countering the Communist Party's subversive activities in the US which were becoming difficult to ignore. The Voorhis Act of 1940 was passed (18 USC. § 2386), which required "registration with the Attorney General of any organization or political subdivision thereof," whose purpose was the overthrow of the government by the use of force and violence. Another 1940 law passed was The Alien Registration Act (known as the Smith Act) which was designed primarily as a safeguard against sabotage or espionage by aliens, and also prescribed penalties for advocating or promoting overthrow of the government by force. The Internal Security Act (McCarran Act of 1950) was another law passed by the legislature that required all "communist-action" and "communist-front" organizations and their members to register with the Justice Department and give full information of their activities, meetings, sponsored broadcasts and sources of financial support. Communist-action organizations were described as those which were "substantially directed, dominated, or controlled by the foreign government or foreign organization controlling the world communist movement." These acts were declared constitutional by the US Supreme Court in 1951 and, along with later similar legislation, became the basis of the prosecution of members and former members of the American communist movement that threatened the nation.

The revelations of the HCUAA hearings, the fiery trials of the leading members of the Communist Party, the espionage cases of Alger Hiss, the Hollywood Ten, and the Rosenbergs, all contributed to even greater concern from the general public. The result was the enactment of the Internal Security Act of 1950 which stated "the Communist Party should be outlawed." Another provision stated that anyone who "knowingly and willfully becomes or remains a member of the Communist Party shall be subject to the provisional penalties of the law." In addition there were the Immunity Laws which provided a method of compelling reluctant witnesses to testify before committees and grand juries, and would limit witnesses' rights to sanctuary under the Fifth Amemndment; this was a powerful tool at the time. Another law enacted was the Communist Control Act of 1954 which was signed into law by President Dwight Eisenhower on August 24, 1954, which finally outlawed the Communist Party of the United States and criminalized membership. It was also aimed at reducing the danger of sabotage of vital industries as well as facilitating prosecution of subversive individuals. Much of this law was directed at Labor Unions that had come under communist domination.

During early trials, particularly involving eleven leading communists in 1947, the first Amendment (free speech) was employed for defense, but was unsuccessful. By the 50s, accused communists began to cloak themselves with the Fifth Amendment (protection against self-incrimination originally designed to counteract torture in English common law). The main obstacle in the use of the Fifth for the communists was the so-called waiver rule. For those who waived their Fifth Amendment rights in deciding to cooperate with authorities, the Supreme Court did not allow its use in order to avoid testifying against others. This could result in a contempt of Congress charge, and a jail term. During this era, a presumption of guilt by those invoking the Fifth Amendment was difficult to avoid, which had far-reaching impact on the careers of reluctant witnesses and their associates; an unfortunate but understandable consequence.

Another important issue with the American public in the 40s and 50s was whether American communists would side with the US or maintain their allegiance to the Soviet Union in case of conflict. Paul Kengor, in a paper entitled "Who's Un-American? Citizenship and the HUAC, Battle of the 1940s and 1950s," reports that Earl Browder, during his testimony in 1944 before the House Committee, declared that he would attempt to plunge this country into a civil war in the event of an armed conflict with the Soviet Union. Records of those hearings indicate that Browder's comments were echoed by hundreds who could be cited from official Communist Party sources.

When the communists invited Paul Robeson, by then a luminary in the leftist world, to the communist-organized Paris Peace Conference in April, 1949, he sang and then gave a speech which dealt, in part, with this same issue. The French press quoted Robeson saying, "We don't want any hysterical stupidity about our participating in a war against anybody no matter whom. We are determined to fight for peace. We do not wish to fight the Soviet Union." The Associated Press included this quote: "It is unthinkable that American Negroes would go to war on behalf of those who have oppressed us for generations against the Soviet Union which in one generation has lifted our people to full human dignity." In 1956, testifying before the HCUAA, Robeson claimed a lapse in memory as to whether his Peace Conference oratory even happened. "I don't remember," he answered multiple times. He did, however, make clear statements as to where his loyalties lay. "I am truly happy that I am able to travel from time to time to the USSR – the country I love above all. I always have been, I am now and will always be a loyal friend of the Soviet Union."

Kengor reminds us that while the issue of whether the communist ranks would refuse to fight continued to be of concern, the Cold War intensified; the USSR took over Eastern Europe, further expanding their "sphere of influence." The regime murdered and jailed untold numbers of their citizens, exploded their first atom bomb, blockaded Berlin, and converted the Buchenwald death camp into a Soviet concentration camp. The loyalty of Americans to their country was a serious concern.

After the war, former communists, some deeply involved in subversive cells and espionage groups, were exposed in a dizzying array, while still others voluntarily came forward. Two of the most important people in the latter group, were former communists Whittaker Chambers and Elizabeth Bentley both of whom had been intimitely involved in the underground apparatus of Soviet espionage. Chambers presented conclusive evidence of the traitorous acts of the leftist icon, Alger Hiss, a high-ranking government official in Roosevelt's administration, and a secret communist. Hiss was convicted of perjury. (More on Whittaker Chambers later).

Not surprisingly, the left mounted a well-orchestrated effort to denounce not only Chambers and Bentley, but also Joseph McCarthy, pro-American Hollywood personalities, government workers, and others who pointed fingers at the communists. The play, *The Crucible*, written in 1952 by Arthur Miller (who later married Marilyn Monroe), was wildly popular with the left, as it not-so-subtly linked the events of Salem, Massachusetts in the 1600s with the House and Senate hearings, further adding to their fictitious narrative.

A later defense used by witnesses called before the HCUAA was that the Communist Party no longer was pursuing the violent overthrow of capitalism and the US government, but simply promoting a new peaceful transformation to their idealistic socialist society. In the beginning, this was an incredible argument to pursue . . . particularly after the decades of militaristic propaganda and expansionist actions of the Soviets in their world-wide quest for communist domination. Nevertheless, this was the new gospel being preached from on high. In 1957, the day Khrushchev gave his famous "Peaceful Co-existence" speech (shortly after the Soviets brutally extinguished the Hungarian revolution in 1956), Earl Browder, twelve years after his removal as head of CPUSA, gave an interview to Mike Wallace in which he outlined his new vision for America. His solution was a unique American form of communism, as opposed to the Russian variety which was developed to convert a backward country, but was not necessary in the US. The new system would be called "Democratic Socialism," a la 2016 presidential candidate, Bernie Sanders. Nevertheless, this new approach was similarly a product of Marxist dialectical methodology; thesis, antithesis and synthesis, American style. This line of thinking is closely aligned with the Cultural Marxist movement that was rooted in the Frankfort School in Germany and flowered in the US in the 60s, under Herbert Marcuse and other radical philosophers in the universities of America.

The Hollywood Ten, a group of prominent Hollywood screen writers and directors, was one of the high-priority targets of the House investigations, and deserves to be discussed in further detail. They refused to answer whether they had ever been members of the Communist Party and were therefore all found guilty of contempt, serving one-year prison sentences. Orville's interviews contain mention of meeting three members of this group, John Howard Lawson, Dalton Trumbo and Lester Cole, during fund raising events for leftist causes.

Hollywood 10 protesters
Courtesy One Step Productions

Later, during their hearings, both my mother and Orville attended rallies and fund raising events for their defense costs. They and other blacklisted writers were influential in subtle ways in the ongoing quest to promote communist ideals in film, while also working to squelch scripts that portrayed religion, capitalism, or America in a favorable light. During the HCUAA hearings in 1951, John Charles Moffitt, a former member of the Anti-Nazi League, a communist front organization, quoted conversations with Lawson, who was the Hollywood Division head of the Communist Party USA, and also the first president of the Writer's Guild of America. He described a statement Lawson made:

> As writers do not try to write an entire communist picture . . . as the producers will quickly identify it and it will be killed at the front office . . . *as a writer try to get 5 minutes of the Communist doctrine, 5 minutes of the party line in every script that you write* [emphasis added].

All of this was in line with Lenin's statement, "of all the arts, for us the most important is cinema." Grigory Zinoviev, head of the Soviet Comintern, ordered that motion pictures "must become a mighty weapon of communist propaganda."

Humphrey Bogart and Lauren Bacall were among many Hollywood stars who formed a support group that traveled to Washington, DC in 1947 to defend the Hollywood Ten, calling themselves The Committee for the First Amendment," but they withdrew when presented evidence validating the charges.

Bogart wrote an article entitled "I'm No Communist" for the March, 1948, issue of Photoplay. In it, he explained that he and other members of the Committee had not realized that some of the Hollywood Ten actually were communists. Bogart, one of the biggest Hollywood stars of his time, was attacked by many liberals and fellow travelers, who claimed he was selling out to save his career. Orville could barely mention his name without showing obvious revulsion.

Bacall and Bogart leading Hollywood 10 protesters to the capitol, 1947

Public domain

The Rosenbergs: But the biggest target of the House committee, and the legal battle that was heard around the world was the spy case against Julius and Ethel Rosenberg and their espionage network.

During the late 30s through the 40s, Julius Rosenberg, with the assistance of his wife, Ethel, organized and ran an espionage ring on behalf of the Soviet government. They were arrested in 1950 on charges of turning over atomic bomb and other military secrets to Moscow, which were later confirmed by Soviet intelligence and testimony from co-conspirators. The couple, convicted in 1951, was executed at Sing-Sing prison in New York in 1953, the last people in the US involved in a treason trial to be convicted and sentenced to death.

Ethel and Julius Rosenberg during trial in 1951

Commonswikimedia.org

During the Rosenberg's incarceration and trial, Orville, my mother, and thousands of pro-Soviet leftists around the world, rose in anger, marching in the streets and crying out for the end of the "injustice" against the Rosenbergs. When the duo was convicted, the depression in the leftist community was palpable and widespread.

I was well aware of the intense activity on behalf of the Rosenbergs. Along with the demonstrations there were fund raising efforts, and I recall being taken to many events at the Unitarian Church and elsewhere. It loomed as one of the most important events of the era, at least as far as the radical left was concerned. For the rest of the country, it was justice being served; a justice that was far kinder than what was happening in their beloved Soviet Union.

The effect of the Rosenberg case on that community was described by Ronald Radosh, an adjunct professor at the Hudson Institute and a leading author on the subject of the Rosenbergs, as "a lynchpin of the American left's argument that the United States government was not only evil during the Cold War years, but was ready to kill regular American citizens because they were against the Truman administration's anti-Soviet policies embodied in the 'Truman Doctrine.'"

There was, at the same time, consternation on two fronts within the Jewish community; on one hand, they were deeply concerned about justice, but on the other hand, there was fear of a backlash against them if the American public felt they condoned spying. According to Marc Tracy, a staff writer with the *New Republic,* the case against the Rosenbergs, and its inherent issue of justice, "obsessed the American Jewish community for six decades," with just about everyone taking one side or the other.

Rosenberg protesters heading to Washington, D.C., gathering at Pennsylvania Station. June 17, 1953. Library of Congress

During the six decades after the trial and execution, the case was kept in the forefront of public opinion with a continuous and ongoing campaign of articles in the old leftist newspaper the *National Guardian,* books written by the Rosenberg's sons, Michael and Robert Meeropol, and a castigating chorus of other leftist writers and commentators. Storylines centered on the well-worn themes that questioned the American justice system and basic American civility; the evil motives of the American government's conspiratorial framing and implicating of the Rosenberg's; a vile anti-Semitic American undercurrent; and the accusation that the Rosenbergs were simply scapegoats in the era of "red hysteria," engineered by the despised Sen. Joseph McCarthy. The supposed innocence of other members of the Rosenberg spy ring, including Morton Sobell, Ethel's brother, David Greenglass, and others, was also touted.

However, the facts clearly flew in the face of any perceived innocence on the part of the Rosenbergs and their cohorts. The official accusations were that William Perl, a brilliant aeronautical engineer and a member of the Rosenberg cell, obtained a massive quantity of technical data from the safe of Theodore Von Karman, the chairman of the US Air Force Scientific Advisory Board. The information included the hovering performance of helicopters powered by jet propulsion; reciprocating engines; high-speed wind tunnel tests; information about the D-558 research airplane; preliminary tests of the NACA 66-006 airfoil; and also data pertaining to the Lexington Report, a detailed study of the feasibility of nuclear-powered aircraft. The tests and diagrams included everything that Von Karman, Americas leading space engineer, was working on. In addition, during Julius Rosenberg's incarceration, government informant Jerome Tartakow, sharing the same cell, reported to the FBI that Julius had bragged about the purloined data and that the documents had kept a four-man team busy for seventeen hours, photographing documents with their Leica cameras.

Since the early 1980s, much has been written by researchers who have studied a wealth of information in regard to the Rosenbergs, and offering counter-arguments to their alleged innocence. The most prominent of these are Harvey Klehr, John Earl Haynes, Ronald Radosh, Steven Usdin and Allen Hornblum, who collectively have authored some six books and numerous articles on the subject. Much of the following is taken from their research and writings, mixed with my own remembrances and independent research.

Composite photo of Rosenberg co-conspirators, David Greenglass (Ethel's brother) (l.) and Morton Sobell (r.) convicted of A-bomb espionage, arriving at the Federal Court to be sentenced. New York. 1951

Major revelations appeared with the release of both the *Venona decrypts* collected during WWII, containing the decoded messages between the KGB and their field agents, and the extensive KGB files released by a Russian defector, Alexander Vassiliev.

Ronald Radosh confirmed through these sources that Julius Rosenberg was a KGB agent who organized and ran an espionage spy ring of college friends, made up of engineers and scientists and that his wife, Ethel, knew of and supported his activities. The archival documents show Ethel Rosenberg hid money and espionage paraphernalia for her husband, served as an intermediary for communications with his Soviet intelligence contacts, provided her personal evaluation of individuals Julius considered recruiting, and was present at meetings with his sources. They also demonstrated that Julius reported to the KGB and that Ethel persuaded her sister-in-law, Ruth Greenglass, to travel to New Mexico to recruit Ethel's brother David as a spy. David Greenglass was working in Los Alamos on the Manhattan project's development of the atomic bomb. In addition, the Venona decrypts regarding Ruth's KGB recruitment states, "*Liberal* (Julius) and his wife (Ethel) recommend her (Ruth) as an intelligent and clever girl."

The information gathered by the spy ring, Radosh writes, was an "extraordinary trove of non-nuclear espionage on radar, sonar, and jet propulsion engines to the Soviets, but the Rosenberg's contributions to the Soviet nuclear weapons program was also important, as it was valuable and practical confirmation of data it was receiving from Klaus Fuchs and Ted Hall, the two major nuclear spies in the Manhattan project."

Morton Sobell, who had spent 18 years in the penitentiary for his collaboration with the spy ring, spent years vociferously and condescendingly promoting his innocence in books and to the media. But in 2008 he suddenly had a change of heart.

In an article in *The New York Times* dated September, 11, 2008, Sobell confessed to journalist Sam Roberts that he had in fact been a Soviet spy; implicated Julius Rosenberg, and admitted they had stolen major military secrets "desired by the Soviets." He also confirmed that Ethel was aware of her husband's activities, which aligned with the Venona decrypts and KGB information. This was certainly a bombshell to the left, however, there was still more to learn. When questioned more deeply as to his spy activities, he hedged a bit before responding, "Yeah, yeah, yeah, call it that." He then added his incredulous conclusion, that, "I never thought of it as that in those terms."

Morton Sobell interview, with poster of Rosenbergs in background, 2008.
NY Times / Redux Pictures

Additionally, he stated that he turned over the information during WWII when we were "allies with the Soviets." This, of course, was a bending of the truth as the year of the theft for which he was indicted was 1948, well into the Cold War period. He also de-emphasized the quality of the stolen data, making the distinction that it was "non-nuclear" and intended to produce weapons that were defensive only. By discounting the massive military information they passed on, Sobell, in his odd and contorted reasoning, did not believe they were guilty of anything close to nuclear espionage.

Three years later, in December, 2010, an even greater bombshell hit squarely into the Rosenberg defenders' midst. During an interview with researcher Peter Usdin, author of *Engineering Communism,* Sobell added important information to the 2008 interview. He now recounted with great specificity his and other members of the ring's involvement in espionage activities. Sitting in his living room under a portrait of Ethel and Julius, he recounted to Usdin his involvement in stealing the documents and what they consisted of:

> On a nonstop photo session over a July 4 weekend in 1948, he, Julius Rosenberg, National Advisory Committee for Aeronautics scientist William Perl, and a fourth man took films of 1,885 pages of classified documents stolen for them by Perl from a Columbia University safe belonging to Theodore von Kármán, at that time the nation's most prominent aerospace engineer. *It included information about the designs and capabilities of every American bomber, designs for analog and digital computers used to automate antiaircraft weapons, and specifications for land-based and airborne radars later used in Korea* [emphasis added.] He thus provided information that advanced the capabilities of the Soviet military machine.

Both Radosh and Usdin also reported on Sobell's role in the transfer of film to the KGB. During the interview, Sobell told Usdin, "We got all the manuals and secrets from Langley Field." On the following Monday morning, Sobell and Rosenberg, "packed canisters of developed 35 mm film in a box that was so heavy one man could barely carry it, took a train to Long Island, *and gave it to the Russians on the platform* [emphasis added]."

Sobell grinned from ear to ear as he described the Leica cameras and apparatus they used to photograph the massive espionage haul and how quickly the documents had to be returned by Perl to Von Karman's safe. The "Leica camera" statement reinforced informant Tartakow's jailhouse conversation with Julius that was so derided by the left at the time of the trial, a piece of information condemned as being part of the government frame-up.

Usdin and Radosh reported that Sobell acknowledged he was engaged in this espionage not because he was anti-fascist, but, as he told them, "I did it for the Soviet Union." His parents were communists who were dedicated to support of the Soviets, his mother even holding Communist Party meetings in the family's apartment when Sobell was a toddler. One of Sobell's uncles ran a communist summer camp in the Catskills and another worked as a secret courier carrying messages between New York and Moscow. Sobell never perceived of himself as anything but a communist. His spying continued until the day he fled to Mexico in 1950 and tried to book passage on a Soviet freighter in an attempt to escape arrest. He was eventually apprehended, however, by Mexican police and returned to US authorities. Not surprisingly, Sobell described it as an unfair "kidnapping."

During the original trial, testimony from another member of the spy ring, Max Elitcher, Sobell's former college roommate, was also enlightening. He told of shaking off an FBI tail on his way to Sobell's home, and accompanying his friend on a late-night excursion to East River Drive in New York City, parking on a deserted waterfront street, and waiting while Sobell delivered a film canister to Rosenberg a few blocks away.

Usdin wrote of other thefts by the spy ring, both during and after WWII:

> The Rosenberg network, especially the agents Joel Barr and Alfred Sarant, passed on the 12,000-page blueprints for the Lockheed P-80 Shooting Star, airborne radars for nighttime navigation and bombing, and other new radar technology. Rosenberg's band of amateur spies turned over detailed information on a wide range of technologies and weapon systems that hastened the Red Army's march to Berlin, jump-started its postwar development of nuclear weapons and delivery systems, and later helped Communist troops in North Korea fight the American military to a standoff.
>
> Both Barr and Sarant fled the U.S. immediately after the Greenglass and Rosenberg arrests, first to Czechoslovakia, and later to the Soviet Union where they were instrumental in establishing the Soviet 'Silicon Valley.'

Radosh's book, *Cold Case: Ethel and Julius Rosenberg*, referred to additional information which he included in an earlier article for the Jewish on-line magazine, *Tablet.* It contained his response to Sobell and the outspoken leftists, who claimed that the information turned over to the KGB by the Rosenberg ring was "harmless," "of little value," or "junk."

As new information found in espionage historian Alexander Vassiliev's notebooks revealed, Greenglass had in fact not only given a primitive sketch of the bomb's lens configuration to Harry Gold, Rosenberg's courier, but later delivered to him the physical mold of a detonator for the bomb. The detonators were built in the shop in which Greenglass worked.

Greenglass clarified in his testimony that the elements of the explosive lenses of the Fat Man bombs used for the Trinity nuclear test and the bombing of Nagasaki were poured into the molds.

Further addressing the "harmless" data turned over, to the Soviets. Radosh wrote, "Moreover, the supposedly 'harmless' material the Rosenberg ring handed over to the KGB included radar specifications and aircraft designs that gave the Soviet military critical information about American capabilities, allowed the Red Army to jam US radar, and contributed to the development of sophisticated Soviet fighters that equaled those deployed by the US Air Force. There can be no doubt that this technology directly led to the deaths of thousands of American soldiers in Korea and Vietnam."

By now, if anyone needs further proof of the treachery of this America-hating cabal assembled by the Rosenbergs, Radosh continued in an article for www.nysun.com in 2014.

As for Greenglass himself, he not only provided the famous sketch of the bomb's lens mold, but as KGB reports indicate, he gave them a "report on a scientific experimentation center for preparing a uranium bomb, with a general floor plan and sketches of individual buildings attached." KGB agent Leonid Kvasnikov described a 33-page letter he received from Greenglass on the preparation of a uranium bomb, the structural solutions for building one, and methods for obtaining Uranium-235, which Kvasnikov called "highly valuable." Finally, not only did he give them the sketch that was displayed at the trial, but he provided the KGB, as their reports indicate, with "a physical sample of material used in the detonator."

This begs an obvious question: If the information was so harmless, why did the entire Rosenberg ring work so hard at the risk of their lives to copy and hand it over to their KGB handlers?

In 1997, Alexsandre Feklisov, the KGB underground operative and agent of the Rosenbergs, wrote in his memoirs that he considered the pair to be "heroes" and described their traitorous behavior "in glowing terms." A photo in his book shows him kissing Ethel and Julius's tomb. Radosh writes that the modern day KGB foreign intelligence arm (the name was changed to the SVR in 1954) "proudly proclaims both Julius and Ethel as 'greats' who served Moscow."

Even Nikita Khrushchev, in his dictated memoir of 1970-74, published in 1990, admitted that the Rosenberg data was instrumental in building the first Soviet atom bomb. A *New York Times* article from September, 25, 1990 quotes the memoirs,

> From Stalin and from the longtime Soviet Foreign Minister, Vyacheslav M. Molotov, the memoir says, Khrushchev learned that Julius and Ethel Rosenberg had *"provided very significant help in accelerating the production of our atomic bomb* ... Let this be a worthy tribute to the memory of those people . . . *Let my words serve as an expression of gratitude to those who sacrificed their lives to a great cause of the Soviet state* at a time when the U.S. was using its advantage over our state to blackmail our state and undermine its proletarian cause [emphasis added]."

Marxist apologists for the Rosenbergs and the Meeropols have also tried to use the argument that the Rosenbergs and Sobell were only "helping a war-time ally against fascism," and that Julius Rosenberg "was ignorant of the Atomic bomb project." Both Radosh and Usdin state that these are absurd defenses considering the fact that "Julius set up his network during the Nazi-Soviet Pact, when the United States and Russia were not allies," and kept the network alive after the war's end during the Cold War. The myth that Julius was motivated by anti-fascist concerns, rather than a desire to serve Stalin, according to Radosh, "is the greatest myth of all." David Greenglass, in an interview with Radosh stated, "He and Julius saw themselves as 'soldiers for Stalin.'"

John Earl Haynes and Harvey Klehr in their book *Spies,* stated that not only did Ethel suggest her brother, David Greenglass, be recruited by the KGB, but even more importantly Julius had recruited a second atom spy, Russell McNutt, precisely because he thought that McNutt would be able to gather atomic bomb information from the plant in Oak Ridge, Tennessee.

Greenglass, who served 9 1/2 years in the penitentiary for his role, worked first at the Clinton Engineer Works uranium enrichment facility at Oak Ridge, Tennessee, and then for the Manhattan Project at the Los Alamos laboratory in New Mexico. He lied on his security clearance application, omitting details of his and his wife's former Communist Party membership dating back to 1942. His testimony was significant in the prosecution of the case against his sister and Julius, testimony that he later repudiated with the excuse that he was protecting his wife and that she was a lot more important than his sister.

The law at the time the Rosenbergs were convicted was Section 2 of the Espionage Act of 1917, 50 *US Code 32* (now 18 US Code 794), which "prohibits transmitting or attempting to transmit to a foreign government information relating to the national defense." But because some still argue that the Rosenbergs would not have been found guilty in a present-day court of law, I quote the same law as it stands today:

> *Whoever, with intent or reason to believe that it is to be used to the injury of the United States or to the advantage of a foreign nation,* communicates, delivers, or transmits, or attempts to communicate, deliver, or transmit, to any foreign government, or to any faction or party or military or naval force within a foreign country, whether recognized or unrecognized by the United States, or to any representative, officer, agent, employee, subject, or citizen thereof, either directly or indirectly, any document, writing, code book, signal book, sketch, photograph, photographic negative, blueprint, plan, map, model, note, instrument, appliance, or information relating to the national defense, *shall be punished by death or by imprisonment for any term of years or for life*, ... [emphasis added].

The code also states another provision that affects Ethel's and the other conspirators' roles. "(c) If two or more persons conspire to violate this section, and one or more of such persons do any act to effect the object of the conspiracy, each of the parties to such conspiracy shall be subject to the punishment provided for the offense which is the object of such conspiracy."

It seems fairly evident that the Rosenbergs violated just about every sentence in the long description above. And the punishment, albeit harsh, is spelled out in no uncertain terms. If the additional data known today were known in 1950, it is also likely that Morton Sobell and others would have joined the Rosenbergs at Sing-Sing.

The sons of Julius and Ethel Rosenberg, Michael and Robert Meeropol, were adopted by relatives at the ages of six and eight; hence, their surname was changed. They have continued a lifelong pursuit of their parent's innocence, putting forth their vehement positions through books, articles and speaking engagements. They began in the 1970s with the assertion that their parents were framed and completely innocent because, "Everyone was saying they were innocent" and "it was part of my reality." But those early assertions steadily eroded over the decades as a result of the Venona and Vassiliev data, not to mention the dramatic admissions of Morton Sobell. This new information was above and beyond the evidence proffered at the trial from witnesses, members of the ring, and from the Greenglass side of the family.

Robert Meeropol, in repayment to the progressive community that "helped him survive," is still deeply involved with progressive politics. He formed the Rosenberg Fund for Children (RFC), "to help children of targeted activists in the US today." Since the second Sobell confession, he has reluctantly accepted the fact that their father was a spy and did not tell the truth to his sons. Rosenberg's last letter to them stated, "Always remember that we were innocent and could not wrong our conscience."

But even with that blow, the brothers continue soldiering on. Their current argument is that "whatever atomic bomb information their father passed to the Russians was, at best, superfluous; the case was riddled with prosecutorial and judicial misconduct; their mother was convicted on flimsy evidence to place leverage on her husband; and neither deserved the death penalty." Their mother, they concluded in particular, had not been a spy, but rather had been framed by the false testimony of her brother, and should never have been tried, much less executed.

Their uncle, David Greenglass, originally testified that Ethel had typed up the bomb and detonator information that was then turned over to Julius. But before his death in 2014, he reversed himself, saying "I frankly think my wife did the typing, but I don't remember." His justification for his trial testimony was that he was trying to save his wife, choosing instead to implicate his sister. The Meeropols believe this is what exonerates their mother, claiming this "false" testimony was part of the "frame-up." But this singular typing incident was only one in a sea of treacherous involvement over many years, which was well documented by the Venona decrypts, KGB documents, and the original evidence.

Today there is really no question as to Ethel's involvement and subsequent guilt, nor is there any question as to the impact of these treasonous activities against our country. But, as Radosh says, the question as to whether she should have been executed may be debated for years to come, but not her innocence.

I can empathize with the Merropols, suffering such a devestating loss of their parents under the harshest of circumstances. However, their continued attempts at a defense in the face of such a perponderance of evidence, have served to strain their credibility, even as they continue to villify the American government for their travails.

Other present-day Rosenberg defenders have continued down this shameful path. In the *Monthly Review* of February 9, 2011 (a magazine founded by Orville's communist friends, Leo Huberman and Paul Sweezy), Radosh cites an article written by leftist activist Staughton Lynd, who offers the incredible defense that the "trial was a sham," and that the Rosenberg's had, "obligations as communists, and as citizens of the world . . . that even if they were guilty, they must be viewed as unadulterated heroes," and that, "If the Rosenberg's helped the Soviet's get the bomb, that might have been justified."

Staughton Lynd, glorified by the left in the late 60s and early 70s, traveled with Tom Hayden and the Communist Party historian Herbert Aptheker, to

Vietnam in 1965–66. The group returned, extolling the virtues of Vietnamese Communism and calling for the immediate US withdrawal from the war.

After years of agitating and lobbying by the Meeropols, the New York City Council, on September 29, 2015, issued a proclamation declaring September 28 (the hundredth anniversary of Ethel's birth), "Ethel Rosenberg Day of Justice in the Borough of Manhattan," and presenting formal statements, including that she was "wrongly executed," it was a "rush to judgment," and that this was a "terrible stain on our country." Radosh's reply in *The New York Times* (Oct. 1, 2015), was apropos,

> The real stain is on New York city's gullible representatives, Revelations over the past 20 years--the Venona decrypts of KGB transmissions to its American agents in the 1940s, and KGB files released by a Russian defector who now lives in Britain, Alexander Vassiliev--showed concretely Ethel's involvement in her husband's espionage ring . . . she helped recruit her sister-in-law, Ruth, who in turn brought her husband – Ethel's brother—David Greenglass into the ring that passed secrets to KGB courier Harry Gold. *It is sad when New York officially honors a woman whose loyalty was to the Soviet Union* ... who martyred herself by refusing to tell the truth, leaving two orphan sons, because she was a firm believer in Joseph Stalin and his totalitarian dictatorship [emphasis added].

Radosh also refers to a statement made by historian Gordon S. Wood who reflected on "the differences between critical history and popular memory, between what historians write and what society chooses to remember." When it comes to the Rosenberg case, many of the old left cannot find it within themselves to let go of their deeply ingrained opinions; they have simply been vociferously expounded upon for too many years, making their distorted and innacurate views the reality they wish to remember.

Viewing the traitorous behavior of the Rosenbergs and their band of vipers from a distance, one only has to return to the requirements of the Communist Party in the 30s and 40s, that incorporated Lenin's following statements and directives: ". . . for revolution it is essential, first, that a majority of the workers . . . *should fully understand the neccessity for revolution and be ready to sacrifice their lives for it* [emphasis added].

A professional revolutionist is a highly developed comrade . . . *who gives his whole life to the fight for the interests of his own class* . . . [emphasis added].

From these comrades, the Party demands everything. They accept Party assignments - the matter of family associations and other personal problems are considered, but are not decisive. If the class struggle demands it, he will leave his family for months, even years. Nothing can shake him [emphasis added]."

It is likely Ethel Rosenberg could have saved her own life by confessing her involvement and reporting the names of other espionage cell members, many of them close friends. But she chose martyrdom by following the dictates of Lenin, Joseph Stalin, and the Soviet cause. The fact still remains that the Rosenbergs led one of the most devastating espionage conspiracies in American history, threatening US security and damaging our international affairs.

Caryl Chessman: The case of Caryl Chessman was not involved with the HCUAA or Senate hearings as the Rosenberg case was, but it had a parallel significance to the radical left as it related to the fairness of the US judicial system.

Chessman was born in 1921, and spent most of his life in and out of prison. In January, 1948, one month after his latest prison release, he committed a series of armed robberies, which also included kidnapping, sexual assault, and rape. He was apprehended and convicted on seventeen of the eighteen counts against him and condemned to death under the "Little Lindbergh Law," in place at the time. The law defined kidnapping as a capital offense under certain circumstances. The left saw his case as another wonderful example of the unfairness of the American judicial system. The goal was keeping it in the headlines; the longer, the better. Orville, my mother, Dr. Fritchman, the Unitarian church members, the ACLU, liberal publications and radicals from all over the world joined in protest to save the life of "the red-light bandit," proclaiming the death penalty "cruel and unjust."

Student protests for Caryl Chessman, c. 1959

This prolonged fight, over twelve years, resulted in my own participation during high school. I remember being fired up over the political fervor and offered spirited arguments in favor of Chessman's innocence and the dreadful injustice being dealt him.

While in San Quentin awaiting execution, Chessman acted as his own attorney, claiming his innocence, and securing multiple stays. The longer the case went on, the more world-wide attention it garnered. Unfortunately lost in the political swirl was the plight of the victims; the rapes, the robberies, the abductions and the terrorization of these innocent citizens seemed to be in the distant background.

Also missing from the discussion was the routine lack of an authentic judicial system in the ever-admired Soviet Union. Where was the American left's outrage at the show trials, at the gulags with their slave labor, and the millions of executed? Regardless of one's support for or against the death penalty, Chessman's trial, appeals, and procedure followed the law as it was written at that time. No such series of appeals and stays would have been possible for Chessman had he been a resident of the beloved USSR. The hypocrisy was glaring.

* * *

CHAPTER 10

COMMUNIST GOALS AND THE NEW SOCIETY

What did the communists target and why? From Orville I learned about the communist tactics of attacking the institutions of America through the continuous and effective use of *agitation*, a term they used with abandon as it was an important and essential tactic emphasized by the Soviet Comintern. The goal was to create chaos, disharmony, and a disturbing undercurrent of unease in all sectors of American life. When people feel that their world is out of control, the communist plan goes, they will clamor for the government to swoop in and relieve their anxieties and fix the perceived problems. That government "fix," however, would be under the control of Moscow. The 1921 *Comintern (Communist International) Guidelines on the Organizational Structure of Communist Parties*, in the *Methods and Content of their Work*, IV, No. 20, *On Propaganda and Agitation*, states,

> In the period prior to the open revolutionary uprising our most general task is revolutionary propaganda and agitation . . . *without particular concern for the concrete revolutionary content of our speeches and written material* [emphasis added].

In other words, the targeted institutions had no particular weighting in terms of what to attack first; an overall, comprehensive campaign was the tool, and disguise was paramount. Any opportunity that presented itself was fair game. What was important was to keep banging the pan with a hammer to drown out anything else, until people were worn down. The targets included the military establishment; "right-wing Hollywood types," the "racist society," the "religious nuts," prayers invoked within any official or semi-official capacity; the corrupt political system that tried to exclude communists; "right-wing" newspapers with their "reactionary" writers; the schools; US foreign and domestic policies; patriotic displays showing love for flag and country; the Pledge of Allegiance; and on to infinity.

With regard to the military a balance had to be struck: a revolution would require arms and weapons, but the propaganda position also opposing war had to be maintained. The Comintern Guidelines, Section IV, *On Propaganda and Agitation,* No. 30, states the two positions,

> For propaganda work in the army and navy of the capitalist state, a special study must be made of the most appropriate methods in each individual country . . . The proletariat rejects in principle and combats with the utmost energy all military institutions of the bourgeois state and of the bourgeois class in general. On the other hand, it utilizes these institutions (army, rifle clubs, territorial militias, etc.) to give the workers military training for revolutionary battles . . . every possibility for the proletariat to get weapons into its hands must be exploited to the fullest.

The brave new communist society/marriage and family: What was the picture of the brave new society as revealed to me in my youth? First, it was to be a society where "want" would be unknown. Everyone would work for the good of the society, each to their own capacity. Of course, Orville and those in his group would be elevated to the ruling clique, because of their work for the party, and their superior intellects. The society would be perfect as envisioned by Marx and Engels. It wouldn't be shackled by false religion, greedy capitalists, or the negativity of American imperialistic ambitions. In addition, group living versus nuclear families was heralded as the mode of the future. Growing up in collective farms with multiple parents and all working for the good of the community was ideal, just like in Russia where sanity surely prevailed. There would be no more unfair land ownership, or fences cutting people off from their neighbors. Besides, what gives anyone the right to own land? Racism would simply melt away and be a non-issue. No want, no greed, no need for prisons, no need for a military, no striving to get ahead at the expense of others. My mother oft stated that the white race would meld together with the "genetically stronger, darker races," and after a few generations the population would be a "lovely shade of brown." This seemed to say that when all the whites were gone, the problems of the world would fade away. It also said to me that my very existence as a white person was a large part of the problem. I doubt, though, that she saw herself as being in the same position.

The press: The reading population of the US, as in most countries, can be heavily influenced by the editorials and columns that are published in newspapers and magazines. Certain publications and writers invariably rise in importance and popularity, and can become the mouthpiece and authority for large segments of the population. Their insights and nuances can be vitally important in shaping what the public perceives as the truth.

In order for leftist ideology to have succeeded, there had to be a strong element of the press that supported it and put air under its wings. There were plenty of writers, newspapers and magazines that stepped into the fray and righteously supported the ideals of the communist world. As early as 1901, Lenin is quoted in his *What is to be Done? Plan for an All-Russian Political Newspaper,* "A newspaper is not only a collective propagandist and a collective agitator; it is also a collective organiser."

Another Lenin quote is also telling about how he uses newspapers, "He who now talks about the 'freedom of the press' goes backward, and halts our headlong course towards Socialism."

It is worth repeating the *Comintern Guidelines on the Methods and Content of Their Work, III. No. 12,* which describes the importance of the press and literary work in furthering communist goals, "Communist *nuclei* are to be formed for day-to-day work in different areas of party activity: for door-to-door agitation, for party studies, *for press work, for literature distribution,* for intelligence gathering, communications, etc. [emphasis added]."

Among the publications that were the mainstay of the left movement, the following stand out as prime examples: *I.F. Stone's Weekly*, *New Masses* (a Marxist weekly periodical), *The Nation,* the *National Guardian, The New York Times*, and the all-important communist organ, the *Daily Worker*. These and others were avidly read by my mother, stepfather, and our family friends. The articles from these publications were held up as evidence and justification for leftist ideology.

The *Daily Worker* was the official Communist Party organ and was required reading by all members. It was published between 1924 and 1957, and laid out on a daily basis the Soviet Comintern thrust and direction in the quest to crush capitalism. It was instrumental in dispersing the massive Soviet disinformation campaigns. The paper maintained a series of correspondents in Moscow, including communists Vern Smith and Janet Ross. In the mid-30s, Smith regularly depicted the Soviet Union in the most favorable light. In so doing, the publication

Typical "Daily Worker" publication.

defended Stalin's Great Terror (Purge) (1936–38), and upheld the Moscow show trials in which evidence was fabricated against "the accused," and extorting their "confessions." Smith also endorsed Moscow's suppression of the Hungarian uprising. He attacked all opponents of Stalinist socialism, including Trotsky, who was assassinated in Mexico on Stalin's orders in 1940. In the 30s, the paper proudly proclaimed that "Communism is Twentieth Century Americanism," and characterized itself as the heir to the tradition of Washington and Lincoln; a further example of communists being portrayed as the ultimate American patriots.

The American Marxist magazine, *New Masses,* which was published from 1926 to 1948, was closely associated with the Communist Party. The magazine was touted as a major force of the American cultural left from 1926 onwards. Whittaker Chambers was the editor in 1931, until he was ordered into the communist underground the following year. By the late 1930s, *New Masses* strongly backed the Popular Front movement (communist coalition) and became an official organ of the Communist Party.

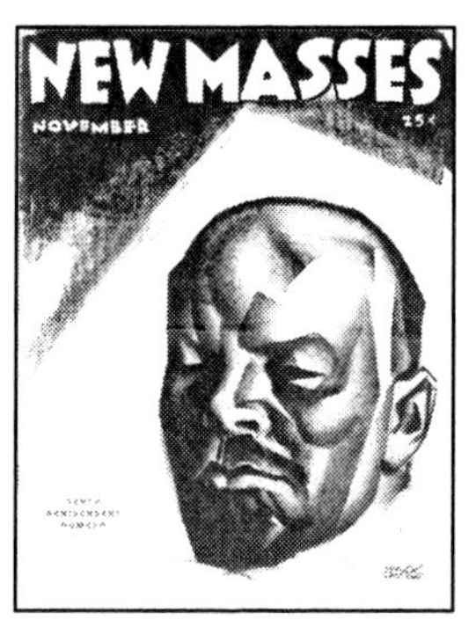

Typical "New Masses" publication with Lenin on cover.

I was only six years old at the closing of the magazine, but Orville maintained a stack of the black-and-white, starkly presented issues, from which he would produce articles to educate me about various political topics. What I recall primarily were articles and poems penned by the black writers Richard Wright and Langston Hughes.

The writer/poet/civil rights pioneer, Langston Hughes, was born in 1902, and became heavily involved very early with the civil rights movement. Like many black writers and artists of his time, Hughes was drawn to the promise of communism as an alternative to a segregated America, and his poetry was frequently published in *New Masses.* He became infatuated with all things Soviet, traveling there in 1932 to make a movie about racism in the US. There he met another black, Robert Robinson, an engineer who had immigrated to Russia in 1930 to work in the Soviet auto industry.

Desiring to leave the USSR and return to the States due to growing concerns for his safety, Robinson had requested permission several times to vacation in Ethiopia as a means of escape, but was regularly denied. Author of *The Forsaken,* Tim Tzouliadis, recounts Robinson's appeal to Paul Robeson for help. What Robinson received was a letter of denial from Robeson's wife, Eslanda, expressing their fear that if Robinson left the Soviet Union and subsequently expressed anti-

Soviet sentiments, it would reflect badly on the Robeson's and put them in a dangerous situation. It had to be sobering for Hughes to learn that Robinson had been stripped of his passport and not allowed to leave. Here was a stark example of the true Russia.

In his autobiography, Robinson described his dread fear of the Soviet KGB; he slept in his clothes nightly for fear he would hear a knock on his door at any moment. In 1974, after 44 years in Russia, including 27 years of attempts to leave, Robinson was finally granted permission to vacation in Uganda. He purchased a round-trip ticket so as to not arouse suspicion, but was then able to gain help to return to the United States, regain his passport, and live in the US for the remainder of his life.

In 1937, Hughes traveled to Spain as a correspondent for various communist African-American newspapers and was also involved in other communist-led organizations, such as the John Reed Club, an organization dominated by the Communist Party. Hughes signed a 1938 statement supporting Joseph Stalin's purges of the Old Bolsheviks, and joined the American Peace Mobilization in 1940 in an attempt to keep the US from participating in WWII. This was during the Nazi-Russian non-aggression pact, and Hughes was following the Moscow party line.

In the same year, Hughes presented a poem in Pasadena, Calif., under the auspices of the "International Union of Revolutionary Writers," entitled *Goodbye, Christ.* It urged Jesus to get out of the way, that the Bible was dead, and was being replaced by "A real guy named Marx Communist Lenin Peasant Stalin. . . . Worker ME—." Typical of Hughes at that period in his life, he glorified his communist/atheist ideology.

In the early 1950s. Hughes was brought before the HCUAA. By that time, he had begun to distance himself from communism and was a cooperative witness. However, he did refrain from implicating others, with the claim that his beliefs were completely his own. He died in 1967.

Richard Wright was born in 1908, and like Hughes, was drawn toward communism in the 30s. In 1932, he began attending meetings of the John Reed Club. He formally joined the Communist Party in late 1933 and as a revolutionary poet wrote numerous proletarian poems for *New Masses* and other left-wing periodicals. Wright moved to Paris in 1946, having left the Communist Party in 1942, and became a permanent American expatriate. Later, he wrote a book, *Black Boy*, chronicling his Communist Party involvement.

American blacks in the 30s and 40s were striving for their day in the sun and their civil rights. Large segments of the general population also wished change. But in the 30s, the CPUSA, responding to the Comintern directives, saw an opening to promote societal division through the civil rights movement. They were very successful in their manipulations, and the remnants are still visible in present day American politics. Many black intellectuals like Paul Robeson, Hughes and Wright responded to the Soviet clarion call, moved by the Soviet constitution that forbade discrimination. However, blacks were not spared from Stalin's periodic disfavor; they were grouped with fellow Westerners as foreigners warranting suspicion and expulsion. Once this was understood, it frequently led to disillusionment with communism and a subsequent distancing.

The *National Guardian*, later known as *The Guardian*, was a periodical I remember as another mainstay of Orville's and my mother's weekly reading requirements. It was a radical leftist independent weekly newspaper established in 1948 in New York City, originally published in close connection with the 1948 presidential campaign of Henry A. Wallace under the Progressive Party banner. Although independent of any political party, the *National Guardian* was initially close to the ideological orbit of the pro-Moscow Communist Party USA. However, in February, 1968, the newspaper's editorial staff was reorganized. The paper shortened its name to *The Guardian* and gradually turned towards a pro-Chinese orientation and support of the Maoist New Communist Movement in the United States. It was last published in 1992.

STOP THE BROWNELL BILLS – SAVE THE CONSTITUTION – WIRE CONGRESS TODAY!

NATIONAL GUARDIAN

World free of major war first time in 15 years — so Ike asks more guns

Typical "National Guardian" publication.

Individual writers committed to the cause became quite influential, especially in painting an unrealistic portrait of the Soviet Union, and having in some cases damaging effects. One of the most infamous of these was **Walter Duranty.** His written words carried great weight with not only the public, but also with the Roosevelt administration. He was the Moscow Bureau Chief of the *New York Times* from 1922-1936 and garnered the Pulitzer Prize for the newspaper in 1932 for a series of stories he authored on the Soviet Union.

Walter Duranty, c. 1930s

Wikimedia Commons

In the prologue of Sally J. Taylor's book about Duranty, *Stalin's Apologist*, she writes, "As Fascism rose in Europe, and Japanese Imperialism threatened the East, Western powers sank deeper into the quagmire of the Great Depression. Against this backdrop, Duranty touted the accomplishments of Stalin's Five-Year Plan, ushering in what would come to be called The Red Decade." This elaborate and false assessment led westerners to believe that what was happening inside Russia "held the key to the future for the rest of the world." This erroneous and malicious appraisal had calamitous repercussions.

Duranty's whitewashed, pro-Stalin reporting, coinciding as it did with the Ukrainian genocide, Stalin's mass starvaton program during 1932–33, the show trials, and Stalin's Great Terror, was unconscionable. After the collapse of the Soviet Union, Ukrainians and allied groups from former Soviet eastern bloc countries unsuccessfully appealed for the revocation of Duranty's Pulitzer award. Years later, even the *New York Times* acknowledged his articles constituted "some of the worst reporting to appear in this newspaper," but to their shame they refused to give up the award, with the feeble justification that giving back the prize would itself evoke the "Stalinist practice to airbrush purged figures out of official records and history."

Nobody suggested purging or erasing Duranty. On the contrary, it is important that Duranty's inexcusable legacy be kept alive as an example of a run-amok, self-absorbed writer and a sympathetic newspaper. (As for the role of the *New York Times* during the eleven years Duranty was the Moscow Bureau Chief, it strains credulity to believe that his articles were simply accepted at face value.)

But it appears that Duranty had cohorts in his fictionalized reporting, as described by the late Dr. James Mace, American historian and expert on the Ukrainian famine:

> In the 1980s during the course of my own research on the Ukrainian Holodomor [famine] I came across a most interesting document in the US National Archives, a memorandum from one A. W. Kliefoth of the US Embassy in Berlin dated June 4, 1931. Duranty dropped in to renew his passport. Mr. Kliefoth thought it might be of possible interest to the State Department that this journalist, in whose reporting so much credence was placed, had told him that, 'In agreement with The New York Times and the Soviet authorities,' *his official dispatches always reflect the official opinion of the Soviet government and not his own* [emphasis added].

I was wryly amused to find that in 2012, PJ Media and their partners, *The New Criterion*, began a yearly award contest entitled the "Walter Duranty Prize for Journalistic Mendacity," specifically given "for what our readers consider the most egregious example of dishonest reporting for the fiscal year."

Duranty's writings, in the final analysis, were nothing more than Soviet communist propaganda thrust upon the American public in the guise of honest reporting. And appearing in a trusted publication gave further credence to Duranty. Probably the most deplorable consequence of Duranty's enthusiastic fabrications about the great Soviet experiment was the loss of the thousands who emigrated as a result, seeking relief from the Depression and eager to participate in the proletarian/socialist struggle. These workers, many with their families in tow, had their passports revoked and, with the exception of a handful, were exterminated or lost in the Soviet labyrynth. Additionally, Duranty's haughty rebukes of writers expressing differing opinions must have added to the plausibility of his words.

In my own mind I liken Walter Duranty, the Pied Piper of pro-Soviet journalism, to Lansford Hastings, "the Pied Piper of Western US migration." Hastings published a book in 1845 describing his famous shortcut across the Great Basin to California. This falsified information led to the disaster that was the Donner Party, who relied on the promising route only to perish in the Sierra Nevada in the disastrous winter of 1846–47. Mr. Hastings had never actually traversed the route he advertised.

In contrast, Duranty resided in Moscow in his position as bureau chief, and was well aware of what life was like there; yet he chose to paint a very different picture for his readers back home. As a result, the pain and suffering he caused touched far more people, over an extended period of time, than Hastings ever did.

The press is a powerful tool, and Walter Duranty's glowing reports created a positive, deep-seated mindset about the Soviet Union in the psyches of many Americans that remained entrenched for the remainder of their lives and even into the next generations. Orville was one of those persons. Duranty's name, and others like Nat and Janet Ross, were held up to me as people who had lived, written and studied in Russia and knew the truth about the great worker's paradise, as opposed to the whining, right-wing detractors who churned out anti-communist propaganda from the comfort of their desks.

George Seldes was an American writer whose career spanned from1909 into the 1980s. He assumed the title of a "free thinker," was heavily opinionated on most topics, and was a lifelong self-described atheist. He was an investigative journalist working on many newspapers and publications and was revered by generations of fellow writers. Orville was very familiar with Seldes' publication, *In Fact* magazine, which was extremely influential in its day (1940-50). He used to refer to Seldes as an upstanding person who was run out of business by red-baiters.

According to John Earl Haines, the author and former researcher at the Library of Congress, "Seldes was actually a long-term secret member of the Communist Party, according to notes of KGB archival files made by Vassiliev in 1993-96." An NKVD intercept in 1940 identified "George Seldes" as a "longtime fellow countryman" (member of the party), however, he denied his membership before the McCarthy Senate hearings.

Seldes' publication partner was "Bruce Minton," which was a cover name for Richard Bransten, a Soviet agent with the code name "Informator." Bransten's wife was another Soviet agent, Louise Bransten, who was a combination secret member of the Communist Party, and also the mistress of NKVD San Francisco station chief, Grigory Kheifets.

When allegations of communist involvement came out against Bransten ("Minton"), Seldes made the absurd claim that he was not aware of Bransten's involvement with the Soviets. But the charade goes on today. The Wikipedia biography on Seldes makes no mention of his or his partner's communist connection. Seldes was given an award in 1980 by the Association for Education in Journalism for professional excellence, and also received the George Polk Award for his life's work in 1981. Either these journalistic organizations were naively unaware or unconcerned with Seldes' troubling and duplicitous background.

George Seldes presented himself to the reading public as a tough but fair, independent journalist; one who had valuable, inside-track information, and was delivering the truth. When not covering political topics, Seldes practiced some admirable journalism, such as being an early reporter on the dangers of smoking, and covering various business issues. But his work in regard to US foreign policy as it related to communist countries must be viewed through the lens of his own communist ideology, which he carefully masked from the public. Seldes died at the age of 104 in 1995.

Isidor "Izzy" Stone's writing career as an investigative journalist spanned the years 1909 to 1989, and he contributed to many publications. Stone was decidedly pro-Soviet in his world view, was associated with the communist "Popular Front," and had formerly been a contributor to the Soviet-aligned *Nation* and the *New Republic*. As a consequence of his pro-communist writing, he was fired from his then-current job at the *New York Post*.

Orville stated in his interviews that when he was working with the National Youth Administration, he often met Stone, who was then writing for the *Nation.* Their meeting place was at the home of Helen Fuller, who later became the editor of the *New Republic.*

Isidor Feinstein "Izzy" Stone, c.1940s
Courtesy, Stone Family

In 1940, Stone moved to George Seldes' magazine, *PM,* and became a stalwart of the paper's pro-communist faction. KGB documents, published in the mid-90s, have now shown that Stone was a paid Soviet spy who had been originally recruited by the NKVD in 1936 and been given the code name "Blin" for "pancake." He was also shown to be a talent spotter, and courier relaying information to other agents. He remained a Soviet spy until 1939, at which point he withdrew due to bitterness over the Nazi-Soviet Pact of 1939-1941, but his sympathies for the Soviets were quickly renewed when war broke out.

The Venona decrypts during WWII showed Stone mentioning to his Soviet handler that he "would not be averse to having a supplementary income." The Soviets insisted that if that should happen, Stone would "have to do his part and really produce." Subsequent intercepts proved that Stone was secretly paid by the NKVD for contributing articles on subjects required by Moscow. As covered in Lt. Gen. Ion Pacepa's book, *Disinformation,* Stone demonized US policies, belittled the FBI, maligned Pope Pius XII, blamed the Catholics for Nazi persecution of the Jews, attacked McCarthyism, and opposed the war in Vietnam, all following the Soviet orthodoxy.

After World War II, Stone welcomed Soviet domination of Eastern Europe and only voiced "tepid criticism of Stalin's brutalities." At the death of Stalin, he voiced disapproval with Eisenhower's "merely official" condolences, stating they were "small-minded and unworthy of a great power." "A magnanimous salute was called for on such an occasion." One of his sympathetic biographers referred to Stone as "an apologist for the hammer-and-sickle."

In 1953, at the urging of George Seldes, Stone founded a weekly periodical, *I.F. Stone's Weekly,* which continued until 1971. It became very influential in liberal circles, and Stone became an icon of the leftist world.

Stone finally professed in 1988, "I was a fellow traveler." The following year, when communism collapsed in Eastern Europe, Stone still could see no conflict between communism and America's "ideals of freedom." He stated, "In a way, I was half-Jeffersonian and half a Marxist. I never saw a contradiction between the two, and I still don't." Once again, with stupefying repetition, we hear the CPUSA mantra that American communists were the true twentieth-century patriots . . . that they were the inheritors of Jeffersonian democracy. What a grotesque distortion of American history. At a minimum, Stone was a paid Soviet agent from 1936–39, cooperated with the Soviets in the 40s, detached himself in 1956, and then, according to the ex-KGB general, Oleg Kalugin, "resumed relations" in 1966, "on Moscow's instructions."

To my mother and Orville, Izzy Stone was an icon, a shelter in the storm. He was the voice of reason and his unending pro-Soviet articles were presented to me as justification for the Soviet sphere of influence, the mistakes of US foreign policy, the benefits of the new Soviet society, and many other subjects.

In his long journalistic career, Stone, like Seldes, did write about some positive issues, the fight for civil rights, as an example. But also like Seldes, the majority of his work in the political realm can now be viewed for what it was . . . leftist propaganda.

Walter Lippmann: In just about any political discussion I had with Orville, a day or two later he would invariably give me an article to support his line of reasoning written by Lippmann or Stone, or something from *The Nation*, *The National Guardian* or the *Daily Worker*. It had the effect of a preacher answering questions with Bible quotations.

Walter Lippmann, c. 1940s

Harris & Ewing Collection, Library of Congress

But Lippmann was special. His column in *The New York Herald Tribune,* from 1931 to 1967, entitled "Today and Tomorrow," was a widely sindicated mainstay in two hundred publications. He was, without question, the most influential journalist of his time. Some term him "The father of modern journalism." To Orville and my mother, particularly during the 40s through the 60s, he was no less than a god, writing eloquently, and mostly against US foreign policies.

Lippmann was a prominent socialist from his youth who, after attending Harvard, "took his socialism with him into his journalism, joining the Socialist Party and the Socialist Press Club." After Roosevelt's election in 1932, he told Roosevelt, "You may have no alternative but to assume dictatorial powers." Lippmann's socialist sympathies toward the Soviet Union remained intact, even with the acceptance of the Nazi-Soviet Pact. In a letter written to Edward C. Carter, Lippmann urged, "cooperation with the European revolutionaries and the Soviet Union in their attempt to build a socialist Europe as a nucleus for a world socialist order, with the obvious corollary of the establishment of socialism in this country." Carter was on the board of directors of the Communist-front organization, the *American-Russian Institute,* and General Secretary of the Institute of Pacific Relations, both of which were exposed by the bipartisan Senate Judiciary Committee as organizations to further communist objectives. FBI files indicate that Carter admitted he was a "fellow traveler;" among the many honors he received, was the "Order of the Red Banner of Labour (USSR)."

In Lippmann's early writings, he stated that the masses functioned as a "bewildered herd" who must be governed by "a specialized class whose interests reach beyond the locality." Later, he wrote, "The elite class of intellectuals and experts were to be a machinery of knowledge to circumvent the primary defect of democracy, the impossible ideal of the 'omnicompetent citizen.'" Not only was this attitude in line with contemporary socialist thinking, but in the right light conjures up the most frightening doctrines of fascism and Russian communism, the notion of a ruling class of intellectuals that would dictate and interpret their ideas to the ignorant multitudes.

Communist, Mary Price, Walter Lipmann's secretary and Progressive Party leader. 1948
AP Images

The *Vassiliev Notebooks* indicate that Lippmann was a "Soviet intelligence source as late as 1944," with KGB cover names "Imperialist" (1941–44), and "Bumblebee" (late 1944 and '45), however, there is no evidence that Lippmann progressed beyond his socialist beliefs to actually become a member of the Communist Party.

Aside from Lippmann's imperial position in the literary world, there are additional disturbing elements to be found. Until 1943, Lippmann's secretary was Mary Price, a Soviet agent. In 1935, she and her sister, Mildred, visited the Soviet Union and were "impressed by the prosperity and efficiency." Upon their return, Mary joined the Communist Party (it is believed her sister was a prior member). The Venona and Vassiliev files show they were designated as secret communists, the same designation given Orville. Mary's KGV code name was DIR. Soviet *Spartacus Educational* quotes her, "I didn't do it for financial reasons or self-aggrandizement, but the whole experience has made a difference in my kind of life and it has made it worthwhile for me."

From 1941 to 1944, she worked for the NKVD and allegedly agreed to furnish to Jacob Golos, controller of the secret apparatus of the Communist Party USA, all the information she could concerning the material Lippmann was writing, along with his contacts, all on behalf of the Soviet Union. Lippmann had extensive connections with the highest levels of the US government, and his files contained a great deal of sensitive information that never went into his columns. The NKVD thus greatly valued Price's work. In addition to her own espionage, Price also recruited Duncan Lee, an officer with the OSS, forerunner of the CIA, as a Soviet source. Price served as his contact and handler, a relationship greatly complicated by the fact that the two had an affair.

Mary Price's apartment in Washington eventually became the rendezvous point for meetings between Golos' courier and the Perlo Espionage Group. There, various members, including Victor Perlo, Charles Kramer, and Edward Fitzgerald, met with Elizabeth Bentley every two or three weeks, delivering stolen intelligence materials. After Price's release from her Soviet handlers, she returned to North Carolina and in 1948 became the head of the state's Progressive Party, where she ran for governor.

The career of Walter Lippmann is complicated and difficult to follow along a linear course. In later years, he moved more to the right, beginning with his opposition to FDR's New Deal and his concern that Roosevelt was placing the American constitutional system in danger by setting illegal precedents; yet a few years earlier he was advising Roosevelt that he may have to assume "dictatorial powers." He also became an opponent of globalism or excessive involvement around the world, as his earlier idealism turned to realism. But at the same time, after Roosevelt's 1946 removal of Henry Wallace as vice president, Lippmann became the leading public advocate of the need to respect a Soviet sphere of influence in Europe instead of a policy of containment.

His influence on American foreign policy was powerful. In the 1960s, he was an articulate opponent on the war in Vietnam, saying it weakened America's ability to fight the true Soviet adversary. As Lippmann's general opinions migrated away from the hard left, Orville's adulation of him waned; still, he gave considerable weight to those opinions that suited his world view; there was a large body of Lippmann anti- US invective from which to choose. History will ultimately be the judge of Lippmann, and his effect on American policy in the 20th century, as more evidence continues to be revealed.

Reflections on the press: What has been the collective legacy of leftist writers Seldes, Stone, Duranty, and many others? In their masquerading as open-minded, courageous men, they appeared to be watchmen for the American citizen. The unhappy truth is that they were heavily influenced and in some cases directed by Soviet Russia. Their histories and influence must be studied in light of what has been revealed in the decades since they plied their trade.

Much of their work was not only inaccurate, but even worse, deceptive, the purpose of which was to shape and mold public opinion, while at the same time covering up subversive activity in the country. Beyond the adverse effects on the population at the time, it also affected me personally. Orville's "teachings" were directly drawn from these writers, who were presented to me during my formative years, as purveyors of truth; the righteous truth, in fact.

The writers mentioned here stand as clear examples not only of the power of the press, but also as a cautionary tale that argues for diligence on the part of the public to be discerning when presented with media reporting of all kinds. There is boundless evidence that today we are being served up a partisan, and even distorted, meal; one-sided, non-probing, and beholden to leftist political interests.

Walter Lippmann, the dean of leftist American writers, epitomized a disturbing and dangerous notion of journalism's purpose: he did not assume that news and truth are synonymous. And as mentioned, his belief was that an "elite class of intellectuals" would communicate to "the bewildered herd" their interpretation of current events. Modern journalism too often subscribes to this philosophy, seeing its role as the interpreter of events rather than presenters of facts.

* * *

CHAPTER 11

THE UNITARIAN CHURCH

After moving to California, Orville and my mother joined the Unitarian Church, not because of any interest in religion, as they were committed atheists, but the Los Angeles church, was a political hub where communists and allied leftists could gather. Orville's earlier view toward Christianity was that Jesus was an absurd fiction created by the rich to repress the poor, and to absolve the rich of all the hypocrisy and bad deeds they indulged in. But later, he conceded to me that Jesus may have lived, but was just an ordinary guy with a robe and sandals who had some good humanitarian ideas. However, anything having to do with the supernatural or mystical realm was nothing more than nonsense and hocus-pocus.

The First Unitarian Church was located in dark, unadorned concrete buildings in a somewhat run-down area of the city. It was headed by Rev. Stephen Fritchman, an outspoken communist sympathizer who was revered by the congregation for his intellectual acuity, his writings, his public speaking abilities, his stand against McCarthy, and his vocal anti- US positions. His church became a magnet for radical leftists. The political gathering place was a natural draw for Orville and my mother, and it became a regular social outing for them. To me,

Rev. Stephen H, Fritchman (l.) and Linus Pauling (r.), La Jolla, California. 1969

From the OSU Libraries Special Collections & Archives Research Center

however, it was a slightly foreboding and vaguely menacing place, humorless and grim.

During the 50s, FBI agents regularly monitored the activities of this institution. In fact, I recall Rev. Fritchman frequently pointing out agents sitting in the rear of the congregation who would nod and wave back. Well-known personalities also occasionally visited, such as Nobel chemist and outspoken atheist, Linus Pauling, opera star Paul Robeson, and others.

Fritchman, a former Quaker and Methodist Minister, wore vestments and maintained a certain amount of religious protocol. There were always a few obligatory pseudo-prayers, but it was explained to me by Orville and my mother that this was only to keep up appearances to maintain their tax-exempt status. Prayers or not, the singular purpose of the church was to promote leftist idealism.

I don't remember meeting a single member of our congregation who believed in God, or considered themselves religious in any way, other than their religious zeal toward political activism. If any were actual believers, however, they would have been considered by Orville and my mother as the saddest dupes of all.

The Sunday sermons were not about worship; they were diatribes against such things as the House Committee on Un-American Activities, the evil ways of our government, and America, in general. This was in keeping with the official goals of the Los Angeles church, to embrace progressive and radical causes as their core focus.

Sunday school activities for the older kids were also based on politics. They sometimes consisted of lectures on such topics as the Holocaust, the callousness of the US, racism in the South, and the exploitation of blacks and the lower classes. The general message was that we lived in a despicable, racist society that needed uprooting, replacement and fundamental change in all areas.

I remember one Sunday, we were transported to a west-side high school where we watched captured Nazi films of old men and women being strapped down on gurneys and rolled into domed crematorium ovens. I vividly recall one old man waving his arms pathetically as he was rolled into the flames. It truly horrified me and gave me nightmares. To this day, it makes my flesh crawl whenever I conjure up the image. It is not that this information isn't relevant to all mankind, especially in a world where Muslim leaders in Iran deny that the Holocaust even happened, but my question is whether viewing of such films was an appropriate activity for young people. I say "no." But it apparently made perfect sense within the leftist/communist agenda, in order to mold young people's minds.

In my junior high and high school years, when a form required the declaration of religious affiliation, I was instructed to write *Atheist* in the appropriate box.

The unwanted attention this caused eventually led my mother and Orville to advise putting in *Unitarian*, which gave the illusion of our being mainstream churchgoers.

As further validation of the value and legitimacy of the church, I was told Benjamin Franklin and other founding fathers had been Unitarians, which gave the impression they, like our family, were atheists, too. As an adult, I learned that the American Unitarian Association wasn't formed until 1825, well after Franklin's death, but the story sounded good and seemed rooted in unimpeachable scholarly trappings. It is true that Franklin occasionally attended services in Boston, officiated by non-Trinitarian ministers, but this was not the Unitarian denomination.

To equate Franklin's strong religious beliefs, evidenced by his statement that Jesus' "system of Morals and Religion was as he left them to us, the best the world ever saw," with that of modern Unitarian thought, or at least the thinking of Rev. Fritchman's church, is disingenuous. In 1790, Franklin wrote to Ezra Stiles, President of Yale, declaring, "I believe in one God, Creator of the Universe. That He governs it by His Providence. That he ought to be worshipped." Orville conveniently left this out of his Franklin comparison, as it didn't fit well with the communist/atheist narrative.

Historically, the vast majority of Americans who identified themselves as Unitarians held strong theological beliefs, as part of a greater Christian worldview. But by the 1950s, many people had come to consider Unitarian/Universalism a separate religion, no longer having any ties to Christianity. The organization had morphed to its present status, which is strongly secular; more a "society" than a church.

Throughout my college years at the University of Southern California, I revered Fritchman, and maintained some level of connection with the church. In fact, Dr. Fritchman presided over my first marriage in 1964. Paul Robeson happened to be visiting Fritchman on a return trip from Russia at the time my fiancée and I were meeting to set up our wedding plans. Still being in awe of Robeson, I asked Rev. Fritchman if he thought the performer might sing at my wedding. I'm relieved now that he was unavailable.

Turmoil struck the church in 1954, when Dr. Fritchman and the congregation refused to sign a loyalty oath in order to preserve their aforementioned tax-exempt status. Loyalty oaths were branded as Hitlerian and anti-American by Fritchman and the left. However, this was during the height of the Cold War and the hearings with the HCUAA, when national concerns regarding espionage and subversive activities aimed at the government were very real, and proving to be warranted. The oath stated that the church would, "not advocate the overthrow of the government of the United States, and of the State of California, by force or violence or other unlawful means, nor advocate the support of a foreign government in the event of hostilities."

This, of course, they couldn't have signed without committing perjury, as there were tomes of recorded sermons over the years with railings against US foreign policy, as well as expressing support for communist countries such as Cuba, North Korea, North Vietnam, the Soviet Union and China. Huge fundraising programs for legal fees were instituted to keep the old and musty church in business while they sorted their issues out with the government, eventually winning in later years when the definition of what constituted a church was relaxed.

Before arriving at the Unitarian Church in Los Angeles in 1948, Fritchman had become a controversial figure in the organization as a result of his confrontational Marxist positions. In retired Unitarian minister Rev. Charles W. Eddis's book, *Stephen Fritchman: The American Unitarians and Communism*, he documents Fritchman's leftist political views and controversial role within the church from the late 30s through 1947.

As late as June 22, 1941, Eddis reports, Donald Harrington, minister of the Community Church of New York, attended a conference where Fritchman voiced strong opposition to the United States going to war against Germany; but by the middle of the week, with the news that Germany had invaded the Soviet Union, Fritchman immediately turned 180 degrees, demanding the US enter the war. This was the common about-face taken by many on the left at the time.

Book cover – "Stephen Fritchman: The American Unitarians and Communism"
Courtesy, Charles Eddis

Eddis chronicles Fritchman's deep involvement with both Unitarian and worldwide youth movements, whose leadership he actively packed with communists. At a 1946 conference for Unitarian youth, dealing with postwar reconciliation, he arranged for Marxist speakers that included lifelong Marxist and MIT mathematics professor, Dirk

Struik, Martha Fletcher, who headed a communist cell in Boston, and Herta Tempi who was a member of the German Communist Party.

Fritchman's other prominent role was as the longtime editor of *The Christian Register*, a prominent publication of the church, where he maintained rigid Stalinist positions. An example of his pro-Russian sympathies was his opposition to the Truman Doctrine, aimed at stopping the spread of communism and the political hegemony of the Soviet Union.

The church as a whole was strongly dedicated to political involvement, and also prided itself on its openness to all forms of religious, quasi-religious, and non-religious beliefs within its walls. Fritchman, however, consistently refused any proposed articles that carried anti-communist opinions, thus squelching any attempts at balance. In 1947, as a result of his intractable behavior, he was ousted from his editor's position.

In regard to this incident, Eddis cites a 1947 manuscript from Melvin Arnold, director of the AUA division of Publications (Unitarian press) entitled *Unitarians Reject Dictation by Political Creedalist*, in he which states:

> As officer, board member, or sponsor of over 25 alleged communist-front organizations during the last ten years, his (Fritchman's) procommunist sympathies were well known, and acknowledged by his friends. His use of the pages of the denominational journal to promote those agencies and their leading personalities was notorious, and evident to anyone knowing the agencies (to be) communist-controlled.

Rev. Fritchman repeatedly denied he was a communist, even when called before the HCUAA hearings in 1949. However, Eddis notes that ex-FBI agent, Linscott Tyler, a congregant of a Unitarian Church in Hingham, Mass., reported Fritchman was a member of the Communist Party, was being closely watched, and his phone wires tapped. Additionally, the Unitarian Universalist History & Heritage Society recounts:

> The Fritchman controversy, however, occurred in the 1940s, when the US Communist Party controlled most communist activity and was itself under the control of the Soviet Union, and ultimately Joseph Stalin. A close scrutiny of the record for those days indicates the high probability that Stephen Fritchman was a valued insider in the Community Party, whether or not he carried a membership card. What he did is clear. Just what he thought he was doing is not.

Rev. Eddis provided me with a video of a discussion before assembled Unitarian Church delegates at the 1978 National Convention, between Fritchman and James Luther Adams, the leading Unitarian theologian of the past century, also a man that can be loosely placed in the socialist/Marxist/humanist arena. The two men appeared to have many of the same political points of view.

The topic of the seminar was "Heresy in Faith." Fritchman described some of his personal history, how after graduation from Wesleyan, he was a socialist under the influence of the Farmer-Labor Party, and then his later growth as a humanist and Marxist. Like Elmer Benson, he boasted of his 760-page FBI file, which brought admiration from the audience. He avoided any of his former militant positions supporting Stalin, Mao, Castro and other communist governments, and contained his remarks to more general Marxist values.

During the talk, both men agreed that what this country needs is a progressive coalition between progressive liberals, progressive evangelicals and leftist Roman Catholics who are promoting Marxism. Fritchman's somewhat rambling soliloquy included his belief that "Marx and Lenin are now respectable" because they are now seen as being in the past and therefore irrelevant. To him, this was unfortunate, but he added that the workers' future efforts will eventually cost the greedy and barbarous capitalists their political and economic power; "that is where the friction lies and where we (the church) will have to be counted." Both men offered their unending antagonism towards capitalism and corporations. Fritchman referred to a quote from communist editor/writer, Paul Sweezy, that capitalism only has another one hundred years before its destruction (from 1978). Both Adams and Fritchman agreed that a "new structure of society is required."

While much more can be added to the profile of Rev. Stephen Fritchman, the foregoing should suffice to demonstrate the rigid and pointed political atmosphere that existed at his Los Angeles church, even though he professed himself a man of strong faith, a supporter of unborn children, and possessing a devotion to radical heresy.

* * *

CHAPTER 12

THE PANTHEON OF ENEMIES

Orville had a long list of political and religious enemies that were subject to unending scorn. The "Jew-hating, fascist collaborators," Pope Pius XII and Cardinal (later Archbishop) Jozsef Mindszenty, were the two international names that topped the list, emphasizing Orville's entrenched animosity toward the Catholic Church. They were deserving of the wrath heaped on them from the communist world. Another cleric occupying the pantheon was Bishop Fulton Sheen, an anti-communist and prominent figure in the promotion of the Catholic Church in the United States.

Unknowingly, I had internalized much of the lessons regarding these religious figures well into my adult life, believing much of what Orville said was accurate. In fact, in the initial draft of my manuscript, I referred to the strong probability that some Roman Catholic priests willfully cooperated with the Nazis. This may be true in some isolated cases, particularly before the war, but after reading my draft, Prof. Paul Kengor referred me to more modern research and writings, including material regarding the Nazi-ordered extermination by Hitler of over one thousand Roman Catholic clerics (primarily Jesuits) in the Dachau death camp, and an estimated three thousand Polish priests liquidated in other Nazi concentration camps. This was all part of a larger plan to eradicate Catholicism in Poland, which had flourished for one

Public execution of Polish priests and civilians by the Nazis, in the Bydgoszcz's Old Market Square on September 9, 1939. Wikimedia Commons

thousand years. In Anna Pawelczriska book, *Values and Violence in Auschwitz,* Hitler is quoted that he wanted his Death's Head forces "to kill without pity or mercy all men, women, and children of Polish descent or language."

Perhaps the most important reference work was Lt. General Ion Pacepa's book on Soviet disinformation, his recounting of firsthand knowledge regarding, among other things, the concerted program by Stalin, and later Khrushchev, to discredit both Pope Pius XII and Cardinal Mindszenty. Reading Pacepa's book and others, I came to understand how badly I had been misled on this topic. It also brought me in touch with the dreadful and lasting power of disinformation, and the false assumptions that I had been led to believe in during my formative years. Although I hadn't heard Orville's ruminations for the past thirty-five years, I realized that the overlay of negativity toward these courageous religious figures had stuck with me all these years later. It was a powerful eye opener.

Pope Pius XII: The head of the Catholic Church, Pope Pius XII, was crowned pope on March 2, 1939, at the very onset of World War II. His papacy was one of the most difficult ever experienced. He had to deal with the fascist Mussolini, who considered the pope a "disease wasting away the life of Italy." Then there was Hitler and the Holocaust, Stalin, the communist attacks against Christianity, and the Soviet takeover of the Eastern bloc countries. In 1945, Stalin engineered a disinformation campaign characterizing Pius XII as "Hitler's pope." While this belief still exists in some quarters, in general, the slanderous worldwide program failed.

Pope Pius XII
Public domain

The staunch anti-fascist/anti-communist resistance, headed by the pontiff, was acclaimed far and wide during and after the war for its courage under extreme circumstances. Jewish groups came forward after the war to recognize and praise Pius for saving tens of thousands of Jews slated for deportation and "progressive extinction." The pope employed brave tactics, hiding Jews in closets, behind blind doors, under stairways, in underground passages of the Vatican, "converting" them to Catholicism (until the ruse was found out), and creating obstacles of every kind against the authorities responsible for the deportations. In addition, Rabbi Herzog of Palestine (father to a future president of Israel, Chaim Herzog) and the chief rabbi of Rome, Israel Zolli, both lauded the pope's efforts on behalf of Jews. In fact, Zolli changed his name to Eugenio, Pius's birth name, to honor him. FDR applauded Pius's actions with statements of honor; Winston Churchill referred to Pius XII as the "Greatest man of our times;" and Albert Einstein stated, "Only the church protested against the Hitlerian onslaught on liberty."

There is so much more that can be written about the courage and steadfastness of Pius XII, including his involvement with the delicate negotiations with Protestant Germans attempting the overthrow of Hitler. But what was important for me was to come to the understanding of the disgraceful disinformation campaign against the Catholic prelates concocted by Stalin, the KGB and their Romanian counterpart, the Securitate.

Cardinal Jozsef Mindszenty: As it turned out, Pope Pius XII's reputation proved too difficult to besmirch. That didn't, however, keep the KGB from going after other important Catholic figures. Hungarian Cardinal Jozsef Mindszenty fit into their plans.

Cardinal Mindszenty was imprisoned in Hungary by the Nazis when the Germans invaded in 1944. His alleged crime was using his church in resistance to German barbarism by shielding countless numbers of Jews scheduled for deportation and extermination. Mindszenty, like Pope Pius, used every means possible to shelter Jews, also offering them temporary conversion to Catholicism.

He was released at the end of the war, but in 1949, during the Soviets regime's takeover of Hungary, he was again imprisoned on charges that he had collaborated with the Nazis during the war. These falsehoods were part of the coordinated disinformation effort of the NKVD, KGB and Romanian DIE under Romanian president, Nicolae Ceausescu, to discredit Mindszenty.

In prison for six years, Cardinal Mindszenty was regularly tortured and forced to sign bogus confessions. Other incriminating documents were later exposed as well-crafted forgeries. The forgers escaped to the West and they described their role in the elaborate forgery factory in Moscow. (In his 1987 memoir, communist journalist, George Seldes, expressed his tacit agreement with all the spurious charges against Mindszenty, disregarding all evidence to the contrary. His communist world view remained unshakable to the end of his life.)

Soviet arrest of Cardinal Mindszenty in Hungary, following trial in 1949.

Mindszenty was eventually freed during the short-lived Hungarian revolution of 1956, but in 1959, when the Soviets again exerted power, he sought refuge in the American Embassy where he lived in safety for 15 years, until the country was freed from Soviet domination following the collapse of the empire. Afterwards, he moved to Vienna and wrote his memoirs, vivid with descriptions of the horrors and Godlessness of both the German and Russian totalitarian states.

Cardinal Mindszenty was certainly no collaborator with Hitler, and to even hint at it is a revolting example of historical tampering. On the contrary, he was a great man who suffered untold hardships, and can only be described by any freedom loving person as a decent, courageous and extraordinary individual who stood steadfast against fascist and Soviet inhumanity. He was, above all, a credit to mankind and to his religion.

In order to understand the attacks against Pope Pius XII, Cardinal Mindszenty, and other Catholic figures, it is crucial to understand the mechanism of disinformation developed and carried out by the Soviet propaganda machine. One of the most valuable resources for understanding this is Lt. Gen. Ion Pacepa. Pacepa, who defected to the United States in 1978, was the head of the Romanian DIE (Soviet Dizinformation Department) under the Romanian secret police, the Securitate, which was the creation of the repressive communist dictator, Nicolae Ceausescu. The Securitate was considered the most ubiquitous and brutal police force in the world at the time. Lt. Pacepa's book, *Disinformation,* details the Soviet's worldwide mechanism to influence and control a multitude of cultural and political areas. As the head of the Romanian arm of that endeavor, Pacepa was required to enforce and guide assignments under Ceausescu. The magnitude of this operation was staggering. Pacepa's quote regarding the size of the operation he directed was, "there were more in the Soviet Bloc working on "dezinformatsiya" than in the armed forces and defense industry."

Some of the tactics of the disinformation program included forging documents and confessions; destroying the reputation of political leaders; denigrating Christianity and Judaism, including the scurrilous attacks on Pope Pius XII and Cardinal Jozsef Mindszenty; defaming American soldiers; infiltrating and controlling the World Council of Churches (WCC); planting four thousand agents of influence in the Islamic world; fanning the flames of resentment against the US and Israel; and convincing the rest of the world that the US government masterminded the assassination of President Kennedy.

The byword for the agency's manual was "you can get anything you want with disinformation." The Soviets developed the methodology to largely displace boots-on-the-ground espionage, seeing it as the best way to affect public opinion and world affairs. The process begins with a seed of truth that is then cloaked in a series of lies and half-truths. The resulting piece of information is then planted within a trusted source, known to the general population, which disseminates it with a credibility that is not questioned. The source may or may not know the validity of the information.

Pacepa's intimate knowledge of all aspects of the clandestine disinformation programs allowed him to expose the ugly methods employed by the Soviet Secret Service and their eastern bloc allies. He later revealed a massive trove of damaging information regarding Ceausescu, which not only precipitated the dictator's downfall, but also made Pacepa a target for assassination by both the Romanian police and the Soviets.

At Ceausescu's trial more than ten years later, the accusations and evidence described in detail in Pacepa's book was instrumental in the dictator's conviction, and was largely responsible for Ceausescu's and his wife's fitting date with the firing squad immediately after the dissolution of the Soviet Union in 1989.

Pacepa's *Disinformation,* along with his first book, *Red Horizons,* are considered the best insider works on the processes of the Soviet disinformation system. They are well worth reading for a firsthand perspective on this still current topic, one that is almost impossible for Americans and others in the West to fully comprehend, let alone recognize.

Bishop Fulton Sheen: There is not enough room in this book to discuss all of the figures in Orville's perceived enemies against communism, but a few more that stand out in my memory are worth discussing. Another Catholic Church prelate that produced copious bile in Orville's gut was Bishop Fulton Sheen who was known for his preaching and especially his work on radio and later television between 1930 and 1968.

Bishop Fulton Sheen in his role as radio and TV religious leader, 1956

Public domain

The Venerable Archbishop Sheen combined his vigorous anti-communist message with an almost equally strong anti-racist message that placed him well ahead of the curve as an advocate for civil rights in the 1950s.But because he was an anti-communist, he was considered by the left as a denizen of the lower order of humanity. Later, in 1967, Sheen became a vocal opponent of the war in Vietnam, but even that didn't accrue to his credit with Orville.

In 1945, largely due to the influence of Bishop Sheen, *Daily Worker* editor, Louis Budenz, converted to Roman Catholicism and renounced communism. He contacted J. Edgar Hoover and offered to provide the FBI with information on former members of the Communist Party. His testimony rocked the party and was devastating to the *Daily Worker*. All told, he was interviewed for three thousand hours by Hoover's agents. Budenz's name became anathema to the party, and to Orville and his friends.

One of Sheen's noteworthy presentations came in February 1953, when he forcefully denounced the Soviet regime of Joseph Stalin, using a reading of Shakespeare's burial scene from *Julius Caesar*, substituting Shakespeare's characters with prominent communist leaders' names including Stalin, Lavrenty Beria, Georgy Malenkov, and Andrew Vishinski. He concluded by saying, "Stalin must one day meet his judgment." The irony was that the dictator suffered a stroke a few days later and died within a week.

J. Edgar Hoover: Among secular personalities, J. Edgar Hoover, appointed director of the FBI in 1924 and who remained in that position until his death in 1972, was another figure who was in the pantheon of American "fascist leadership." Orville described Hoover to me as a paranoid, closet cross-dresser, a consummate showman who kept dossiers on American political leaders of both parties, and therefore controlled the government with his robotic, crew-cut agents. Orville had a wry smile on his face when telling these questionable stories.

Hoover was a complicated man in many ways, but let it not be forgotten that he was greatly admired and appreciated by FDR, President Lyndon Johnson, and the American public at large. The Kennedys, however, didn't like Hoover because of the dossier he kept on Jack's infidelities, including his relationship with Mafia leader Sam Giancana's girlfriend, Judith Campbell Exner. To me, or any American citizen for that matter, there were certainly areas of concern, such as Kennedy's alleged ties to the Mafia and its relationship to the planned assassination of Fidel Castro, as well as his chronicled affair with Marilyn Monroe, with its own mob overtones.

It is apparent Hoover was obsessed with his job. His top priorities were rooting out Nazi and communist influences in the US government and fighting organized crime, while building the FBI into a modern, advanced institution. He has been derided by the American left for years, including the diatribes constantly recited by Orville. But once again, Hoover's concerns about the high degree of communist influence in the government, in scientific circles, and in the media and the entertainment industry, were borne out through testimony by former communists, and the many Soviet documents and files that have come to light.

William F. Buckley, Jr.: With his bird-like features, rapier wit, and enormous intellect, William F. Buckley, Jr. represented a conservative fortress that was the bane of communists the nation over. Orville disliked the very mention of his name. Buckley's weekly TV program, *Firing Line,* aired from 1966–1999. In addition, he founded the publication, *The National Review*, in 1955, and added to his exposure with a nationally syndicated newspaper column. These three media vehicles helped propel him into the role of the conservative conscience of the Republican Party for over thirty years. The power of his message, and his charismatic persona were instrumental in paving the way for Ronald Reagan's election in 1980.

William F. Buckley meeting with President Reagan in the White House, 1986

Public domain

Historian George Nash stated Buckley was, "arguably the most important public intellectual in the United States in the past half century." His core message was described as a, "fusion of laissez-faire economics, melded with traditional American political conservatism, and anti-communism." Buckley was a constant thorn in Orville's side and he belittled him as nothing more than a "pseudo-intellect" and "puppet of big business;" a machine that simply spit out unintelligible gobbledygook. He was characterized as the handmaiden of J. Edgar Hoover, the CIA and American imperialism. But Buckley's intelligent and cultured presentation created a difficult wall to penetrate, which irked Orville to no end, feeling as he did that communists and leftists had garnered the corner on intelligent thought. Having the Catholic Buckley throwing darts at communism and leftist ideology was almost unbearable.

Whittaker Chambers: A former high-level American communist, Whittaker Chambers (1901–1961), was perhaps the most hated figure in Orville's pantheon of "criminals." He was labeled a "turncoat," a "consummate liar," a "stool pigeon," and was considered beneath pond scum. Chambers and Elizabeth Bentley, who Orville spoke of with similar epithets, were two of the foremost people to testify before Congress about communist party intrusion into the US government. The damage done to the party as a result was enormous.

Chambers attended Columbia University, fertile ground for the recruitment of young communists. He left the university in 1925 after causing some literary controversy. Shortly afterwards, he met a member of the communist underground (an even deeper layer of espionage), with whom Chambers and his wife became good friends. He became a Marxist and joined the Communist Party that same year. He also launched into a vigorous study of communist literature and, after reading a work by Lenin, became deeply affected by the crisis of the middle class and his own family, "a malaise from which communism promised liberation." Chambers' biographer, Sam Tanenhaus, wrote, "Lenin's authoritarianism was precisely what attracted Chambers; he had at last found his church."

When I read Chambers' extraordinary book, *Witness,* I saw several parallels with Orville's life; specifically, Orville's involvement with the Lutheran seminary and his preaching, and his transformation to socialism and communism because of his Bible education; the institution of communism became his new church, too. Chambers wrote for and edited the communist publications the *Daily Worker*, and *New Masses,* combining his superb literary talents with the goals of communism. In 1932, he was recruited into the Communist underground, and shortly after, his main controller became Josef Peters. Peters introduced Chambers to Harold Ware, the head of the communist underground cell in Washington. The members of that cell included Lee Pressman, Alger and Donald Hiss, John Abt, Charles Kramer, Nathan Witt, Marion Bachrach, Nathanial Weyl, and Victor Perlo; all of them members of Roosevelt's New Deal administration. Chambers became the courier between New York and Washington for stolen documents, all delivered to Boris Bykov, the Soviet GRU station chief.

So many of these names were those of intimates or closely associated Communist Party functionaries of my mother and Orville, all of them working so assiduously toward the dissolution of the US government, and each of them ardent Stalinists promoting domination by Moscow.

Chambers carried on his espionage activities from 1932 until 1938. During that period Stalin's Great Terror was underway and Chambers became frightened, fearing for his life, and with good reason. Others around him who had become disillusioned were "invited" back to Moscow and were purged. He ignored several orders to travel to Moscow. Not surprisingly, his communist faith was weakening. He began concealing clandestine documents as a way of hopefully preventing the Soviets from assassinating him and his family. And one day in 1938, he went to work and then vanished, taking his family into hiding, the stolen documents having been concealed and safeguarded with relatives. After a year in hiding, which included living in his car and frequent moves, he was able to resurface, and later became an editor at *Time* magazine.

Nine years later, in 1948, Chambers was called to testify before the HCUAA where he gave up the names of those who were part of the underground "Ware Group," including Alger Hiss, one of the most prominent of the New Dealers, and a man who had presided over the United Nations Charter Conference. The furor and backlash of the leftist community was momentous. It created serious questioning of the government infiltration at all levels.

Whittaker Chambers testifying before the HCUAA, 1948
Public domain

While the statute of limitations had run out to try Hiss on espionage charges, he nonetheless was tried for perjury. Chambers' testimony was crucial and damning, and Hiss was found guilty, for which he served a substantial sentence in the penitentiary. Although he professed his innocence to his deathbed, Hiss's espionage activities have since been proven beyond any doubt through the released Soviet and US Army documentation. Chambers' testimony, at the time vociferously ridiculed by the left as lies, has been found to be highly accurate.

Chambers was a tragic, but truly great man. He was courageous, kind, eloquent, and a brilliant word-crafter. His book, *Witness,* has been considered one of the outstanding autobiographical works of the twentieth century. Not only that, but it also served as a warning about the dangers of communism. He died of a heart attack in 1961 at the age of 60. In 1984, President Ronald Reagan posthumously awarded Chambers the Presidential Medal of Freedom for his contribution to "the century's epic struggle between freedom and totalitarianism." In 1988, Interior Secretary Donald P. Hodel granted national landmark status to the Pipe Creek Farm where Chambers lived. In 2001, members of the Bush Administration held a ceremony to commemorate the hundredth anniversary of Chambers' birth. Speakers included Chambers' close friend, William F. Buckley, Jr.

* * *

CHAPTER 13

MARXISM AND THE CULT OF PERSONALITY

Marxist and communist ideology as a religion is a fact that is often overlooked, but the power of which should not be minimized. The faithful and even blind devotion, particularly in regard to Stalin, exhibited by Orville and his fellow travelers was further made manifest, and perpetuated, by the "cult of personality" so purposefully cultivated by China, Russia and other totalitarian regimes.

In China, the epitome of communism as a religion was Mao's *Little Red Book*, which became the bible of the bloody and inhuman Cultural Revolution. It contained Mao's philosophical interpretation of *The Communist Manifesto,* with quotes defining Maoism, known as a form of Stalinism. These pronouncements gave authority for the death by purges, starvation, and executions of some 30 million innocents in the decade between 1966 and 1976.

Chinese propaganda poster from the Cultural Revolution, showing image of Mao smiling down on revolutionaries displaying their Little Red Books, c. 1969

Included in the genocide were those arbitrarily designated as "enemies of the state," including university professors, statesmen, artists, writers, and others; simply put, anyone who did not agree with Mao fell into this category. They were publicly humiliated and murdered, many by marauding, club-wielding youths fervently seeking to "cleanse" their society of "bourgeois revisionists."

As Mao's rule progressed following the Cultural Revolution, owning and carrying the book at all times became an unofficial requirement for every Chinese citizen. During this turbulent and frightening time, violating this unofficial rule would have been seen as a sign of divergence from Mao's leadership, which could lead to ostracism or even death.

Studying the book was mandatory in order to advance in college, the military, the bureaucracy, the science community, and most other fields.

Chinese Red Guards mandatory reading from Little Red Book during the Cultural Revolution, c. 1969

Glasshouse Images / Alamy

At public gatherings, military exhibitions, workers' rallies, et cetera, adherents would wave The *Little Red Book* over their heads in ecstasy, showing joy, and chanting ritual slogans, along with cries of condemnation to enemies of the state. Photos of such gatherings, which show such religious devotion, are chilling.

The *Little Red Book* became so holy that for some possession of the book itself became a psychological burden; it couldn't be disposed of, and if it became inadvertently stained or soiled, it likely would have caused considerable offense.

Although largely abandoned in the 80s, the *Little Red Book* is still studied and admired by some segments of the Chinese population to this day, and even by some in other countries who find its leftist message inspiring.

Monument of Joseph Stalin leading soldiers, Prague. 1955. Destroyed, November, 1962.

Public domain

A similar cult of personality existed in the Soviet empire, where thousands of statues, images and paintings of Stalin hung in virtually every public space and household. Huge images and placards were prominently displayed during the interminable military and worker marches. His writings and grandiloquent titles were part of a successful program to raise Stalin to godlike stature, in the same vein as the Roman Caesars and Egyptian Pharaohs.

Although somewhat tempered after his death, Stalin's memory still lingers in the minds of many Russians with awe and reverence that extends far beyond normal admiration, regardless of evidence of his treacherous regime.

East German military women parading with images of Stalin. Creative commons/German Federal Archives

In Cambodia, Pol Pot constructed his own lawless doctrine with a sadistic regime whose reign of terror took place between 1975 and 1979; a bloody outpouring where, by some estimates, one-quarter to one-third of the Cambodian population was exterminated. His gift to the Cambodian people was total collectivism based on the doctrine of Pol Pot-ism, the Cambodian version of fundamentalist Maoism, spoken in the name of the ominous Angkar, a faceless and lawless organization developed to indoctrinate, control, and terrorize the populace. This new societal construct aimed to elevate Pol Pot to an exalted stature spread by his Khmer Rouge cadres through the use of slogans, maxims, advice, instructions, watchwords, orders, warnings, and threats. Henri Locard's book, *Pol Pot's Little Red Book,* reports stories from survivors, interspersed with historical commentary and contextual analysis, thoroughly exposing the horrific foundation upon which it was based.

Hitler, of course, laid out his "religious" ideas about society and German nationalization in *Mein Kampf,* which became a type of bible for many, including the SS and Nazi Party officials who fawned over the Fuehrer's godlike words and image and relished in the magnificent public assemblies he orchestrated.

One of the most egregious present-day examples of the cult of personality and worship is the dictatorship of Kim Jong-Un in North Korea. Beginning in 1948, three generations of the Kim family has required total loyalty and reverence by the subjugated populace. This ruling dynasty created a government known worldwide for its political purges and Russian-style gulags.

The first modern leader of North Korea, Kim Il-Sung (1948–94), changed Korean history books to include the declaration that his actual birthplace was on a volcano, the place where the mythical father of Tagun, the founder of Korea, descended from heaven five thousand years ago. thus creating a divine association.

At the massive statues of Kim Il-Sung and his son Kim Jong-Il, in Pyongyang, people can be seen bowing in reverence at the flower-festooned bases of the monuments, whose figures with outstretched arms and warm smiles belie the brutal, totalitarian control of all aspects of life in North Korea. (Similarly in Russia, the murals and statues of Stalin bore the smiling countenance and open arms of the warm "Uncle Joe.") Journalist Mark Bowden, observing similar devotions to Kim Jong-Un today in North Korea, has reported that, "The multitudes stand and clap at the merest glimpse of him" and, "Men and women weep for joy when he smiles and waves."

North Koreans bowing in reverence to statues of Kim Il Sung and Kim Jong Un

Public domain

* * *

PART V

THE SCIENCES

CHAPTER 14

DARWIN, COMMUNISM, AND RELIGION

The Marxist education I received was deeply committed to promoting a doctrinaire ideology in regard to the beginning of the universe, human evolution and the necessity for the societies of the world to abandon religion. This was based on their interpretation of Charles Darwin's theories, expounded in his 1859 book, *On the Origin of Species by Means of Natural Selection or the Presentation of Favored Races in the Struggle for Life,* which introduced the theories of "natural selection," "survival of the fittest," and also purported to prove that man, and not God, was the ultimate authority. Darwin was the foremost example of a man who was able to shake off the shackles of religion and thus be able to let his mind develop new scientific theories.

Orville was always quick to use Darwin in defense of communism. He would carefully spell out how Darwin's ideas were so relevant, how they justified communist ideals and how religion was nothing more than a cruel invention to control the masses. This, he stated with conviction; however, my mother would sidestep the word "communism" and replace it with "progressive ideas."

Charles Darwin
Public domain

Both Orville and my mother were very clear about the accuracy of Darwinian Theory; bolstered by acquaintances in the scientific arena, mostly associated with their close friend, botanist Prof. Harry Highkin. I followed in lockstep with that belief for many years, maintaining Darwin as the benchmark for a person who exhibited sober and unfettered thinking. The abstract theory coupled with the intellectual respectability of Darwin seemed to all fit quite nicely together for me. I recall heated discussions in my dormitory at Menlo College, and later at USC, where my imperious and deprecating rhetoric was voiced in full passion. The larger ramifications of Darwin's ideas did not become truly clear to me until much later in life, but at the time of my enthrallment, I really knew very little about the man, his methods, or even how well his theories had held up in the world of science over the prior hundred years (now over 150 years). I also had no idea how important it was in the development of the expanding political Marxist and communist doctrines.

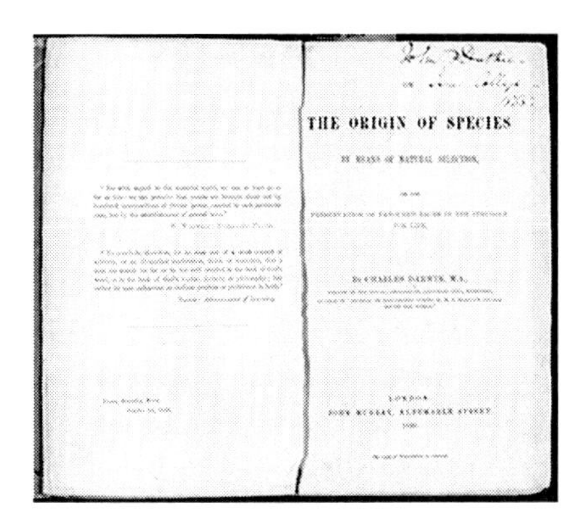
THE ORIGIN OF SPECIES

First edition of Charles Darwin's "Origin of Species by Means of Natural Selection," 1859.

Public domain

What I did know was that invoking Darwin's name was a powerful political statement that I agreed with; an impregnable fortress of truth that seemed so logical that only a dunce would dare disagree.

During the writing of this work, this section was, by far, the most difficult and lengthy subject to discuss due to its complexity and importance to Marxist ideology. It delves into not only Darwin and his life, but touches on some of the significant evolution and origin-of-life theories put forth by subsequent generations of scientists including work in the fields of genetics, molecular biology, evolutionary biology, sociobiology, evolutionary psychology, archeology, geology, paleontology, mathematical population genetics, intelligent design, political science, and other areas. It is a bewildering world with fierce opponents on all sides, battling for recognition and their position in their tight-knit scientific and philosophical communities. Accusations of "pseudo-science" and irrelevancy are hurled at each other by the various camps in defense of their turf.

But unfortunately, and unknown by the general population, much of this antagonism has been fostered and enflamed by the rigid protocols of radical politics and the battle to have the scientific community conform to leftist ideology. This might seem strange to many as most people envision science and politics as being separate fields. What does the polio vaccine or the study of moon rocks have to do with communism or capitalism?

I also wish to be clear that I am not promoting any of the myriad theories about the origins of life, the process of evolution or non-evolution, or intelligent design (ID) concepts. My own opinions notwithstanding, my thrust here is to illuminate elements of leftist orthodoxy that have become woven into the fabric of scientific, and evolutionary studies, and which also figured so prominently in the attitudes expressed in our household. Readers can decide for themselves what school to follow, whether or not political ideologies should have a role in evolutionary science or, conversely, whether various ID hypotheses (supernatural or not) should be expelled from study by the scientific community.

Darwin's link to Marx, Lenin, Stalin, Hitler and Mao: This section cannot be underestimated due to its fundamental importance, past and present, to Marxist philosophy. The appearance of Darwin on the international stage was of vital importance in the selling of communism to the world. To Karl Marx and his co-author, Friedrich Engels, Darwin's ideas had the effect of a miner discovering the Comstock Lode. Marx and Engels produced *The Communist Manifesto* in 1848 eleven years before Darwin's publication of *Origin*, but Darwin's ideas regarding the triumph of the strong and the subjugation of the weak was a powerful addition to this new idealistic philosophy. It provided Marx and Engels with a "scientific rationale" to deny creation and by extension, to deny God, both fundamental to their socio-political theories. It also neatly applied "natural selection" to politics and economics; to socialism and communism; and ultimately to the higher and final order of government that would supplant the lower order of primitive capitalism just as capitalism supplanted feudalism. In addition, it also supported Marx's concept of perpetual "class struggle," as reflective of nature.

After reading *Origin* when first published, Marx wrote to Engels, stating, "This is the book which contains the basis in natural history for our view."

It is interesting to note that while Karl Marx was developing his principles aimed at the abolition of religion, destruction of capitalism, and his visions of a new society, he lived with his devoted family in impoverished circumstances. Marx Historian, Mary Gabriel, in an article entitled "Marx's Not-so-Marxist Marriage," reported that his wife, Jenny, "may not have understood what she was getting into when she married Marx, and the sacrifice of the

"Manifesto of the Communist Party" by Karl Marx and Friedrich Engels.

countless privileges she might have expected as a Prussian aristocrat." She bore him six children, three of whom died early. Their housemaid also bore Marx a son, who then grew up within the family. Author Gabriel noted also that in later years the family was living in a squalid flat in London, after being expelled from European country after country for his revolutionary writings. This seemingly grim existence may likely have contributed to the later suicides of two of his three remaining offspring, daughters Eleanor at age 43, and Laura at age 66. Laura and her husband, Paul Lafargue, committed double suicide, deciding "they had nothing left to give to the [communist] movement to which they had devoted their lives." Eleanor died tragically by ingesting Prussic acid after learning of her faithless lover's marriage to another.

Paul Lafargue's suicide letter strikes me as a testament to the hard, secular Darwinian world view that permeated Marx's dogma, and that I was so familiar with in my youth. Lafargue expressed his wish to not live beyond seventy, as he felt he would be a burden to himself and others, "I fixed the exact year for my departure from life. I prepared the method for the execution of our resolution. I die with the supreme joy of knowing that at some future time, the cause to which I have been devoted for forty-five years will triumph. Long live Communism! Long live the Second International."

Lenin spoke at the pair's funeral in Paris. Author Joseph Hansen, in the introduction to *Leon Trotsky My Life*, noted Lenin's remarks at that function, which illustrated the cold-hearted devotion he demanded from his followers, "If one cannot work for the Party any longer, one must be able to look truth in the face and die like the Lafargues."

In the same vein, the Darwinian philosophy, adapted to communist class struggle, was laid out by Engels in his eulogy to Marx, "There were no catastrophes in history as there were none in nature. There were no inexplicable acts, no violations of the natural order; God was as powerless as individual men to interfere with the internal, self-adjusting dialectic of change and development."

This stated, in essence, that there was no right or wrong in man's behavior, any more than a hawk picking up a squirrel for breakfast or a tiger lunching on a zebra. In nature, there was no obligation to be kind or tolerant, and man was to be judged in the same fashion. Any acts of assassination, extermination, or societal mass murder could now be explained as merely the resulting truths of the dialectic arrived at by logical arguments. These truths were argued as immutable laws, blessed by Darwin and, using nature as a guide, it is an easy jump to develop a political philosophy from this line of amoral thought to eliminate the less fit and herd people into box cars headed for extermination camps (Nazis), or to send off millions to Siberian gulags.

Even Lenin showed his admiration for Darwin by keeping a singular piece of art on his office desk, a "kitsch statue of an ape contemplating a human skull, while sitting on a stack of books; one being *The* Origin of Species." Modern copies of that same sculpture are readily available online.

Biographer and militant atheist, Yemelian Yaroslavsky, mentions in his 1940 book on Stalin that while an ecclesiastical student he (Stalin), "began to read Darwin and became an atheist." In 1922, Yaroslavsky formed an organization called the "League of Militant Godless" (LMG) which was given special powers to dictate the ground rules of the national campaign to eradicate religion. By 1928, anti-religious education began in the first grade.

Stalin's atheism permeated his dictatorial regime which included the purging of religious figures; examples such as Archbishop Andronic of Perm, who was forced to dig his own grave and was buried alive, and Bishop Germogen of Tobolsk, who was strapped to a paddle wheel of a steamboat and mangled by the rotating blades. Nuns and priests were killed in unimaginable ways: beheaded, scalped, crucified, cut to bits by swords, having limbs chopped off, boiling in tar, and whatever other torture could be thought up. Also employed were prison and labor camps, and punitive psychiatry incorporating psychological punishment and mind control experimentation in order to force abandonment of religious convictions. It was estimated that fifty thousand clergy had been executed between 1917 and the end of the Khrushchev era (1964).

During Stalin's purges of the Great Terror, 1937–38, Church documents record that 168,000 Russian Orthodox clergy were arrested. Of that number, 100,000 were shot. Between 1927 and 1940, the number of Orthodox churches in the Russian Republic fell (demolished and converted to such uses as bath houses, granaries, night clubs and museums of atheism) from 29,584 to fewer than 500 (98.5 percent).

The most hauntingly tragic example was Stalin's ordered destruction of the great mid-nineteenth-century Eastern Orthodox Cathedral of Christ the Savior that stood a few blocks southwest of the Kremlin. The grand structure was the scene of the 1882 world premiere of the 1812 Overture composed by Tchaikovsky. It was to be replaced with a grand building complex to be named the "Palace of the Soviets." WWII thwarted this plan.

Destruction of Christ the Savior Cathedral by order of Stalin, 1931
Keston Institute, Baylor University.

In 1947, the All-Union Society for the Dissemination of Political and Scientific Knowledge was established. Its purpose was to run houses of scientific atheism in Soviet cities. By 1957, the school system enhanced atheistic materials in its curriculum, including a textbook that contained the declaration, "Religion has become the medium for the spiritual enslavement of the masses," a theme often evoked by Orville.

In 1960, the Central Committee brought back the practice of atheistic tutors visiting known religious believers to try and convince them to become atheists. If recalcitrant, it was brought to the attention of authorities and their transgressions were made public. In total, victims of Soviet state atheistic policies resulted in the murder of an estimated 12 to 20 million Christians.

Darwin scholar, Dr. Jerry Bergman, wrote in *The Dark Side of Charles* Darwin, that Stalin's brutal childhood started him on his way to his equally brutal worldview, convinced by Darwin that "mercy and forbearance were weak and stupid." As a result, Stalin was able to kill with a "coldness that even Hitler might have envied and in even greater numbers."

Mao was also of the same stripe. What happened in China mirrored the atrocities of the Soviet Union at an even more militant and belligerent level. Researchers have stated that Mao regarded Darwin as the foundation of Chinese scientific socialism.

The eventual horrors that emanated from this "scientific" worldview adopted by the Nazi's, the communists, China's "scientific socialists," and other totalitarian regimes are almost indescribable. In the Soviet Union alone, the government created failed harvests, famine, social and political repression, religious persecution, mass murder, and placed neighboring countries under heel. A quote from Beate Wilder-Smith discusses the horrors of Hitler's Germany in regard to their absorption of Darwinian law, "The Nazi's were convinced, as are the communists today, that evolution had taken place, that all biology had evolved spontaneously upward, and that in-between links (or less evolved types) should be actively eradicated. They believed that natural selection could and should be actively aided, and therefore instituted political measures to eradicate the handicapped, the Jews, and the blacks, whom they considered as underdeveloped."

Adolph Hitler, reflecting Darwinian thinking, wrote the following racist sentiment in *Mein Kampf,*

> If nature does not wish that weaker individuals should mate with the stronger, she wishes even less that a superior race should intermingle with an inferior one; because in such cases all her efforts, throughout

> hundreds of thousands of years, to establish an evolutionary higher stage of being, may thus be rendered futile.

The justification for this godless world was that it was "scientific," i.e., "proven," and therefore immune from discussion. Not including Hitler's atrocities, the communist leaders alone, using Kengor's apt description, "left a wake of more than 100 million corpses from the streets of the Bolshevik Revolution to the base of the Berlin wall," (some estimates are much higher) a number that far outpaced the fourteenth century, so well described by Barbara Tuchman in *A Distant Mirror,* when over 50 percent of Europe's population succumbed to wars and the black death.

The line of human victims, not including those killed in WWI and WWII, resulting from totalitarian communist/socialist regimes of the twentieth century, if pressed tightly together and shoulder to shoulder, would stretch five to six thousand miles in length, approximately the distance from Los Angeles to London. In all of these regimes, there was no suggestion of pity toward the helpless and unfortunate, nor was there forward thinking of the horrors that would continue, seemingly forever. It was simply godless nature doing what it does best: kill or be killed in order to survive, and ultimately thrive.

Darwin's impact on science education and the scientific community: Darwin's theory of evolution became so rooted in left academia that by the mid to latter part of the twentieth century the term theory became practically nonexistent; it was now seen as undeniable fact; it was in essence, "settled science." Those with higher education who might question Darwin were viewed by Orville, my mother, and myself (as with most leftists), with their usual disdain and dismissal. The companion view of atheism as a stated fact was also part of their belief system. Those in the religious realm were already discounted by Orville, simply dismissed with the charming label of "Christers."

Neither my mother nor Orville had a single friend that was religious. In the area of science, practitioners who either held a belief in a creator or left the subject of creation to unknown processes that might have required intelligent design, were also derided as sub-intellects, which unwittingly included many of the greatest minds in human history (Einstein, Planck, Boyle, Tesla, Born, Pasteur, Newton, Kepler, Copernicus, and on and on). Unwittingly, this also may have periodically included Darwin himself who as a young man attended Cambridge to be a clergyman. But it also would depend on what period of his life we are talking about, what his frame of mind was at any moment, and to whom he was communicating. After about age 40, he wavered back and forth about his religious beliefs, but later in life consistently referred to himself as an agnostic.

It is evident that the left rigidly controls the scientific community at the university level, both nationally and internationally, with virtually no input from scientists holding views reflecting intelligent design (ID) or any hybrid theories that might include both Darwinian and ID concepts. This has come about over the long history of America's colleges, which were at first 100 percent devoted to the specific religious groups that founded them.

Over time, they transitioned into the European concept of universities with non-religious orientations, and offering graduate degrees. This shift from religious to secular education was greatly accelerated by the federal government and state aid that was far greater than what churches could contribute, thus, one by one, secular education took root. This transition is well detailed in *The Soul of the American University: From Protestant Establishment to Established Nonbelief*, by historian, George M. Marsden, a professor at the University of Notre Dame. The universities have also maintained an iron grip on the lower levels of education with their power to influence the publication of textbooks that are in line with secular beliefs.

The rage against ID is that it is a cover for "Creationism," and is therefore "letting God in the door." But any reasonable study of the varied world of ID paints a far more complex picture. As Ben Stein depicted in his documentary *Expelled: No Intelligence Allowed,* a massive wall has been built around the scientific community that actively expels scientists who even mention the concept of ID from the universities. By doing so, many new scientists, whose careers have not been allowed to advance because of their perceived "backward and unscientific ideas," have had their reputations destroyed and their research marginalized as irrelevant and kooky.

But new theories regarding the origin of life on our planet are far different than what they were a scant few generations ago. Some are far removed from the settled science I saw in junior high, intended for general education, which portrayed lightning impacting the bubbling "primordial soup," spontaneously generating life. With the modern understandings of microbiology, which is a vast world of which Darwin had no understanding, and the massive intricacy of a single DNA molecule with its complex helix spiral and infinite complexity, few scientists are as positive as to how life began, as they were a few decades ago.

In this arena, the notion of "Directed Panspermia" (seeded life from some unknown extraterrestrial source or civilization) has been thrown out for consideration by such leading people in the field as physicist, Stephen Hawking and biologist Richard Dawkins. All in all, it amounts to conjecture with no substantiation and or testability. At the same time, if panspermia can be contemplated by noted scientists, then the possibility of an incomprehensible super intelligence behind earth's origins, also put forth by a few noted scientists, should logically be part of the discussion; to not do so is a gross abdication to leftist politics.

The oft-quoted astronomer Fred Hoyle, noted for his theory of stellar nucleosynthesis, rejected the Big Bang theory, and though previously an atheist, came to the idea that a "super intellect" with a "guiding hand had monkeyed with physics." He also stated that even the random appearance of the simplest cell had as much likelihood of spontaneously being created as a "tornado sweeping through a junkyard and assembling a Boeing 747 from the materials within."

But the tragedy of it is that the universities of the world, their presidents, department heads, and professors, are drawn from the secular agnostic/atheist ranks almost exclusively which largely prevents research and acceptance of colleagues with alternative views. Scientific publications also exhibit the same censorship. A well-known example relates to Dr. Richard Sternberg, editor of the *Proceedings of the Biological Society* of Washington, D.C, who came under intense scrutiny and persecution for publishing an article by Dr. Stephen Meyer concerning the inability of the materialistic theory of evolution to account for the information necessary to build novel animal forms.

While a search on these topics readily produces myriad examples of this exclusionary environment surrounding the evolution issue, the fact remains that the general public and millions of students world-wide have not been aware of the conflict in the halls of science over Darwinian Theory. They have been taught that evolution is an established fact only opposed by the ignorant.

Darwin, eugenics, and attitudes toward women: Darwin's belief in eugenics cannot be left unmentioned, a direct precursor to Hitler's policies of the twentieth century. His book, *The Descent of Man, and Selection of Sex*, is laced with noxious ideas, such as his dismay not only at the "weak" propagating, but also the idea of preservation of the weak and sick by vaccinations; they should naturally have died off. Among many illustrative Darwin quotes are the following:

> We must bear in mind without complaining the undoubtedly bad effects of the weak surviving and propagating their kind.
>
> Hardly anyone is so ignorant as to allow his worst animals to breed.
>
> The advance of man from a former semi-human condition to the present state requires . . . *natural selection eliminating the weak and inferior humans and leaving superior humans to continue populating the earth* [emphasis added].

> At some future period, not very distant as measured by centuries, *the civilized races of man will almost certainly exterminate and replace throughout the world the savage races.* [emphasis added]

To underscore the importance of eugenics in Darwin's sphere, Bergman cites author Dennis Sewell who wrote *The Political Gene: How Darwin's Ideas Changed Politics,*

> In the years leading up to the First World War, the eugenics movement looked like a Darwin family business. Specifically, Darwin's son Leonard replaced his cousin Galton (who was lauded by Darwin) as chairman of the national Eugenics Society in 1911. In the same year an offshoot of the society was formed in Cambridge. Among its leading members were three more of Charles Darwin's sons, Horace, Francis and George. The group's treasurer was a young economics lecturer at the university, John Maynard Keynes, whose younger brother Geoffrey would later marry Darwin's granddaughter Margaret. Meanwhile Keynes' mother, Florence, and Horace Darwin's daughter Ruth, sat together on the committee of the Cambridge Association for the Care of the Feeble-Minded . . . a front organization for eugenics.

Darwin also had a belief in the bizarre and false concept of "pangenesis." This theory put forth the idea that human bodies produced "gemules" which grew in the organs that could be passed on to offspring which would, in turn, alter life from generation to generation.

He also had a strong belief about "underdeveloped humans" (e.g. blacks and women) that permeated his writing. His "scientific" analysis regarding women was that they had smaller brains; they were "eternally primitive," and childlike; biologically and intellectually inferior to men; less spiritual; more materialistic; and "a real danger to contemporary civilization." These ideas, according to Prof. Evelleen Richards, Historian of Science at the University of NSW Australia, contributed to the "nourishing of several generations of scientific sexism."

Darwin's health and state of mind: Since Darwin's utterances and writings have been elevated to God-like status by most of the scientific world, it does not seem unreasonable to also examine his health and state of mind, which Darwin himself spent much time describing and dealing with. Returning to Bergman's *The Dark Side of Charles Darwin*, he notes Darwin's self-documented psychological ills,

> His (Darwin's) mental problems were so severe that he became an invalid at . . . around age 30. They included various combinations of psychological symptoms including, severe depression; insomnia; incapacitating anxiety; fits of hysterical crying; depersonalization; visual alterations (seeing spots); malaise; vertigo; shaking; tachycardia; fainting spells; shortness of breath; trembling; nausea, vomiting; dizziness; muscle twitches; spasms and tremors; cramps and colics; bloating and nocturnal flatulence; headaches; nervous exhaustion; dyspnea; skin problems; tinnitus; and sensations of loss of consciousness and death.

All of these Darwin wrote about incessantly, battling his demons on a daily basis. Only with great anxiety was he able to leave his house. He was childlike in his relationship to his wife who became in essence his mother.

While suffering these unimaginable infirmities, he became painfully aware that his theories were upsetting the society he lived in. After all, what Darwin concluded in his theory of natural selection was the purposelessness of life, an ideology that conflicts with every religion on the face of the earth. Evolution stresses that no meaning exists in life other "than doing what is needed to survive and pass on life."

Bergman also stated, "Darwin was keenly aware that admitting any purpose whatsoever to the question of the origin of species would put his theory on a very slippery slope."

This might well have brought on some of Darwin's internal consternation, given the dismal projection of that theory on mankind's existence. His concern was validated during the next century.

Darwin also expressed fears that his theories were not accurate, admitted he had no proof, and that they were dangerous. In a letter to Asa Gray, Darwin wrote, "I am quite conscious that my speculations run quite beyond the bounds of true science."

Definitions of science in the mid-nineteenth century varied somewhat from modern understanding; nevertheless, this is a powerful statement.

Another aspect of Darwin's personality was unpleasant at best. Dr. Bergman discusses the well-documented sadistic tendencies Darwin displayed toward people and animals. The commonly held image is that of a placid and kindly man who patiently applied scientific principles and pondered the vast epoch of man, carrying the weight of the world on his shoulders. However, the image doesn't fit well with the reality.

Bergman quotes Darwin's own words, "As a little boy, I was much given to inventing deliberate falsehoods, and this was always done for the sake of causing excitement." Darwin also admitted to stealing solely for fun. Bergman also stated, "A clearer example of his sadistic impulse was when a young boy, Darwin 'beat a puppy . . . simply from enjoying the sense of power.'" Through his university years and later, he was abnormally fixated with killing birds and other animals.

Guns and shooting became an obsession far and above the norm of the average nineteenth-century gentleman's recreational pursuit. He also kept voluminous yearly records of the animals he killed. He became an expert shot, as well as becoming adept at killing birds and rabbits by throwing rocks, all for the pure pleasure of it. He described his laboratory as a "chamber of horrors," where he practiced dissection on live animals including birds and rabbits, before anesthesia "when ripping out the innards of animals caused them to suffer greatly." At one point, he murdered a 10-week-old "angelic little fantail, and a pouter," and described in detail their slow deaths as a result of his experimentation with various poisons. In later life he apparently felt some remorse, but it had been a long time coming.

On his five-year Beagle voyage, he waded onto the Brazilian coast, and his fellow crewmember described Darwin excitedly beating birds to death with his geological hammer, fascinated by their stupidity. He had also purchased a rifle and two pistols before the journey and looked forward to some battles with natives and the possibility of shooting the "king of the cannibal islands." This was years before he began to write about his theories of evolution.

Some leftist scientists cite Bergman's research as ad hominem (attacking a person's character) and not related to one's scientific work; therefore, they claim, it is irrelevant. But it was Darwin's fourteen thousand letters and his books that chronicled his maladies, along with his concerns about the relevancy and accuracy of his research. When contrasting Darwin's statement, "The love for all living creatures is the most noble attribute of man," with Darwin's thoughts and behavior, it brings into question his overall stability, making it difficult to separate the man from his scientific output.

* * *

CHAPTER 15

THE PALEONTOLOGICAL RECORD AND LACK OF TRANSITIONAL FOSSILS

The fundamental premise underlying Darwin's theory of evolution was that, through the eons of time, inferior species evolved into superior species through natural selection. The resulting science textbooks have taught evolution through progressive drawings showing fish growing feet, adapting to the land and developing step by step to higher species. Also prevalent are the sequential drawings of lemurs, chimpanzees and gorillas marching upward in stages, eventually to modern man. But a major stumbling block was recognized by Darwin himself, one that has persisted to the present. Darwin asked, "Why then is not every geological formation and every strata full of such intermediate links? Geology assuredly does not reveal any such finely-graduated organic chain; and this perhaps is the most obvious and serious objection which can be urged against my theory."

In short, in order for the theory of evolution to prevail as Darwin perceived it, transitional examples of evolving macro species must certainly exist. We would fully expect to find fossils of fish with rudimentary feet, and examples of further stages, on their way to becoming mammals. Yet the fossil record, numbering today in the area of one-hundred million identified and cataloged examples in the world's museums actually show the opposite of Darwin's theory, namely no evolution. This incredible growing record covers the approximately 1.5 million species (estimates range from 5 to 100 million in total) of all past and present forms of life, with no transitional examples among them.

Prominent scientists questioning Darwin's theories: As I have delved into this compelling topic, I have studied numerous compendiums of quotes by scientists regarding the importance of paleontology to evolution. I have chosen to focus on those compiled by Shawn D. Pitman, MD, who has taken efforts to exclude quotes taken out of context. Luminaries in the field who stress the importance of paleontology include Sir Gavin de Beer, director of the British Museum, Yale paleontologist Carl Dunbar, and Pierre-Paul Grasse, chair of Evolutionary Biology at Sorbonne University and past president of the French Academie des Sciences and one of the most eminent French zoologist of the twentieth century. Grasse still believed in Darwinian evolution at some level, but was unsure of the actual mechanism. His affirmative statement about the importance of paleontology is definitive, "Why, because it is the only way of obtaining factual evidence supporting any of the theories proffered . . . Any other explanation is conjecture."

Another Grasse statement speaks to the general consensus on the subject,

> Today [1977] our duty is to destroy the myth of evolution which keeps rapidly unfolding before us . . . Naturalists must remember that the process of evolution is revealed only through fossil forms. A knowledge of paleontology is, therefore, a prerequisite; only paleontology can provide them with the evidence of evolution and reveal its course or mechanisms . . . that is why we constantly have recourse to paleontology, the only true science of evolution.

Other noted scientists confirming the lack of evidence for transitional forms of species-to-species in fossil history include some of the most important paleontologists and geologists in the field. For example, David M. Raup, geologist, curator and dean of science at the Field Museum of Natural History in Chicago, which houses the world's largest fossil repository, who stated,

> A large number of well-trained scientists outside of evolutionary biology and paleontology have unfortunately gotten the idea that the fossil record is far more Darwinian than it is. *This probably comes from low-level textbooks and semi-popular articles*. . . Also, there is probably some wishful thinking involved [emphasis added].

The director of the Botanical Institute at Lund University, Swedish geneticist, Prof. Heribert Nilsson, also stated, "My attempts to demonstrate evolution by an experiment carried on for more than 40 years have completely failed."

Colin Patterson, senior paleontologist at the British Museum of Natural History, and Director of the American Museum of Natural History, in a letter to Luther D. Sunderland, author of *Darwin's Enigma: Fossils and other Problems,* stated,

> I will lay it on the line – *there is not one such fossil for which one could make a watertight argument (for evolution)* [emphasis added]. The reason is that statements about ancestry and descent are not applicable in the fossil record. Is Archaeopteryx the ancestor of all birds? Perhaps yes, perhaps no: there is no way of answering the question. It is easy enough to make up stories of how one form gave rise to another, and to find reasons why the stages should be favoured by natural selection. But such stories are not part of science, for there is no way to put them to the test.

By any accounting, Patterson is one of the world's top evolutionists of the past several decades. He has recently called evolution "positively anti-knowledge," and in another address he called evolution "story-telling." In a presentation on November 5, 1981, at the American Museum of Natural History in New York, Patterson stated,

> It does seem that the level of knowledge about evolution is remarkably shallow. We know it ought not to be taught in high school, and perhaps that's all we know about it...about eighteen months ago . . .*I woke up and I realized that all my life I had been duped into taking evolutionism as revealed truth in some way* [emphasis added].

Mark Ridley, zoologist at Oxford University and a leading writer on evolution stated, "In any case, *no real evolutionist whether gradualist or punctuationist, uses the fossil record as evidence in favour of the theory of evolution* as opposed to special creation [emphasis added]."

George Gaylord Simpson was noted by many as the twentieth century's foremost paleontologists. He was also a confirmed atheist and evolutionist. In his book, Tempo and Mode, he wrote, "The regular absence of transitional forms is not confined to mammals, but is almost a universal phenomenon, as has long been noted by paleontologists."

Nevertheless, Simpson had other explanatory theories in his defense of evolution theory, one being Darwin's explanation of the "poorness of the geological record," and yet another theory, he himself called "controversial and hypothetical" that he named "quantum evolution." But the fact remains that today, 65 years after Simpson's work was published, and 156 years after the publication of *Origin,* no macro-transitional evidence has been found.

H. S. Lipson, professor of Physics, University of Manchester Institute of Science and Technology, UK, and author of *A Physicist Looks at Evolution* wrote, "I have always been slightly suspicious of the theory of evolution because of its ability to account for any property of living beings (the long neck of the giraffe, for example). I have therefore tried to see whether biological discoveries over the last thirty years or so fit in with Darwin's theory. I do not think that they do. *To my mind, the theory (evolution) does not stand up at all* [emphasis added]."

More names of prominent scientists who reject the validity of species-to-species transitions include:

Michael Ruse, philosopher of science and biology stated, *"Darwinian Theory is based as much on philosophical assumptions as on scientific evidence* . . . For many evolutionists, evolution has functioned as something with elements . . . akin to being a secular religion [emphasis added]."

Mary Leakey, paleoanthropologist, during an AP interview on October 10, 1996, said, *"All of these trees of life with* their branches of our ancestors, *that's a lot of nonsense* [emphasis added]."

Niles Eldredge, Ph.D, geologist, and curator in the Department of Invertebrates at the American Museum of Natural History is quoted by Phillip Johnson in his book, *Darwin on Trial,* "We paleontologists have said that the history of life supports (gradual adaptive change), all the while knowing that it does not."

Charles Darwin himself made a number of statements questioning his own work in light of the failure to produce transitional forms in the fossil record,

> *When we descend to detail, we cannot prove that a single species has changed;* nor can we prove that the supposed changes are beneficial, which is the groundwork of the theory [emphasis added].

There is undeniable scientific evidence that species do come and go, dinosaurs being a prime example. However, evidence that one species evolves to another has proven hard to come by. Further clouding the theory of transitional or intermediate species is the fossil record from the ancient Cambrian period of 540–500 million BC. Invertebrate fossil species from this geological time period appear fully formed and complex, with no transitional forms preceding them. Some of the species represented include snails, starfishes, jellyfish, reptiles and birds. Additionally, these have been found in locations as diverse as Canada and China.

Another example appeared in 1938, when a fisherman made a catch of a coelacanth at the mouth of the Chalunna River on the east coast of South Africa. This was the same species of a fossilized fish believed for some time to be extinct for 70 million years. Evolutionists had held it up as the forerunner of amphibians. But with the appearance of this fish and the subsequent capture of many more like it, that glimmer of hopeful proof faded.

What will be the long-term effect on the science of evolution with regard to the fossil record? Perhaps if contrary investigation was permitted within the hallowed halls of the scientific community without demonizing those who study alternate theories, it might just lead to other fruitful discoveries. What is scientific study, after all, if not an ongoing series of wide-ranging hypothesis and testing? Without the freedom to allow scientific findings to change what we know about the world, we would still believe that the world is flat. One thing is certain: the search for truth in science is stifled when guarded and shaped by a closed society.

Fakes, frauds and misrepresentations. By the beginning of the twentieth century and even before, the lack of physical evidence to support evolution, particularly within the paleontological record, gave impetus to attempts at filling the gap. These resulting fakes, frauds, and misrepresentations were initially accepted in the rush to prove the theory. The consequence, however, was that many of these were incorporated into school textbooks, and remained there for decades, some into the recent 2000s. The so-called validation of Darwinism was therefore reinforced, along with the underlying ideology of Marxism and atheism.

Darwin's photographs and illustrations. In 1872 Darwin published *The Expression of the Emotions in Man and Animals*. The goal was to show, with the help of photography, that human emotions evolved from some lower animal type. By supposedly showing that all human expressions were shared by the animal kingdom, Darwin claimed proof and further expansion of his theory of evolution. The difficulty with this approach was the revelation that the photographs and attendant illustrations had been manipulated, posed and otherwise "created."

As described in Bergman's book, the use of photography at that time went largely unquestioned, and was seen as an objective medium for showing objects as they really were. Darwin compiled his photos in a number of ways. One marked example was an etching from *Expression*, entitled "Horror and Agony," that was copied from a photograph by Paris physiologist Professor Duchenne, who was known to use electrodes to stimulate facial muscles in patients. The subject in the photo was a mental patient enduring just such treatment, although the etching commissioned by Darwin only showed the man's face without the more disturbing elements.

Other illustrations included drawings made to look like photographs, with various features highlighted to enhance the facial expressions. Another technique used the layering of photographic negatives to achieve the desired result. Rather than capturing genuine and natural expressions of emotion, Darwin utilized various forms of manipulation to "prove" his point.

Piltdown Man. One of the most famous examples of a fraud was the Piltdown Man, "discovered" in 1912 by amateur archaeologist Charles Dawson, and Arthur Smith Woodward, curator of the British Museum's paleontology department. This artifact, reputed to be the skull of a 500,000- to 1-million-year-old man, caused a sensation around the world. It was hailed as the "missing link" between ape and man for over forty years; clear-cut confirmation of Charles Darwin's theory of evolution.

But in 1953, it was determined that the skull was part of an elaborate hoax which cleverly combined a medieval cranium, and a stained chimpanzee jaw. It was revealed that Dawson had actually created some thirty-eight other fakes over the years leading up to this incident, hoping to gain acceptance into the scientific hierarchy, and ultimately the prestigious Royal Society.

Fully two generations of students absorbed the "scientific" knowledge that came with this fraud. Although I was only eleven years old when the truth came out, Piltdown Man was nonetheless part of the "settled science" of my mother and Orville's youth, and had already fed into the ideology that they passed onto me.

Haeckel's embryos. Earnst Haeckel (1834–1919) was a serious proponent of Darwin who advanced his theory of evolution throughout Germany. From the springboard of Darwinism, Haeckel developed further theories of the evolution and development of species, writing extensively on the subject and later becoming a professor of comparative anatomy. He gained notoriety for his creation of illustrations and woodblock prints of vertebrate embryos, purporting to show the preponderance of original similarity of species that then diverged into various animal forms. Over time these became widely accepted as evidence for evolution, and were included in biology textbooks both in the US and abroad, remaining in some as late as 2014. His theories were frequently debated during his lifetime and were eventually discredited.

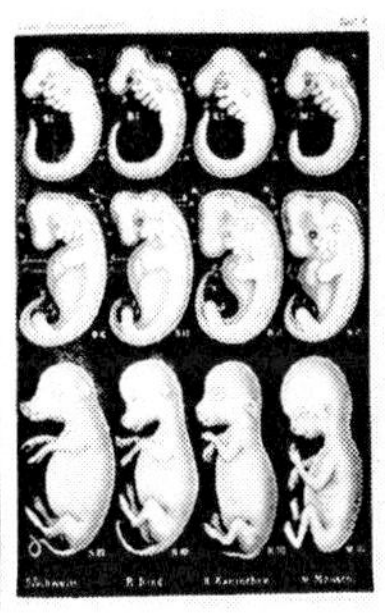

1874 illustration from Earnst Haeckel's book "Anthropogenia" showing stages of embryos of fish (F), salamander (A), turtle (T), chick (H), pig (S), cow (R), rabbit (K), and human.

The most recent investigation in regard to Haeckel was performed by Dr. Michael Richardson, an embryologist at St. George's Hospital Medical School, University of London, and his team, in the late 1990s. Richardson's work documented embryo growth in nine species, following their developmental stages as laid out by Haeckel. The results were that none of the embryos and their resulting growth looked the same at the same state of development as indicated in Haeckel's famous woodblock prints. In fact, the differences were quite remarkable. In a 1997 interview with The Times of London, Dr. Richardson stated, "This is one of the worst cases of scientific fraud . . . they are fakes."

Haeckel was also a key figure in "scientific racism," believing in the superiority of some races over others, as well as holding views on the elimination of society's "lesser" individuals, in line with the emerging study of eugenics. His ideas and concepts bolstered the future Nazi and communist regimes that would follow.

In the end, although Haeckel's views regarding embryo development and evolution no longer carry authority, the inclusion of his illustrations over generations has had the effect of persuading a vast audience of an implied legitimacy.

Lucy. The discovery of Lucy *(Australopithecus afarensis)* in 1974 in Northern Ethiopia by Dr. Donald Johanson and Tom Gray, while not a fraud or a fake, can be placed in the column of serious misrepresentations. Lucy was destined to become one of the most famous (and most controversial) finds of all time. *National Geographic's* September 20, 2006 issue hailed her (a 40 percent partial skeleton) as "Perhaps the world's most famous early human ancestor." Johanson was more succinct, "These new hominid fossils . . . constitute the earliest definitive evidence of the family Hominidae," the upright walking "missing link" that was so sought after. And it resulted in instantly making Johanson's career.

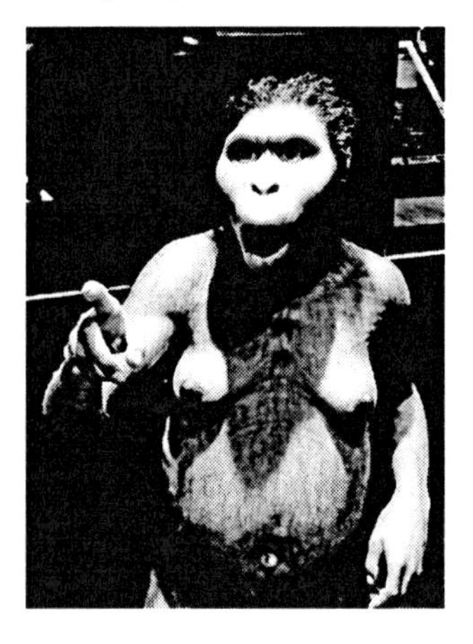

Lucy exhibit, showing human characterization, National Museum of Nature and Science, Tokyo, Japan.

In the exuberant aftermath of the discovery, countless magazine articles were written, and exhibits were rapidly erected at multiple venues such as the New York Museum of Natural History, the American Museum of Natural Sciences, the Museum of Man in San Diego, the National Museum of Anthropology in Mexico City, National Museum of Nature and Science in Tokyo, the University of New Mexico, Michigan State University and the huge $17.1 million-dollar ode to evolution at the St. Louis Zoo (since removed), inclusive of an animatronic figure of Darwin and an exhibition of a contemplative Lucy looking more human than ape, and most provocatively, walking upright with modern hands and feet. A traveling exhibit showed Lucy in the same manner.

However, as prominent researchers gained access to the fossils (or replicas thereof), Lucy's "hominid" status began to be seriously questioned. Some of the notable aspects included her gorilla-like appearance, small brain size, V-shaped jaw, large teeth, conical chest, undeveloped locking mechanism in her knees (related to walking upright), the microwear on her teeth which indicated she was a fruit eater, and wrist bones that were locked and stable, indicating a knuckle-walker. The shape and size of the pelvis, as reconstructed from the fractured pieces, even suggested that "she" was possibly a "he." Lucy was, in fact, very similar to a modern chimpanzee, a separate species from that of humans.

As time passed, with more contradictory evidence coming to light, Johanson, in his 1981 book, *Lucy: The Beginnings of Humankind*, written with Maitland A. Edey, admitted to having bias.

> There is no such thing as a lack of bias. I have it; everybody has it . . . If you are working back at around three million, as I was, that is very seductive, *because you begin to get an idea that that is where Homo did start*. You begin straining your eyes to find Homo traits in fossils of that age . . . logical, maybe, but also biased. *I was trying to jam evidence of dates into a pattern that would support conclusions about fossils which, on closer inspection, the fossils themselves would not sustain* [emphasis added].

After the dust had settled some fifteen years later, Dr. Johanson commented in *National Geographic* magazine (March, 1996), "It is hard for me now to admit how tangled in that thicket I was. But the insidious thing about bias is that it does make one deaf to the cries of other evidence." In the same publication, Johanson also admitted that "Lucy has recently been dethroned."

Even since the unearthing of Lucy in 1974 and new archeological findings over the intervening period, the same problem exists that plagued Darwin, namely the paucity of physical evidence to document his theory. Dr. Richard Leakey, former chairman of the Kenya Wildlife Service, and a second-generation member of one of the world's foremost families in the field of paleontology, archeology, and anthropology, reported the reality of this situation in his 1978 book, People of the Lake.

> If someone went to the trouble of collecting together into one room all of the fossil remains so far discovered of our ancestors (and their biological relatives) who lived, say, between 5 and 1 million years ago, he would

> need only a couple of large trestle tables on which to spread them out. And if that were not bad enough, a not unusually commodious shoebox would be more than sufficient to accommodate the hominid fossil finds of between 15 and 6 million years ago.

Through the years, Leakey has added many comments regarding this persistent gap in the fossil record, such as the following contained in his 1981 book, *The Making of Mankind*, all the while maintaining his faith in evolution. Notice his use of the word "hope."

> Biologists would dearly like to know how modern apes, modern humans and the various ancestral hominids have evolved from a common ancestor. Unfortunately, the fossil record is somewhat incomplete as far as the hominids are concerned, and it is all but blank for the apes. The best we can hope for is that more fossils will be found over the next few years which will fill the present gaps in the evidence.

As I have been researching this field of evolution science, I keep returning to the world of forensics I was involved with for so many years and the fact-finding that is so critical to the outcome of legal cases. Physical evidence plays a large role in determining what aspects of a building were incorrectly constructed. "Destructive testing," the process of opening up areas of a structure that have shown signs of failure, allows us to see the sequence of the construction. Detailed photography, and in some instances taking samples of building materials, provides the documentation needed to tell the story of what went wrong and why.

Relating this to the science of evolution, we find the "theory" having morphed into accepted "fact," with very little physical evidence to support it. Gaps are often filled in with speculation of how a species "might" have lived, or how "adaptation" "probably" came about due to X, Y or Z.

In my experience in the courtroom, experts who rely on conjecture and subjective reasoning at the expense of concrete evidence, will easily be disregarded by judges and juries looking for the truth of what actually occurred on a project. And while expert testimony and opinion can be considered evidence, there are judicial requirements which state that, "the expert's technique or theory can be or has been tested—that is, whether the expert's theory can be challenged in some objective sense, or whether it is instead simply a subjective, conclusory approach that cannot reasonably be assessed for reliability." (Federal Rules of Evidence, Rule 702)

My example from the courtroom is echoed by David Pilbeam, Harvard professor and curator of paleoanthropology at the Peabody Museum of Archaeology and Ethnology, with his statement that appears in Leakey's *The Making of Mankind,* "If you brought in a smart scientist from another discipline and showed him the meagre evidence we've got he'd surely say, 'forget it; there isn't enough to go on.' Leakey added his opinion, "Neither David nor others involved in the search for mankind can take this advice, of course, but we remain fully aware of the dangers of drawing conclusions from the evidence that is so incomplete."

The fossils being found are definitely factual in their own right, worthy of display, scientific study, and even speculation with regard to their relevant connection with modern Homo sapiens. But when these speculations and broad conjectures suddenly become a form of settled science, without dissent, and are authoritatively published in textbooks, as well as the basis for vast museum exhibits and other forms of public education, something has gone awry. It is instructive to recall Dr. Leakey's two "large trestle tables," and one "not unusually commodious shoe box" of physical findings, even though, to be generous, today we might be able to add a table or two.

* * *

CHAPTER 16

MARXISM AND MODERN EVOLUTIONARY SCIENCE

Among leading members of the scientific community over the past few decades, there are those who have freely confessed that they have a need to believe in the concept of evolution beyond any demonstration of fact or conventional scientific method of analysis.

These people are said to be employing an *a priori* approach (formed or conceived beforehand), which in regard to science is potentially limiting and prone to false conclusions.

If, for instance, one was to introduce a political ideology into their scientific investigations, such as King John's version of feudalism, a sixteenth-century Japanese war lord's interpretation of governance, American Indian tribal politics, or John Rockefeller's version of capitalism, one might reasonably recognize the resulting theories as being more philosophical than scientific. At the very least, it would raise serious questions for a sensible person, let alone an impartial scientist. For example, I have strong doubts that Einstein employed politics in his development of the theory of relativity, or that Louis Pasteur did the same in his development of the small pox vaccine.

Stephen Gould in his office at Harvard

Dorothy Greco

A perfect example of this *a priori* approach to scientific investigation is the work Stephen J. Gould and Niles Eldredge and the mixing of their theory of evolution with their leftist politics, militant atheism and "radical science."

With Darwinian theory being seen as a significant foundational ingredient offering a scientific validation of Marxism, the inconvenience of a lacking paleontological record, in order to sustain the theory presented an untenable obstacle.

In 1972, as a response to this dilemma, Gould and Eldredge put forth a new theory that sought to be an answer to the missing transitional fossil record. Not surprisingly, the inspiration for the new theory came from Hegel and Marx, and was called "Punctuated Equilibrium." This new Marxian theory bypassed the Darwinian concept of slow change, and postulated that long periods of equilibrium in life forms were jarred by world-wide catastrophes or unknown cataclysmic events, in line with Marx's concept of revolutionary upheaval. After these convulsions, the natural dialectic of thesis, anti-thesis and synthesis in nature would foster entirely new species that would reign until the next event.

Gould was very proud that his theory coincided with a Marxist interpretation of societal evolution, as he clearly explained,

> Alternative conceptions of change have respectable pedigrees in philosophy. Hegel's dialectical laws, translated into a materialist context, have become the official 'state philosophy' of many socialist nations (Russia, China and others). These laws of change are explicitly punctuational, as befits a theory of revolutionary transformation in human society. In light of this official philosophy, it is not at all surprising that a punctuational view of speciation, much like our own, but devoid (so far as we can tell) of references to synthetic evolutionary theory and the allopatric model (when species become isolated), has long been favored by many Russian paleontologists. It may also not be irrelevant to our personal preferences that one of us [Gould] learned his Marxism, literally, at his daddy's knee.

Needless to say, this new theory invigorated leftist-oriented scientists who were growing uncomfortable with the deficiencies of Darwin's original theories. But even now, almost a half-century after Gould's and Eldridge's answer to the aforementioned problem, the same paleontological issues exist that Darwin faced. Surely evidence of some form of transition in the fossils of macro species resulting from these upheavals must exist. Alas, it does not.

Instead, this new general theory bypassed the fossil record, offering an elaborate construct that included the miraculous appearance of new species, which either sped up or even bypassed the evolutionary cycle. The theory relies more heavily on conjecture than scientific evidence. This is inevitable when attempting to meld Marxist political philosophy with science, an impossible and undesirable task. Still, leftist scientists continue the exercise.

I recently came across an American Indian proverb which says "If you notice that the horse you are riding is dead, you should dismount." Gould dismounted the dead evolutionary horse, but climbed onto a second expired steed by the name of Marx.

Gould had strong opposition including British Darwinist, John Maynard Smith, who had little positive to say about the man's ideas. "The evolutionary biologists with whom I have discussed his (Gould's) ideas tend to see him as a man whose ideas are so confused as to be hardly worth bothering with, but as one who should not be publicly criticized because he is at least on our side against the creationists."

In addition, noted journalist and author Robert Wright, Richard Dawkins, and E. O. Wilson, were involved in the development of an opposing theory entitled "Sociobiology," which developed an elaborate theory explaining human morality within a Darwinian framework. However, this was in direct opposition to Darwin's (and Gould's) theory of pitiless, purposeless natural selection, as the only reality. This conflict illustrates the scientific warfare that is still underway between the various theorist camps.

Wright's statement about Gould was, "Among top-flight evolutionary biologists, Gould is considered a pest – not just a light weight, but an actively muddled man who has warped the public understanding of Darwinism."

Typical edition covers of "Science for the People"

Gould, who died in 2002, was legendary not only for his admirable prose, but also for his ability to claw his way to the top of the scientific community; and this was despite his theories having been met with great resistance. But he was a great self-promoter, and his methods worked. As a result, the proud Marxist and militant atheist became the acknowledged spokesperson for the scientific community in regard to evolution, taking joy in scalding ID proponents from his Harvard pulpit, and anyone else who challenged his viewpoints.

The Socialist publication Solidarity published an extensive biography on Gould, not only describing his left political biases, but also his involvement with the militant Marxist group "Science for the People." Their periodic magazine of the same name gave voice to their leftist agenda for science. Gould was also on the advisory boards of the journal Rethinking Marxism, and the Brecht Forum, sponsor of the New York Marxist School.

Over the years Gould began to push the outer limits of "science," mixing philosophy with political ideology. This school of thought was described as "Evolutionary Biology," which delved deeply into the social aspects of civilization and away from a strict application of science. With supreme confidence in his reputation as a leading scientific figure, Gould apparently came to believe that he could decide which factors warranted a place in his research and which could simply be discarded, thereby creating his own field of study free of conventional restraints.

Here he describes his new philosophy,

> *Science is no inexorable march to truth*, mediated by the collection of objective information and the destruction of ancient superstition. Scientists, as ordinary human beings**,** *unconsciously reflect in their theories the social and political constraints of their times.* As privileged members of society, more often than not they (scientists) end up defending existing social arrangements as biologically foreordained (biological determinism) [emphasis added].

Here, he states the startling belief that scientific exploration does not have to be reconciled with either facts or religious interference (ancient superstitions). One could perhaps argue the latter, but not the former. Objective information (facts) is the foundation of truth. Subjective arguments, however, frequently and unfortunately, invade the domain of evolutionary scientists. If objective information can be ignored or discarded with this "scientific" approach, what is left?

But Gould wasn't finished yet. In a 1997 essay for *Natural History* magazine, entitled "Non-Overlapping Magisteria" (NOMA), and later in his book *Rock of Ages* (1999), Gould put forward what he characterized as "a blessedly simple and entirely conventional resolution to the supposed conflict . . . between science and religion." As described in *American Scientist*, June, 1999,

> It was a simple, humane, rational, and altogether conventional argument for mutual respect, based on non-overlapping subject matter, between

> two components of wisdom in a full human life: our drive to understand the factual character of nature (the magisterium of science) and our need to define meaning in our lives and a moral basis for our actions (the magisterium of religion).

Despite the earmarks of an honest attempt to promote respect and harmony between science and religion, it was in truth a distinct separating of the two, with religion being relegated to its own "box." The additional goal was to remove an obstacle which many scientists felt was blocking the path to truth, namely "creation science" and its companion the study of intelligent design.

Expanding on his "magnanimous" stance toward religion, Gould was quoted in 1999 with the following. "I am not, personally, a believer or a religious man in any sense of institutional commitment or practice. But I have great respect for religion, and the subject has always fascinated me, beyond almost all others (with a few exceptions, like evolution and paleontology)."

One has to wonder what his "respect" and "fascination" with religion meant to him when he made statements such as this one for the *Skeptical Inquirer*, winter 1987/88. It sounds more like the impetus for the development of NOMA,

> Creation science has not entered the curriculum for a reason so simple and so basic that we often forget to mention it; *because it is false, and because good teachers understand exactly why it is false.* What could be more destructive . . . than a bill forcing our honorable teachers to sully their sacred trust by granting equal treatment to a doctrine not only known as false, but calculated to undermine any general understanding of science as an enterprise? [emphasis added]

What we see in NOMA is a seemingly rational, sensible, and high-minded approach to reconciliation, with the ulterior motive of excluding and cutting off contrary opinions and beliefs, all in the name of true science. It brings to mind a similar enterprise undertaken by Orville in the 40s. He formed the innocuous-sounding Independent Voter's League of Minnesota (the state affiliate of the National Citizens Political Action Committee) that appeared as a centrist organization of independent voters, whether liberal, conservative or progressive, who were seeking commonality. The organization, however, was yet another communist-driven front whose goal was to draw unsuspecting people from the mainstream into the influence of the left.

The bigger issue with Gould's non-overlapping of science and religion is how to define what would go into the religious box and what would go into the science box. I can imagine a panel of government experts having an ecumenical conference every few years deciding that issue. Would scientific studies that touch on the improbabilities presented in regard to life springing up from nothing be part of science or religion? And what of valid and growing studies regarding the age of the earth? The cries for "settled science" can be heard far and wide, to the detriment of man's quest to continue exploring and questioning.

The Radical Science Movement: Further affecting the world of scientific study as far back as the 30s and 40s was the development of the Radical Science Movement in England. This undertaking had its roots in the older left generation of scientists, many of whom were giants in that brotherhood and closely associated themselves with the communist scientific community in the Soviet Union and China. At the forefront of the list was the renowned J.B.S. Haldane, the leading militant atheist scientist of his day; a man deeply involved in communist activities in the 30s, during the era of Stalin's Great Terror. He was the editor of the Communist Party of Great Britain's official newspaper, the *Daily Worker*. Other notables included Hyman Levy, British mathematician, who was a member of the Communist Party from 1931 to the mid-50s; Joseph Needham, British biochemist, who spent much of his life in China and whose biographer stated was piteously duped by his communist spymasters and agents; Lancelot Hogben, the Marxist socialist and evangelical atheist, who later switched to "Humanism;" and J. D. Bernal, molecular biologist, Marxist, and militant atheist, who joined the Communist Party in the 20s and held blind allegiance to Stalin and the Soviet Union from then on. He endorsed the Marxist "Proletarian science" of Tromfin Denisovich Lysenko, Stalin's autocratic head of Soviet Science and genetics. Geneticists working under Lysenko's rule who veered from this official doctrine found themselves imprisoned and many were executed for their "bourgeois science."

Bernal's grotesque eulogy on the death of Stalin in 1953 is unfathomable with today's understanding of Stalin-Soviet atrocities. His insatiable appetite for Communist propaganda had no bounds, calling Stalin, "The greatest figure of contemporary history." He also stated that shallow Western thinkers who made accusations against Stalin were merely showing their "utter ignorance."

The modern Radical Science Movement was founded by Richard Lewontin, Leon Kamin and Stephen Rose whose views were cultivated during the turbulence of the 60s and 70s. All three of them were militant Marxists. The group grew to include many of the scientific luminaries of the later phase of the 20th century, and many who endorsed Gould and Eldredge's theory of Punctuated Equilibrium. The result was that the scientific field took on a distinctly political focus; a further melding of Darwinism and Marxism.

Lewontin, was a colleague, friend and fellow professor at Harvard with Gould, and they co-authored many articles together. Lewontin, like Gould, was a member of the radical science movement group Science for the People. His pursuit of scientific thought and exclusion of contrary facts largely mirrored Gould's,

> We take the side of science in spite of the patent absurdity of some of its constructs, in spite of its failure to fulfill many of its extravagant promises of health and life, in spite of its tolerance of the scientific community for unsubstantiated just-so stories, because we have a prior commitment to materialism [emphasis added].

Lewontin continued,

> It is not that the methods and institutions of science somehow compel us to accept a material explanation of the phenomenal world, but, on the contrary, that we are forced by our *a priori* [previously formed opinions] adherence to material causes [anti-supernatural] to create an apparatus of investigation and a set of concepts that produce material explanations, no matter how counter-intuitive, no matter how mystifying to the uninitiated. Moreover, that materialism is absolute, for we cannot allow a Divine Foot in the door.

Lewontin's and Gould's approach to science in general, and the study of evolution in particular, could not be clearer: science is not necessarily a path to truth based on facts; objective information can be dismissed; materialistic results are required even if it's counterintuitive; and *a priori* conclusions and science mixed with social and political ideology is completely acceptable.

The foregoing, to me, is perhaps the starkest example of what resulted from basing one's entire world view on Marxism and its practice, communism. As I have described in multiple ways, my upbringing was an exercise in seeing every single aspect of life and society through a communist lens. Not only did it promote an undercurrent of inhumanity, but it even usurped scientific thought, one area that should always remain an arena of open discussion and research from all sides.

The further tragedy is the exclusion from Science's "hallowed halls" of anyone examining theories that might touch on the unexplained or unexplainable, whether you call it religion, science fiction, or superstition. Ultimately, it exposes the liberal lie of supreme tolerance and openness; in practice, the left can only accept adherence to their own established doctrine. Darwin's theories may have appeared over 150 years ago, but the political and scientific ramifications I have described have become the norm in American schools; a disturbing reality.

* * *

PART VI

REFLECTIONS

CHAPTER 17

REMEMBRANCES FROM MY YOUTH

All of the experiences I have discussed to this point show one persistent theme: the omnipresent world of politics coloring all major facets of our family's life. But aside from the large topics of politics, religion, the government and so on, the same outlook permeated even smaller areas of daily life.

Baseball and golf: The best memory I have with Orville occurred in May of 1951, just before moving to California. I remember the date because it was when Orville took Peter and me out of school to see Willie Mays play at the Minneapolis Miller Ballpark. This was just before Mays was brought up to the major leagues with the New York Giants. Although the historical value of black Americans breaking the color barrier was probably lost on me at that age, I still remember how exciting it was to go to that game.

The author, age 9 (l) and brother Peter, in Little League, Hermosa Beach, California, 1951. Shotwell family archives

Baseball was clearly the best part of both my brother's and my relationship with Orville, beginning when we moved from Minnesota to California. When I was age eleven to twelve, he managed our Little League team. He had an affinity for the sport, appreciating how it grew up from the streets and sandlots rather than being a snooty man's pastime. He also enjoyed the attention (according to my mother) from my being an all-star pitcher. I excelled at that position, certainly adding to my love of the game.

But like everything else, Orville's approach to coaching Little League carried political overtones. As the teams were being formed, there was some consternation that I did not fully understand, but it had to do with Orville's charge of discrimination against the Japanese and Latino players, aimed at one of the influential members of the Little League board. I never knew the whole story, but among the kids there was no racial bias of any kind; we were just friends playing ball. What seemed clear was that Orville felt justified in stirring things up and then acting as the arbiter of "justice," however, there would be little accommodation for the complexity of emotions that might exist among the participants. It wasn't that long after the war, and there were people who had been touched by the internment camps, as well as those who had fought against the Japanese. It was a complex situation requiring finesse and thoughtfulness.

At any rate, Orville increased the percentages of Japanese and Latino kids on our team, perhaps to right a wrong, whether real or perceived; it's unlikely, however, that he would have felt the same benevolence to kids of German ancestry.

Orville's inconsistent approach to praise and blame was on display a few years later during my first year in high school. It was either on Memorial Day or Pearl Harbor Day, when a few of the Japanese students ran a Japanese Zero flag up the school flag pole, burning the rope so it was difficult to remove; a naïve and unfortunate prank. As for we kids, Asian, white and Latino, in our sad ignorance we all thought it was great fun. We were all just good American buddies. In fact, the class president was from a Japanese family.

Understandably, though, members of the Foreign Legion and others in the community were furious. On the other hand, Orville expressed his displeasure with those who were critical of the prank, the veterans, who were a constant target of scorn.

The other sport that I was able to share with Orville, albeit less intensely than baseball, was golf. He loved the game, and could feel good about participating in it knowing the "common man" had access to municipal courses; no need to be a rich capitalist with a country club membership. Most Saturdays he would absent himself to play, sometimes giving us a few dollars to do the household chores he was neglecting. When I was older I played with him a few times, but mostly hacked my way around. I know that Orville played as a guest of some member friends at the private Saticoy Country Club in Ventura County, and really liked it, but sadly he had been unable to bring himself to join as he felt it was too "bourgeois;" a poignant reminder of how all-encompassing one's ideology can be.

The Boy Scouts: To most people, the Boy Scout organization was just a healthy involvement for youth around the world, teaching young men about self-reliance, participation in community activities, learning various outdoor and social skills in regard to cooperation and appreciation of their fellow scouts and adult leaders. It involved young people from all strata of life and from all nationalities, not only in local troops, but in relationship to the larger scouting community.

I wasn't much of a scout, being far more interested in baseball and basketball, but because my older brother was a member, at age eleven I joined the local scout troop, too. But whatever carefree fun I might have experienced was to be short-lived.

Wearing the scout uniform and occasional parade-marching with the flag was part of the focus on love and appreciation of country. After all, this was only eight years after the end of WWII, when patriotism much in the general public's hearts. Reciting the Pledge of Allegiance and occasional group prayers at meetings was also an integral part of the Boy Scouts at that time. These activities infuriated Orville and my mother and we were instructed not to participate in them. In fact, they made a federal case out of it, in keeping with their "in your face" political views. Sadly, I became a pawn in the expression of their dissatisfaction with the organization.

The local Boy Scout council sent a contingent to our home to try to figure out a way to avoid conflict and allow me to remain a scout, while still remaining true to scout principles and regulations. Orville strutted around the living room, book in hand, quoting Patrick Henry and Jefferson, and making fun of the pathetic scout leaders who were there on my behalf. I listened to the goings-on in the adjacent hallway. To make matters worse, an executive with the Boy Scouts who attended the meeting was our next door neighbor; his sons and I played Little League together. In fact, he was the assistant manager of our Little League team. I don't recall a resolution being reached at that meeting, only that I quit the Boy Scouts soon after.

The Stantons – A bright light: I met Ed Stanton in the eighth grade, and he became my closest school friend. His wonderful family turned out to be my salvation; although I'm sure they had no sense of that at the time. They lived in an attractive, understated, lovely home with a view across the Santa Monica Mountains. I stayed overnight at Ed's fairly often, and we were together at school and most weekends in one fashion or another. Ed's father was a strong, responsible, upright businessman. Ed's mother, Rose, was a loving woman, attractive, well dressed, and kind. She was always looking after the well-being of her family. She would make breakfast in the morning, and when I was there she even asked me what I'd like to have! This was unheard of at home, except on a very occasional Sunday. Rose smiled a lot, always had thoughtful words and never seemed to be grinding her ax over others' shortcomings. I never observed the kind of turmoil and suffocating environment I was used to at home.

When I was in the presence of Rose Stanton, I felt my world was centered and the stars had aligned. It was this woman, over a half-century ago, who offered me a glimpse of a life that I wished for myself. I'm sure she was not aware of the impression she and her family made on me. Since her death in 2011, I maintain a photo of her on my desk, with the dear, loving smile I recall so vividly.

Of course, I didn't or couldn't discuss my family's political perspectives, even with the Stanton's, as I was told it was dangerous to do so; you never knew who you were really talking to, and besides, what you said could be reported. But Ed, always calm, seemed to understand my feelings, even though his family experience was nothing like mine and he wasn't totally aware of the political issues in our family. Just the fact that he listened was the true mark of an unbelievable friend.

It took a number of years, some serious counseling, and a failed marriage to achieve my goal. That new life took root in 1976, when I married Gwyneth, and we formed the type of family that I had hoped would happen one day.

I was aware that this example of an American institution carried little value for my mother. Her attitude about our marrying was of a perfunctory nature; well, that was just what you did; nothing particularly special. An illustration of this indifference was that, for the first three years of our marriage, my mother, living about eight blocks away, only babysat our first child once; and rather than coming to our house, we had to bring the baby and all the equipment to her 4th floor condominium. That particular role was not in her repertoire, and we did not ask again. As for Orville, with whom I remained in contact over the years after his divorce from my mother, extending himself to meet and get to know my young family was similarly avoided. When he and I would meet, it was always away from our homes. This allowed him to just be himself without having to interact with others, which might require accommodations and false chit-chat.

I led two lives: In contrast to the picture of misery that was drummed into my head, we were living in a beautiful community, surrounded by mostly healthy, smiling, happy people who populated California in the 50s. The US was in one of the greatest bursts of economic growth ever witnessed in human history, the postwar Eisenhower years. Outside of the home, I loved my friends, enjoyed athletic events, and was a co-founder of a high school social club. We had a corresponding sister club that we had been friendly with since junior high.

But at the same time, I could act like the perfect young communist; for instance, from about the age of thirteen to seventeen, when I wrote a paper for a history class about China or Russia, Orville would thoroughly brief me on the subject. I wrote well, and could articulate the class struggles and the adulation of communism in these countries. Little of what I wrote was truly internalized; I just did what was expected of me. In retrospect, I don't really know what I thought or believed at the time.

The lack of a sense of closeness in our home, combined with the pervasive negativity, gave me a gnawing discomfort when I was there. I kept communications with my mother as minimal as possible and engineered my routine to avoid interaction. During the week, Orville left early in the morning and returned late. On Saturdays, he was generally off playing golf, also avoiding the home as much as possible.

During several summers, I lived on the east coast with my father and occasionally with my grandparents. In contrast to my West Coast life, we hardly ever discussed politics; it was blissful.

The result of these factors was that I basically shut out much of what went on with our dysfunctional family. I also drifted apart from my brothers. After my older brother Peter eagerly left for college, happy to vacate the family, I took over his "bedroom." It was a small, windowless basement area where the furnace was located, with black building paper tacked up over the studs. It was wonderful to be physically separated from the family. Lucky for me the pilot light on the furnace never malfunctioned. I probably didn't know any better, but my mother never expressed any misgivings about the safety of having her sons live down there.

What I felt was an overall numbness and disconnect with my feelings, not knowing what I wanted to do with my life. Perhaps it was fortunate that I was so unhappy, since it galvanized me into examining my experiences and doing something about it as an adult.

My brothers' response: My brothers and I all reacted negatively from the years spent with my mother and Orville, albeit to varying degrees. After Peter escaped the suffocating family, he rarely came back for visits. After dismissal during his first year at Swarthmore College for violating various school policies and poor grades, he immersed himself in the subcultures of New York City and San Francisco. Over the following years, he traveled around the world, working enough to keep himself going. Returning to New York, he worked as an apartment building superintendent while continuing his work on various books and papers. He eventually became an acknowledged historian of the Chinese game "Go" and lives with his wife in Santa Fe, New Mexico.

My younger half-brother, Bjorn, on the other hand, probably suffered the most, being eight years younger, and still at the tender age of nine when his parents divorced. With Peter and me out of the house, he lived alone with our mother. When our grandfather joined them in California, the environment became challenging for them all.

Bjorn had been a pretty unhappy and stubborn child, who was not well-equipped to handle his problematical parents or his own emotions. By age twelve, he became inappropriately involved with classmates, and during his junior and high school years became incorrigible. At one point he was sent off to Juvenile Hall, and later a boarding school in northern California. He fully embraced the alternative lifestyle of the late 60s, getting deeply involved with the gay world, drugs, and leftist politics.

The author (l) and brother Bjorn, c. 1952. Shotwell family archives

He pulled things together for a few years, working in high-level restaurants, getting architecture and landscape architecture degrees and working in a few architectural offices. But his life took another turn when he contracted HIV at about age 35. He lived with that for twenty-eight years, along with Hepatitis C for twenty years. This became overlaid with depression, drugs, and alcohol.

After his death in 2013 at age 63, I read a surprising passage in one of his journals. He was 48 when he wrote, "I've had every opportunity since childhood to pave a road to success and happiness. I had good schools, good hobbies, gardens to work in, a safe environment, and I got involved in liberal politics as an activist which led me to rebel and hang out with less than desirable dope smoking teenagers. The pot led to jail which led to worse situations." I knew he had had a difficult road, but I found this description especially poignant.

Over the last five or six years of his life, I was in close contact with him, and often listened to his rages against the world. I found out after his death that he had relied on heavy amphetamine use to maintain what to him was a semblance of a hold on reality. He died alone in his apartment in Portland, Oregon, and I couldn't help feeling that he was finally released from the tragic and unhappy burdens of his life.

* * *

CHAPTER 18

WHY DID MY MOTHER AND ORVILLE RESPOND TO COMMUNIST IDEOLOGY?

Probably the most persistant question I am asked when describing who my mother and stepfather were, what they actually believed, and the political environment I was raised in, is how and why they came to make the decisions they did? How did they come to such a deep, religious belief that the likes of Josef Stalin and Mao were the bearers of light and the answer to all of mankind's problems?

The reply to this question seems to lie within the areas of individual makeup, personality flaws, perceptions of reality, and persuit of pure idealism. Both Orville and my mother had an inability to deal with or admit to any personal flaws, and instead looked to the world around them; a world they saw as filled with confusion and faulty thinking that could be fixed with the right system . . . a new society with its everflowing fountains of goodness, caring, and love ... elements lacking in their own lives. Using the benevolent words of the communist ideal they could rationalize their personal inabilities by focusing on a far more important goal; fixing humanity and the world.

Rather than looking at people and the world the way it actually was, and working within those confines, they embraced an ideal world which became their reality. But as author and newspaper columnist, Dave Richardson, states in his book *Transparent* about foundational assumptions that control people, that way of thinking was flawed. Orville, and to a degree my mother, assumed that commmunism was fair to all, that Lenin, Stalin and Mao were benevolent figures, visionaries who could see the ideal and had the political power to mold it into reality. They also assumed that the evils of capitalism and American democracy were rigid and could only be changed by Marxian violent upheaval and destruction.

In order to realize their ideal, they had to deny what was plainly before their eyes. Richardson states, "For idealists, the physical world is either not real or is unimportant. It is only a stage to play out the pursuit of their ideal." In Stalin's case, the US would be the next venue for communist revolution. Orville and his friends bought into this idealism with their all, choosing their course of action as outlined by the Comintern rules and Moscow's requirement for party membership. Nazi Germany endeavored to perfect their own ideal society; whatever force was required to achieve the ideal could not be condemned as improper; they were seeking a perfect world and who could argue with that? In Germany, the ideal of the superior Aryan race was used to carry out the plan for Hitler's new perfect society. In Russia, similar to the Ayrian concept, the new archetypical ideal that would emerge from their society would be "The New Soviet Man."

Orville was always looking to this perfect world somewhere out in the either. In his interviews, he interjected a quote from Henry Steele Comager, "I like the dreams of the future better than the history of the past."

My mother and Orville shared the belief that Stalin would end the inequities of the world with the installation of communism worldwide. But there was an inherent problem in that belief; in order to realize the dream, one had to set aside the inevitable horror that would come to the non-believers. Anne Applebaum, in her book, *Gulag,* describes the various elements that characterized Lenin's and Stalin's blueprint for that dream: both leaders arbitrarily meted out death sentences; they aggresively disrupted an entire society's set of values; demonized lifetime accumulations of wealth and experience as being a liability; glamorized robbery of individual property as "nationalization;" and viewed murder as an acceptable part of the struggle to attain the "dictatorship of the Proletariet."

History continually reminds us that the greatest attrocities in human history have been committed by totalitarian idealists and those seduced by that idealism. Orville was typical of the true believer, both downplaying the dark side of implementation, and even denying its existance, in order to remain focused on the ideal. But it nonetheless was there, lurking under the surface.

Whittaker Chambers summed it up when he said, "What man can call himself a Communist who has not accepted the fact that Terror is an instrument of policy, right if the vision is right, justified by history?"

It was no different in Germany, where the downtrodden citizenry reached out to Hitler to fix their broken world after WWI and create a new German ideal, a glorification of a history that never was, and a thousand year, world-wide Third Reich, filled with Aryan purity and a political system of socialism, an ideal that never had any chance of becoming a reality. The pursuit was costly; their cities were destroyed and their populations desimated, along with their dreams.

Can any rational person come to the conclusion that the pursuit of idealistic societies has been worth the 75 million lives lost in WWII, or the accumulative 100 million, or more, lives lost in the twentieth century due to the madness of totalitarian communism?

Anne Applebaum does a good job summarizing a simple answer to the riddle of why westerners like Orville and my mother could stomach such an abysmal ideology as Stalinist/Leninist communism:

It is not only the far left, and not only the Western communists, who were tempted to make excuses for Stalin's crimes that they would never have for Hitler's. Communist ideals---social justice, equality for all---are simply far more attractive to most in the West than the Nazi advocacy of racism and the triumph of the strong over the weak. Even if communist ideology meant something very different in practice, it was harder for the intellectual descendants of the American and French revolutions to condemn a system which *sounded*, at least, similar to their own.

Joseph Epstein coined the term *virtucrat* in a 2014 article which describes part of Orville's sense of himself, stemming from his perceived lofty intellect. This was derived from the "virtuousness" of his Christlike political opinions, as shown in his turning to communism partly because of the biblical teachings of sharing and the words of Jesus. To him life was a Manichaean battle between good and evil, and communism would declare victory over this issue. He was on a biblical crusade to destroy evil, but sadly it required evil to do the job.

My mother's situation was somewhat different. She always dealt with life in generalities. Perhaps she didn't completely understand the extreme level of hardcore communism in which Orville, Charlie Kramer, Sol Adler, Nat and Janet Ross, Harold and Faye Glasser, Johnnie Jacobson, Roger Rutchick, Beenie Baldwin and others were so deeply involved. But even if her involvement was conducted in the tangential role of a girlfriend, and later a wife, adhering to Orville's doctinaire political direction, she still took an active stance in supporting the ideal. One telling example was changing her April 30 birth date to May 1st to coincide with the May Day celebrations of the communist revolution in Russia.

From the earliest days of her relationship with Orville, after her divorce from my father, my mother was allowing clandestine meetings of communists in her home that she knew clearly were illegal and dangerous. She described how she offered her house to him for "a lot of secret meetings," held with "important people." She explained the advantage of the locale: "I was just Orville's girlfriend, and I was single and had no attachments. Who would suspect me of being involved with any secretive activities?" Apparently not yet considered "in the fold," she did not sit in on the discussions; she felt, at that time, that she "had nothing to offer," Regardless, in her infinite naiveté, she didn't think the FBI could find them. I mentioned that she had two children upstairs during these meetings (me and my brother) and there could have been a raid. In fact, I suggested that she and Orville could have been hauled away. She sloughed it off.

It wasn't in my mother's makeup to see the big picture or even her own involvement on a day to day basis. When she was about eighty-nine years old and entering into her final six years with slowly increasing dementia, I interviewed her about various times in her life. While talking about Orville (a large and frequent topic), she said to me, with a slightly coy smile, "Do you think he was a communist?" She had never before raised the issue, but seemed willing to broach it now. I was surprised to hear it because for her, the issue of communist party membership was something whispered about but never voiced out in the open; more secrets even to the last. I said, "of course he was," and we both laughed. I think there was some relief that the long-held secret was out, the secret that we had been instructed to never talk about.

I went on to ask her if she thought the country would have been better off if Orville and his allies gained control. Her immediate answer was "no," followed by the perplexing, "but they had a lot of good ideas, better than the other side. They were very bright and intellectual." She reminded me of the ladies riding out in their surreys from Washington with picnic baskets and dressed in their finery, to view the grand Battle of Bull Run in 1861, at the start of the American Civil War. In the naiveté of the time, they were expecting an afternoon's exciting performance, having no comprehension of the chaos and bloodshed that was to follow just a few hours later.

What communism offered my mother and Orville, with its unrelenting discipline, was an ordered world that seemed to align the universe for them. It was also like a secret club of intellectual superiors, and even must have carried a level of intrinsic excitement. The way out of their discontent was strict political order and subsurviance to their unattainable ideal. As history has shown, the political path that they chose was badly flawed and unfortunately answered none of the fundamental problems and resentments accumulated during their lives.

My mother's world, post-Orville: My mother continued her involvement with liberal/leftist politics even after her divorce from Orville. She would march down to any street protest that took place on a given weekend. But there was never a well-defined discourse on the issues at hand. I only heard the usual generalities about fighting for people's rights, freedom for the oppressed, and the like.

She claimed, as had Orville, that she read a "balanced press," but it was difficult to see. Her daily ritual was to sit at her dining room table, sipping coffee until midday, and reading the *Los Angeles Times*, and the *New York Times*, both well known by the 70s and 80s for their left bias. Her one conservative publication, *The Wall Street Journal*, was only perused for stock information on the recommendation from one of her financial advisors. The opinion pages would never have been opened. She lived in affluent West Los Angeles, adjacent to the Mediterranean-style Shangri-La of Westwood Village, on a stretch of Wilshire Boulevard dubbed "The Gold Coast." She fit right in, with resources resulting from her sporadic real-estate work, and her well-invested inheritance, which provided a very comfortable existence.

I asked her once if the Russians and Joe Stalin had been successful in overthrowing the US government, did she ever consider that she might have been one of the first to be dragged out of her tasteful condominium and executed in the street; after all, the new communist government, as they did in Russia, the Balkans, Eastern Europe, and elsewhere, would not look kindly upon her wealth. They would want to make room for other more deserving families. She dismissed the idea as ridiculous, and simply too absurd to contemplate.

One of the most prized benefits of her comfortable economic situation was her ability to travel extensively, beginning in her fifties. She would rent out her condominium for three months at a time and head out on her own, with little in the way of an itinerary, and leaving only the occasional American Express address for receiving letters from home. While many of her trips were to known tourist destinations that were relatively safe, she also ventured into some pretty dicey areas, such as Afghanistan, and rural Morocco, where being a single female on her own was not the wisest choice; some of her tales were pretty hair-raising. My mother also travelled to her much-admired Russia, coming home and telling us about all the happy Russian people she encountered. In contrast, we had friends who travelled there with a theater troupe to put on performances of *Fiddler on the Roof*, staying with local families. Upon their departure, our friend gave his host a carton of cigarettes as a thank you. The man actually cried at receiving such a precious commodity. My brother Peter also made a trip to Russia, and encountered a population numbed by widespread alcoholism; people drowning their sorrows at the end of every day. A far different picture, and this from a strong-minded liberal.

When my mother died in 2013, she had come to the end of a steady five-to-ten-year decline from dementia. During those last few years, she would repeatedly tell us that the best thing she had ever done was to "have my three sons." She would go on to describe taking Peter and me all around on the streetcar for 10 cents, and having all sorts of fun. Her new "memories" were of a loving family, and a lovely experience as a mother. This was undoubtedly a comforting, but unfortunately false, narrative as those younger years were tumultuous.

I became her conservator and guardian, relieving her of any daily responsibilities, and when I would visit her at her assisted-living facility she was actually affectionate with me, smiling and holding my hand when we walked; something she did not do when I was growing up. This was an unexpected benefit for me, allowing me to experience my mother with some warmth before the end of her life. In fact, I truly believe those last years turned out to be the happiest for her, with no cares about politics, no TV news, no protests to attend, and a release from persistent negativity.

Mother and author, 1976. Shotwell family archives

* * *

CHAPTER 19

FINAL THOUGHTS

Some of the comments I have made about my mother, primarily in regard to her political perceptions and how they affected my life, might seem harsh, which I wish to temper with a bit of Christian charity, even though she would have brushed off the notion.

On the positive side, due to her somewhat zany personality, we were exposed to places and events that a more normal upbringing might not have included, such as our extensive summer travels across the country following different routes each year. I never cared for sleeping in campgrounds, under picnic tables, or in cow pastures, but it was educational. Through all of her ups and downs, and her difficulties with the men she chose to be involved with, she persevered with her boys as best she could. Another person might have abandoned us or given up hope, but she dug in her heels and went forward. I am also grateful for her giving me life, although its course is far removed from the one she charted for herself.

Some credit is also due Orville. Despite the unfair and unforgivable political indoctrination, he kept us sheltered and put bread on the table for the twelve years he and my mother were married, and that certainly must be recognized. His involvement with us through baseball created at least a bit of a bridge, and on weekends he was always willing to meet at the Little League field and work with us. I am thankful for those memories.

Looking back, I realize that, for whatever reason, I had the ability to develop and benefit from close friendships and an active school/social life outside my home; those things allowed me to navigate through those early years. As an adult I made a priority of gaining balance, and pursuing the life I envisioned for myself. It wasn't easy but I feel, after all, that I faired pretty coming from where I began, culminating in the forty wonderful years with my wife Gwyneth.

I also feel like I have miraculously fallen into a divine gap measured in time and place. Simply due to the arbitrary year in which I was born, I didn't have to face the bitter cold and death at Valley Forge during the Revolutionary War, or the horrifying battlefields of the Civil War. I didn't have to suffer gas attacks in France during WWI, or claw my way under fire up the slopes of Mount Suribachi on the island of Iwo Jima; or desperately try to stay on my feet to avoid being bayoneted and discarded on the Bataan Death March. I didn't have to be on a landing craft, storming the beaches of Normandy, with thousands falling all around me, fighting the Germans or the Japanese during WWII, nor did I have to be huddled in fear on Pork Chop Hill in Korea, or fighting in the jungles of Vietnam.

For that matter, I also didn't have the misfortune of living a life of suffering through the barbarism and hopelessness of the Mao and Stalinist regimes, or ending up in one of Hitler's crematoriums at Treblinka. As a citizen of the United States I am eternally grateful to the men and women who did serve in the military, who have made, and are keeping, this country free and safe.

The sense of security that young people have today is an incomparable blessing. But it is also a danger if it is coupled with the belief that this security will simply go on forever. Democracy is fragile and more difficult to achieve than other forms of government. There has never been another country like the United States. Representative democracy was a new idea forged by the founding fathers, and they knew perhaps better than most that it would be a constant struggle to maintain; they understood human nature. Socialist and communist governance can appear appealing in the beginning; a seemingly benevolent leader impresses with promises of taking care of everyone's needs: "From each according to his ability; to each according to his needs," the slogan most closely associated with Karl Marx.

On the face of it, it sounds so "reasonable." But once human nature takes over, as it always will, and the people who are industrious begin to recognize that those considered "in need" wish to bear no responsibility for their own well-being, resentments begin to build and things get messy. Those without will seek "redress." That's when the true nature of a Hitler, Himmler, Goebbels, Mussolini, Mao, Lenin, Stalin, Pol Pot, Kim Il-Sung, Castro, Chavez, or a Peron, will appear, and the "utopia" will slowly transmogrify into a stifling, iron-handed totalitarian environment, often under military control. Winston Churchill said it well, "Socialism is a philosophy of failure, the creed of ignorance, and the gospel of envy. Its inherent virtue is the equal sharing of misery."

A moving example is *The Forsaken,* by Tim Tzouliadis, which recounts the experience of thousands of Americans who immigrated to Russia during the 1930s, both to take part in Stalin's five-year plan building towards a worker's paradise, and to escape the Depression. This very readable, thoroughly referenced work clearly shows the transformation from the promised, wonderful-sounding utopia, to a nightmare that lasted well into the latter part of the twentieth century.

What has gradually occurred in this country since the 1930s, and has gained momentum in the last two to three decades, is the persistent belief that America is somehow a heartless, mean and egotistical country, guilty of perpetrating "crimes against humanity" as one young lady, sitting next to me on an airplane stated. Ignored in this belief system is the reality that the US rebuilt Europe and Japan after the war, while continuing to expand our economic freedoms. The environment created has resulted in millions of people clamoring to come here to escape oppression in their countries of origin. Their desire is not to be taken care of by the government, but rather to have the opportunity to create a life using their abilities to the fullest. Having opportunity does not equate to a guaranteed outcome; life has no guarantees; but the freedom to pursue life on one's own terms allows all kinds of possibilities.

Perhaps my biggest regret is that I did not choose to share this part of my early life with my daughters, that I did not convey more about my unusual growing up years, rife with indoctrination, and my subsequent turning away from that ideology as a result of my varied life experiences.

As described in my prologue, I might never have returned to those days had it not been for the rise of Barack Obama in 2008. As I saw and read about Obama's mentors, I was very disturbed by what was reported. There was Black Liberation Theology reverend, Jeremiah Wright, Obama's pastor for twenty years, seen in videos ranting "God damn America." Black Liberation Theology is a Marxist-type movement whose precepts include a theology that "accepts only the love of God that participates in the destruction of the white enemy," and that "the State of Israel is an illegal, genocidal . . . place." Obama distanced himself from Wright when these things came out, and claimed that he had never heard such sermons. But who could believe this? Not only had the Obama's been long-standing members, he and Michelle were married by the good reverend, who Obama thought of as an uncle.

In *Dreams from My Father*, the memoir Obama wrote when still in his 30s, he mentioned an influential person by the name of "Frank" some twenty-plus times, but never included his last name. This strong mentor was Frank Marshall Davis, a card-carrying communist and editor of communist newspapers in both Chicago and Hawaii. Obama's grandfather put the two together during Obama's teenage years in Hawaii, and the relationship continued until he went off to Occidental College in Los Angeles.

Once in college, Obama described how he sought out the Marxist professors and radical students with whom he felt the most comfortable. As a young man, that type of philosophy and behavior isn't all that unusual; but the fact that he has never disavowed those beliefs must necessarily cause one to accept that he still holds to that ideology. In his presidency, several of his closest working associates were from families embedded in the militant left of the 30s through the 60s. Whether they like the characterization or not, the leftists of today are descendants of the leftists of the past and the current president is a product of forces of long-standing leftist ideology. History repeats itself, over and over, with each generation.

Populist sentiment has been growing in this country for some time but without, I feel, a true understanding of how the implementation of such an ideology would play out. Countries like Venezuela and Argentina provide a strong example of once-prosperous upwardly mobile nations that have been reduced to massive poverty, sky-high inflation, and loss of personal liberty, under the guise of government benevolence. It is at once a tragedy to behold, and a cautionary tale for a free country like the US

The real challenge is in recognizing what lies beneath the "comfort" and "surety" of a populist agenda. One will find a drive for power, and control over the individual, fueled by the belief that people are incapable of directing their own lives. The failures of that agenda speak for themselves. The fact remains that the United States, throughout its history, has provided the most freedom and opportunity for the most people; unlike any other nation. Nothing is "perfect," there is no such thing. But the founders understood that the natural order is for men to be free to pursue their lives without the yoke of tyranny that is government control. Orville and my mother never got that message.

Another regret is that I was unable to confront Orville with the facts that have emerged over the past twenty years; he was gone by then. Most likely, though, it would have been a meaningless exercise, so devoted was he to his doctrine. And what new facts have we learned? We now have the invaluable evidence that we have gained from the *Vassiliew Notebooks*, the *Mitrohkin Archives*, the released records of the government Venona Project during WWII, the confession of Morton Sobell, the extrordinary autobiography written by Whittaker Chambers, and many other books and manuscripts by ex-communists about their experiences. In retrospect, the benign liberals who were duped and dragged along by their more militant comrades might have had quite a different take on their political endeavors had they had this information.

When considering the effects of the leftist writers and publications that so vociferously painted the rosy pictures of the Soviet Union and their cause, do we ever hear the heart-felt apologies for covering up or otherwise distorting the truth about the atrocities of the communist dictators? And do we hear from those who battled and ridiculed the House and Senate hearings of the 40s and 50s regarding communist infiltration into the government, now found to have been well justified?

Where are the past and contemporary leaders of the left and their media friends coming forth to admit they were badly misled and wrong, and guilty of misleading others; those who formerly spent their waking hours trying to tear apart the US government and the country's institutions? Unfortunately, they are very quiet on these subjects, because most still see the US in the same light that my mother and Orville saw it. A newspaper can write a retraction fifty years later about a true monster like Walter Duranty, but of what benefit is that in contrast to the damage created at the time. Where are the mea culpas?

The philosopher George Santayana's well known quote rings true to me: "Those who cannot remember the past are doomed to repeat it." It is my strong belief that today's growing populist political environment in the US is evidence of exactly what Santayana described.

As I have been writing this narrative over the past few years, I have been reminded of various incidents that stand out to illustrate my thoughts. One in particular will serve as a closing statement. When my mother was about eighty-five years old, and planning to move to a wealthy retirement community in Laguna Woods, California, I helped her choose a condominium in the luxury tower of the development. Although we did not recognize it at the time, her dementia was already beginning. But even then, her acerbic, leftist worldview was still firmly rooted in place. We found a wonderful unit with a perfect northern exposure on the fourth floor that looked out at the beautifully manicured entry courtyard. Framing the view across the beautifully planted sunny flowerbeds and lofty treetops were the fluttering American and California flags. It was a truly beautiful panorama; a picture postcard at its best. Upon seeing the flags, my mother immediately hardened, and refused to even consider the unit. With a dismissive snort, she stated emphatically that there was no possible way she would purchase a unit where she had to look out at an American flag every day. To her it was anathema, an unwelcome sign. Had it been the hammer and sickle of Soviet Russia fluttering on the soft breezes that wafted in from Laguna Beach, I believe it would have been a heartwarming and delightfully picturesque addition to the view.

Coming Full Circle: The focus of this book has been on the radical liberal political philosophy of communist agitation and subversion practiced by my stepfather, mother, family friends and associates. My father, on the other hand, represented the more benign form of liberalism described earlier, a form of traditional Democrat liberalism that has unfortunately been receding greatly in the past decade.

My intention has been to give the reader an intimate insider view of how radicals view the world in all its many facets, and to show how those convictions have not only continued, but have seen a revival in this country, that is shaping modern culture and politics.

After being immersed in red for much of my early life, and finally emerging, the underpinnings of radical politics strikes me as inherantly a form of madness. I never understood it so completely until I read psychiatrist Dr. Lyle Rossiter's book, *The Liberal Mind,* where he disects the various forms of leftist political thinking from mild to radical. Through my own transition from the far left to the right side of the political spectrum, I found it fascinating and helpful in sorting out my own past. It also helped me to better understand how the current trend of the left has twisted itself into such a self-defeating and self-loathing form of modern political expression.

In his book, Rossiter deals with what the radical liberal *is* and *is not* passionate about, eloquently capturing in totality the perceptions and values that I experienced and believed during the years of my "immersion in red." He writes,

> What the liberal mind *is* passionate about is the world filled with pity, sorrow, neediness, misfortune, poverty, suspicion, mistrust, anger, exploitation, discrimination, victimization, alienation, and injustice. Those who occupy this world are 'workers,' 'minorities,' 'the little guy,' 'women,' and the 'unemployed.' They are poor, weak, sick, wronged, cheated, oppressed, disenfranchised, exploited, and victimized.

Rossiter goes on to explain how radicals bear no responsibility for their problems; that none of their agonies and complaints are attributable to faults or failings of their own, poor choices, bad habits, defects in character, low frustration tolerances, and on and on. All of this they blame on faulty social conditions such as poverty, disease, war, ignorance, unemployment, racial prejudice, ethnic and gender discrimination, capitalism, globalization. And, of course, all of it inflicted by generic entities such as "Big Business," "Big Corporations," "greedy capitalists," " US Imperialists," "the rich," "the wealthy," "the powerful" and "the selfish."

Contrasting with the list of how the modern liberal mind views their fellow man, he also describes the values that the liberal mind *is not* passionate about: "Their] agenda does *not* insist that the individual is the ultimate economic, social and political unit: it does not idealize individual liberty and the structure of law and order essential to it; it does not defend the basic rights of property and contract; . . . it does not preach an ethic of self-reliance and self-determination

. . . It does not advocate moral rectitude or understand the critical role of morality in human relating."

Rossiter goes on to touch on other topics that do not enter the radical liberal agenda. The ones that stand out to me, and were decidedly lacking in Orville's "teachings," were a celebration of the genuine altruism of private charity, the ethics of consent, or the blessings of voluntary cooperation. Instead, in Orville's world, the government would decide how resources were distributed, making voluntary participation inconsequential.

These topics are endless grist for the liberal mill; for persistent never-ending protests and for political policies that promise to fix all the ills and inequities of society. They promise to round off the hills and fill in the valleys of each and everyone's life, until their ideal is achieved, secured with binding laws that will maintain their vision of human societal perfection. What is always left out of this equation is the immutable fact of human nature which defies control unless forcefully coerced.

Orville could speak for hours on morality and his support of the have-nots, with his chest swelling, while at the same time seeing acts of lying, cheating, subversion, obfuscation, espionage, and ultimately redistribution of wealth, as being wholly acceptable. As Lenin once said, "There is no morality in politics, there is only expedience."

Again, Rossiter explains,

> The liberal cure for this endless malaise is a very large authoritarian government that regulates and manages society through a cradle to grave agenda of redistributive caretaking. It is government everywhere doing everything for everyone . . . Through multiple entitlements to unearned goods, services and social status, the liberal politician promises to ensure everyone's material welfare, provide for everyone's healthcare, protect everyone's self-esteem, correct everyone's social and political disadvantage, educate every citizen, and eliminate all class distinctions.

And finally, he describes how these liberal intellectuals see themselves as heroes of the proletariat in this great societal melodrama, people that could take credit for providing society with whatever they wanted or needed even though they had not "produced by (their) own effort any of the goods, services or status transferred to them," but had instead "taken them from others by force."

The foregoing paints, very succinctly, what I lived and breathed. It is an agenda that has proved a failure and worse, whenever and wherever it has been implemented. Margaret Thatcher encapsulated this basic truth with a single blunt and straightforward sentence, "The problem with socialism is that you eventually run out of other people's money." Socialism is, moreover, but a stepping stone to the radical politics that disregards individual liberty, and has brought untold human suffering to millions in the name of benevolence.

I have come along way since my formative years immersed in Marxist/socialist ideology, as a witness to its deceptive character and insidious workings. As a result I am forever grateful to the various forces and experiences in my life that allowed me to shed my past and enter into the realm of truth.

Mike and Gwyneth Shotwell at Filoli Gardens in Woodside, California, 2012.

Shotwell family archives

* * *

CPSIA information can be obtained
at www.ICGtesting.com
Printed in the USA
FSOW01n0233221116
27545FS

9 781944 212520